Effective Education of
African American Exceptional Learners

Effective Education of African American Exceptional Learners

New Perspectives

Edited by

Bridgie Alexis Ford
Festus E. Obiakor
James M. Patton

pro·ed
8700 Shoal Creek Boulevard
Austin, Texas 78757

pro·ed

© 1995 by PRO-ED, Inc.
8700 Shoal Creek Boulevard
Austin, Texas 78757-6897

Library of Congress Cataloging-in-Publication Data

Effective education of African-American exceptional learners : new
   perspectives / edited by Bridgie Alexis Ford, Festus E. Obiakor,
   James M. Patton.
       p.   cm.
   Includes bibliographical references and index.
   ISBN 0-89079-619-X
   1. Afro-American children—Education.   2. Exceptional children-
-United States—Identification.   I. Ford, Bridgie Alexis.
II. Obiakor, Festus E.   III. Patton, James M.
LC2731.E44   1994
370'.8996073—dc20   94-38147
                                                                    CIP

Production Manager: Alan Grimes
Production Coordinator: Karen Swain
Art Director: Lori Kopp
Reprints Buyer: Alicia Woods
Editor: Debra Berman
Editorial Assistant: Claudette Landry

Printed in the United States of America

1   2   3   4   5   6   7   8   9   10   99   98   97   96

Dedications

To my community of family support system—my mother, Cherrie, grandmother Thompson, LaMar, Adrienne and the "kids," the Sharps, Janette, Barbara, Clotine J. Mays, F. Williams, and my talented goddaughter Charlyn—for their unconditional support and encouragement.

To Papa, Mama, my brothers and sisters in Nigeria, and to Pauline, Charles Jr., Gina, and Kristen for their love and kindness.

Without the strength, love, spirit, and beauty of all members of my family, especially my two truly gifted children, Asha and Ade, this book would not have been conceptualized and brought to fruition.

Contents

Foreword

CULTURE, ASSESSMENT, AND VALID TEACHING FOR THE AFRICAN AMERICAN STUDENT

Asa G. Hilliard III
Fuller E. Callaway Professor
Department of Educational Policy Studies
Georgia State University,
Department of Educational Psychology/Special Education
Atlanta, Georgia

In 1904 Alfred Binet was commissioned by the minister of public education in France to develop techniques for identifying those children who were performing poorly in the regular schools and who might need some type of special education. The "IQ" test that he developed is now a well-known part of the history of psychology. Less well known is the fact that Binet called for and made specific recommendations for special education pedagogy that he called "mental orthopedics."

Implemented in special classrooms, these mental orthopedics were reported by Binet to have resulted not only in improved academic achievement, but in improved intelligence as well. By intelligence he meant the capacity to learn and to assimilate instruction. Therefore, intelligence could be taught. It could develop and expand. Binet appeared to be intrigued by the possibilities of remedial instruction.

Binet's test was introduced into the United States by Goddard. However, it was Lewis Terman of Stanford University who first modified the Binet test for widespread use in the United States. Terman's modifications were major; he did not simply translate the Binet test. But more important, he made changes in the underlying assumptions, purpose, and uses for assessment. For Terman, the test was to be used to rank test takers on the basis of their global scores, to label them, and to provide them with a special education that was appropriate to the label. Because intelligence was thought by Terman to be fixed, clearly Terman's revised test was not intended to be a diagnostic instrument, and his educational treatments were not intended to be remedial. Few psychologists and educators seem to understand this basic set of differences between Binet and Terman.

Terman's fundamental detour from Binet actually set the stage for the development of two paradigms for thinking about assessment, treatment, and the relationship between them. Yet in contemporary professional practice, these two paradigms are seldom explicit. As a result, some professionals actually attempt to function using inconsistent and even contradictory models for professional practice. For example, using a test that was designed to provide global ranking as if it were a sophisticated diagnostic tool is a gross misuse of the test. The IQ literature, including the technical manuals for IQ tests, do not support their use as diagnostic devices. For example, "predictive validity" refers to the accuracy of a guess about a person's rank in a distribution of achievement test scores. There is no body of literature on "instructional validity" of IQ tests, referring to how the test can be used to produce high academic achievement.

The two competing paradigms may be loosely labeled custodial and remedial. The *custodial* paradigm is rooted in the assumption that mental abilities are fixed. Under this model, testing is used to rank students and to give them a label based on that rank. Users of IQ tests in schools also assume that three or so unique or distinct pedagogies (treatments or teaching strategies) exist in the schools (high, medium, and low tracks, or programs for students considered gifted, average, and impaired) and that instructional *benefits* accrue to children because of placements and special services. Under this model, if assessment is valid, children are not expected to change their rank or to master higher than predicted criterion levels of achievement.

On the other hand, the *remedial* paradigm poses almost opposite positions. Under it, assessment is diagnostic. The discovery of deficiencies is for the purpose of prescribing valid remedial treatment or teaching strategies. Under this model, there is no certainty when it comes to forecasting future achievement of children, either in terms of rank or in terms of criterion levels of performance. In fact, the goal under the remedial paradigm is to destroy the predictive validity that is the mainstay of the custodial paradigm. The goal is to awaken in children intellectual powers that are masked or even suppressed, to nurture those powers, to produce growth in capacity.

There have been many court cases and public policy meetings on matters pertaining to equity in special education. Rarely if ever have those considerations been conducted with an explicit recognition of the existence of two competing models. As a result, court decisions, public policies, and professional practices reflect confounding of the models. For example, in the landmark federal court case in the ninth district court in California, the case of *Larry P. v. Wilson Riles* (1979), Judge Peckam expressed a leaning toward a remedial model. He wanted educational treatments that did not leave misclassified (low scoring) students in dead-end cases that yielded no remedy for the difficulties. Yet his ruling allowed for tests to be used, if disproportionate placement could be eliminated, whether or not such tests led to valid remediation in classrooms.

Another example of the confounding is evident in attempts by the San Francisco Unified School District and the Chicago School District to move to a remedial model. Both districts, however, are still required to operate under state and national rules that were designed for a custodial model—that is, the use of labeling to get supplemental funding.

In recent months and years, many articles and position papers have been circulated that paint a picture of the state of the art in assessment and special education. Several important findings appear to have general support. Among them are the following:

- No consensus exists on what is a learning disability. Each state has its own definition. Nevertheless, the learning disabilities classification is the most rapidly expanding category in special education.

- Teaching approaches are similar when the treatment of children is provided in the various special categories.

- No evidence exists indicating that children who are placed in special categories achieve any better than they do in regular classes.

- No evidence exists to show that data from assessment are used in the design of day-to-day instruction in classrooms.

These findings raise serious questions about the whole system of assessment, placement, and treatment in special education. The National Academy of Science (NAS) panel report asserted forcefully that assessment's value, and by implication special education's value, must be justified on the basis of increased benefits for children. To date, the evidence for benefits has been hard to find, to put it mildly. Yet there are many developments in both assessment and remedial instruction as well as in the links between them that suggest a vital and valid role for professional educators.

If psychology and specialization in teaching are to play any meaningful and professional defensible role in the structure and operation of teaching and learning, those roles must meet the standard called for in the NAS report. Simply put, children must gain significant benefits from professionals' services or there is no need for those services.

Thus, teaching and learning, as well as psychology—the primary helping profession that supports teaching and learning—already are having great difficulty measuring up to the task of providing significant benefits to children. This is before and independent of issues of services to the African population. Bias or lack of validity in assessment and weak academic achievement results from teaching are merely more acute when African populations are served than when European populations are served.

These issues have been noted for many years. Almost always the complaints of African scholars and other plaintiffs have been ignored. Hence, litigation has been the primary vehicle for remediation of what to some is an intolerable situation. The African population shares some concerns with other ethnic groups such as Hispanics, Indians, Asians, and even some European immigrant populations. Africans also have experienced a unique set of circumstances. Several centuries of domination are directly responsible for many of the negative practices and results seen in psychology in education.

Two interrelated conditions explain some of the problems seen with African children in the schools. On the one hand, slavery, segregation, and racism are political variables that have educational components. Carter G. Woodson wrote the classic statements on how the education process was used to cripple Africans. On the other hand, independent of the political environment, cultural diversity presents its own necessities.

The calculated, sophisticated, pervasive, and deliberate miseducation process by the dominant European population toward the African population has been well documented and analyzed. However, few educators seem to understand its meaning and value in explaining the low academic performance of Africans in the schools today. The political process made use of cultural strategies! Primary among these cultural military strategies was the suppression and denial of African ethnicity. It was well understood that ethnic (cultural) identity produced solidarity and resistance by dominated populations. As a result, educators placed emphasis on the African's social class (socioeconomic status) or "racial" (pigment) identity. For many designers of the education process, this was a conscious strategy. At any time that Africans have sought to function collectively and independently on their own behalf, they have been brutally oppressed or diverted.

This whole thing would be of little interest here now except that this treatment of culture is at the base of difficulties in some aspects of professional practice. The cultural reality of African people remains strong in the majority of the African population. It is invisible even to many Africans who practice the culture. Yet the culture is there. It is meaningful. It is vital. But one must be in a position to observe it. This requires formal training in the academic disciplines that focus on cultural reality. Cultural linguistics and cultural anthropology are two examples. There already is a literature on African culture in these and other areas, yet not even a handful of psychologists or educators are aware of the literature. Fortunately, there are a few professionals who have lived the culture. Although they could benefit too from additional formal study, at least there is a greater chance that they will perceive the culture of African clients in a valid way, than if they were alien to it.

If the only goal is to raise student achievement, however, formal study and understanding of the mechanism of oppression or the functioning of culture, and the interaction between oppression and culture, may not always be necessary. The simple fact is that there have always been educators who had no trouble producing academic achievement with student populations, African and others, whether or not they were culturally distinct. Race, minority status, socioeconomic status, and other variables are not factors that predict what students can learn. More likely than not, they predict how schools will treat children.

The fact that traditionally low-performing students, poor African children in particular, can be taught so well by some teachers, Africans and others, without special training and without the help of psychologists and special educators, places a special burden on the psychologist and special educator to justify the need for special assessment and intervention.

Valid assessment is possible. By that I mean assessment that is tied validly to instructional strategies that work, instructional strategies that add power to ordinary successful teaching, instructional strategies that justify special assessment and intervention. However, professionals often must look beyond the mainstream of current professional practice to find them.

Sometimes it is good to listen to the professionals who have less vested interest in the status quo than is true of the majority of us. Some of the less vested professionals have much that is valid to offer. Some have already solved vexing "problems" related to student achievement. Some have unique points of view, unique analyses.

This book brings together the voices of some of those who have long experience, and who at a minimum have experienced African culture. Some have also begun the process of formal study of that culture. The field of psychology and special education desperately needs a book such as this one. The perspectives are special and, from my experience, add validity that is badly needed.

While the focus of the book is the African American student, the principles embedded in the approaches presented here can inform approaches to the study and service for any other ethnic group.

SUGGESTED READINGS

Backler, A., & Eakin (1993). *Every child can succeed.* Bloomington, IN: Agency for Instructional Technology.

Blagg, N. (1991). The special education paradox: Equity as the way of excellence. *Harvard Educational Review, 61,* 2.

Coles, G. (1987). *The learning mystique: A critical look at "learning disabilities."* New York: Fawcett Columbine.

Gould, S. J. (1981). *The mismeasure of man.* New York: Norton.

Guthrie, R. (1976). *Even the rat was white: A historical review of psychology.* New York: Harper and Row.

Hehir, T., & Latus, T. (Eds.). (1992). Special education at the century's end: Evolution of theory and practice since 1970. *Harvard Educational Review,* Reprint Series No. 23.

Heller, K., Holtzman, W., & Messick, S. (1982). *Placing children in special education: A strategy for equity.* Washington, DC: National Academy Press.

Hilliard III, A. G. (1976). *Alternatives to IQ testing: An approach to the identification of gifted "minorities" students* (Final Report), Special Education Support Unit, California State Department of Education. (ERIC Document Reproduction Service No. ED 147 009)

Hilliard III, A. G. (1991). *Testing African American students.* Morristown, NJ: Southern Education Foundation.

Hilliard III, A. G. (1992). Behavioral style, culture, and teaching and learning. *Journal of Negro Education, 61* (3), 370–377.

Hilliard III, A. G. (1993). The immigrant and the pedagog. In R. Samuda & S. L. Woods (Eds.), *Perspectives in immigrant and minority education.* New York: Lanham.

Holloway, J. (1990). *Africanisms in American culture.* Bloomington: Indiana University Press.

Holloway, J. E., & Vass, W. K. (1993). *The African heritage of American English.* Bloomington: Indiana University Press.

Hoover, M. R., Dabney, N., & Lewis, S. (1990). *Successful black and minority schools: Classic models.* San Francisco: Julian Richardson Associates.

Larry P. et al. v. Wilson Riles et al. (1979). C-71-2270 FRP, 9th Federal District Court of California.

Lidz, C. S. (1987). *Dynamic assessment interfactional approach to evaluating learning potential.* New York: Guilford.

Lipsky, D. K., & Gartner, A. (1990). *Beyond separate education: Quality education for all.* Baltimore: Brookes.

Nobles, W. W. (1973). Psychological research and black self-concept: A critical review. *Journal of Social Issues, 29*(1) 11–31.

Salomon, G. (Ed.). (1992). "Special Feature: New directions in technology-mediated learning." *Educational Psychologist, 27*(3).

Sizemore, B. A., Brossard, C. A., & Harrigan, B. (1983). *An abashing anomaly: The high achieving predominantly black elementary school executive summary.* Pittsburgh, PA: Pittsburg University, Department of Black Community Education. (ERIC Document Reproduction Service No. ED 236 275)

Skrtic, T. (1991). The special education paradox: Equity as the way to excellence. *Harvard Educational Review, 61*(2).

Spitz, H. H. (1986). *The raising of intelligence: Selected history of attempts to raise retarded intelligence.* Hillsdale, NJ: Erlbaum.

Wilson, A. (1991). *Awakening the natural genius of black children.* New York: African World InfoSystems.

Woodson, C. G. (1919). *The education of the Negro prior to 1861.* Washington, DC: The Associated Publishers. (Reprinted by A & B Books Publishers, Brooklyn, NY)

Woodson, C. G. (1933). *The miseducation of the Negro.* Washington, DC: The Associated Publishers. (Reprinted by Ams Press, New York)

Preface

This book is written from a proactive and productive perspective. We understand that the design and delivery of effective and authentic educational services to African American youth with exceptionalities necessitate a comprehensive understanding of conditions that can actively promote or inhibit access to quality services. The current state of affairs reveals that African American youth confront multidimensional educational problems within the educational system.

In writing this book, we reaffirm that traditional and contemporary civil rights reforms, general education reforms, and federal mandates designed to eliminate discriminatory practices or inappropriate special education placements have not resulted in systematic access to quality educational services for African Americans. In addition, we reaffirm that neither the traditional monocultural education approach nor the presently constructed multicultural approach places African American children as primary foci. There appears to be a deliberate omission or half-hearted inclusion of African Americans in education programs.

Traditionally, African Americans, perhaps more than any other visible racial group, have associated education with liberation and empowerment. The tremendous value placed on education historically in the African American community "as a way out" has been chronicled in African American literature, music, art, psychology, sociology, and education. Yet, the larger society has most often responded to the historical educational request of African Americans by labeling them as being a threat, as being maladaptive, as possessing deficits, or as being invisible. The portrayal of the African American as a positive and healthy human being represents an exception to the usual negative images generated by mainstream American society. This struggle has almost become endemic. Furthermore, efforts to ameliorate problems confronting African Americans with exceptionalities seem to be even more greatly thwarted by the usual negative assumptions and perspectives. In writing this book, our mission was not simple; however, as the saying goes, "It is a challenging job, but somebody has to do it."

We strongly believe that the goal of providing quality education to *all* African American students demands a serious reframing and redefining of theories, research questions, and educational models. It was imperative that professionals make a shift away from the usual negative, self-defeating, deficit perspectives used by too many educators, service providers, and other professionals. From our perspective, the first step toward the delivery of effective services for African American youth is for professionals to begin to change their conceptualization of "what is" and "what is not." Our effort has been toward promoting the actualization of positive, well-meaning education for African American learners.

Our initial goal in preparing this book was to bring together African American scholars in the fields of regular and special education, psychology, and communication. As we became more involved with this book, we discovered that we had to include not only scholars, but also teachers and service providers. We were able to combine both research and pedagogy, a rare occurrence in books today. Our conviction is that if the public school is to make a meaningful difference in providing quality education for African American students, systematic adoption and implementation of practices that afford African American students opportunities for academic excellence to their fullest potential must exist.

The information contained in this book builds on and refines historic ideas of other scholars. In addition, it presents original critical perspectives pertaining to theory and practice. We are convinced about the uniqueness of this book: This text represents the first work of its kind. It assumes an accurate, balanced, and holistic framework in presenting and examining salient issues related to African American learners with exceptionalities. As a whole, this book centers on the active involvement of African American families and resources within African American communities. We note that these factors are crucial in the provision of effective educational services for African American youth.

In Part I, Assessment and Identification Practices, the reader has the opportunity to explore and examine issues surrounding these practices for African American students with exceptionalities, including those with gifts and talents. Part II, Antecedent Factors Surrounding Complementary School Learning Environments, includes the following topics: self-concept models for African American exceptional students; communication patterns of African American learners; curricular and pedagogical procedures for African American learners with academic and cognitive disabilities; cultural framework for educating students classified as having emotional or behavior disorders; and the restructuring of teacher education programs to enhance leadership and teaching skills of professionals regarding inclusiveness for African Americans. In Part III, The Home–Community–School Pyramid Connection, the contributors investigate the roles of African American parents and communities. They address the restructuring of the balance of power and/or networking between professionals, African American parents, and communities. Finally, Part IV, Alternative Models, features two exemplary models presently providing effective educational services to African American youth. Embedded in this examination are the philosophical, curricular, and pedagogical bases for the Foreign Language Immersion and Cultural Studies School in Detroit, Michigan, and the Marcus Garvey School in Los Angeles, California.

As readers will discern, our fundamental and guiding catalyst for the creation of this book is our commitment to effective delivery of empowering services to African American youth and their families. We have provided readers with the philosophy, research, and practice outline that will lead to an enlightened, positive, and healthy perspective needed to appropriately guide the education of African American learners with exceptionalities. Undoubtedly, consultants, researchers, general and special educators, and graduate and undergraduate students will find this book an excellent resource.

Books of this nature are impossible without the wonderful support and assistance of colleagues and friends. We sincerely thank our contributors for their time and energy in writing their respective chapters. In addition, we thank Bob Algozzine, Dorothy Aramburo, Helen Bessent Byrd, Frances Carroll, Melvyn Cornelius, Grace Dawson, Doris Duncan, Geneva Gay, Cassondria Greene, Asa Hilliard, Milton Hinton, Rosa Lockwood, Earl Mello, Bruce Ramirez, Donald Wharry, Naomi Zigmond, and the members of The Council for Exceptional Children–National Black Caucus of Special Educators for their encouragement and dedicated support. Next, we thank Parthenia Smith Cogdell, Harold Dent, Ruth Diggs, Gladys Johnson, John Johnson, Reginald Jones, Robert Marion, LaDelle Olion, and Allen Sullivan for their pioneering efforts as advocates, researchers, scholars, and practitioners in the area of effective services for African American youth and their families. We want to acknowledge the thoughtful suggestions of Robert Marion and Veda Jairrels, who reviewed the manuscript. To the editorial staff of PRO-ED and James R. Patton, we thank you for having a 21st century vision. Finally, our sincere gratitudes go to our colleagues in our respective institutions, and especially to Roberta Reese and Karen Matthiesen at The University of Akron for their untiring secretarial support and Merlyn Persad, a committed and gifted graduate student.

B.A.F.
F.E.O.
J.M.P.

List of Contributors

Mary Gresham Anderson, PhD
Department of Special
  Education
The University of Maryland at
  College Park
College Park, MD 20742

Joy L. Baytops, MA
Programs for the Gifted
Office of Elementary and
  Middle School Instructional
  Services
Va. Department of Education
P.O. Box 2120
Richmond, VA 23216-2120

Helen Bessent Byrd, PhD
Department of Special
  Education
Norfolk State University
2401 Corprew Ave.
Norfolk, VA 23504

Ineala D. Chambers, MA
Foreign Language Immersion
  and Cultural Studies School
8210 Cameron St.
Detroit, MI 48211

Tempii Champion, MA
Department of Communication
  Disorders
University of Massachusetts
Amherst, MA 01002

Norma J. Ewing, PhD
Pullian Hall Room 27
Southern Illinois University
Carbondale, IL 62901

Bridgie Alexis Ford, PhD
Department of Counseling and
  Special Education
University of Akron
Akron, OH 44325-5007

Beth Harry, PhD
Department of Special
  Education
The University of Maryland at
  College Park
College Park, MD 20742

Janice Jackson, MA
Department of Communication
  Disorders
University of Massachusetts
Amherst, MA 01002

Asa G. Hilliard III, PhD
Urban Education
Department of Educational Pol-
  icy Studies and Department
  of Educational Psychology/
  Special Education
Georgia State University
Atlanta, GA 30303

Thomas E. Midgette, PhD
University of Arkansas
Department of Psychology
136 Graduate Education
    Building
Fayetteville, AR 72701

Festus E. Obiakor, PhD
Division of Psychology and
    Special Education
The Teachers' College
Emporia State University
Emporia, KS 66801

Anyim Palmer, PhD
Marcus Garvey School
9120 South Harvard
Los Angeles, CA 90047

James M. Patton, PhD
Academic Programs
The College of William
    and Mary
Williamsburg, VA 23185

Harry N. Seymour, PhD
Department of Communication
    Disorders
University of Massachusetts
Amherst, MA 01002

Gwendolyn Webb-Johnson, PhD
Department of Educational
    Curriculum and Instruction
Texas A&M University
College Station, TX 77843

PART I

Assessment and Identification Practices

CHAPTER ONE

Assessment of African American Exceptional Learners: New Strategies and Perspectives

Thomas E. Midgette

In this chapter I discuss assessment of African American exceptional learners. First I cover the historical, legal, and theoretical bases of assessment, highlighting relevant legislations and educational reforms. Next I examine the philosophies, purposes, and practices of assessment. Then I examine a paradigmatic shift in assessment from a deficit model to a difference model. In addition, I address issues relevant to assessment practices for African American children and outline the Programmatic Education Plan (PEP) and the importance of parent involvement.

ASSESSMENT: A DEFINITION

Assessment refers to the gathering of relevant information to help individuals make well-informed decisions. Assessment in education and psychology involves the collection of information that is relevant in making decisions regarding appropriate goals and objectives, teaching strategies, and program placement. Meaningful assessment ought to be an ongoing process, individualized and programmatic.

Educational and psychological assessments involve more than simply administering and scoring tests and reporting test scores.

They involve the careful analysis of the information provided by various instruments, techniques, tests, and other expert sources, which results in making appropriate decisions (Mehrens & Lehmann, 1991; Walsh & Betz, 1990). For assessment to be successful, it must be pragmatic and involve the use of culturally reliable and valid instruments and techniques, depending on the specific purpose for the assessment (Hilliard, 1980; Samuda, Kong, Cummins, Pascual-Leone, & Lewis, 1991). Before any assessment is done, two issues should be addressed: the legal and philosophical bases and prerequisites for testing.

Historical, Legal, and Theoretical Bases

Assessment or evaluation has been defined by the Phi Delta Kappa National Study Committee on Evaluation (1971) as "the process of delineating, obtaining, and providing useful information for judging decision alternatives" (p. xxv). Assessment involves professional judgment and allows teachers, parents, educators, and administrators to make a judgment about the desirability or value of something. Mehrens and Lehmann (1991) contended that "whoever makes a decision, and whether the decision be great or small, it should be based on as much accurate information as possible" (p. 5). They added that "assessors have the important responsibilities of (1) determining what information needs to be obtained, (2) obtaining accurate information, and (3) imparting that information in readily understood terms to the persons responsible for making the decisions—students, parents, teachers, college admissions officers, government officials, or judges" (Mehrens & Lehmann, p. 6). Often these decisions are classified as institutional and individualized. As Mehrens and Lehmann pointed out, these educational decisions based on assessment and evaluation (done correctly) should enhance learning because it aids both the teacher in teaching and the student in learning. In addition, assessment results ought to aid the parents in engaging their children in learning.

Potential Problems with Assessing the Exceptional Child

Mehrens and Lehmann (1991) identified at least five difficulties in evaluating children with exceptionalities:

First, most of the standardized aptitude and achievement tests have been normed using average children, that is, the norms have been developed on the basis of performance of children who are not at one extreme or the other, such as hyperactive, emotionally disturbed, or hard-of-hearing. Second, observation is one of the most important tools that can be used to diagnose children with exceptional needs. Observations can be challenging because each observer's view may be subjective, confounding and sometimes unreliable. Third, children with exceptionalities such as learning difficulties or behavior problems may vary greatly in their behavior. Fourth, when dealing with the exceptional child, one is dealing with the extremes, and thus from a traditional measurement perspective, may not be quite as reliable if obtained when dealing with the average child. Scores will reflect differences, but these scores are quite unreliable and difficult to interpret or imply causality. Fifth, another problem associated with testing of the exceptional child is the question whether modifying the directions or stimuli—such as using braille for the visually impaired; oral procedures for the blind; nonverbal directions for the deaf—affects the validity of the test. (pp. 437–438)

A movement toward equality of educational opportunities and access for the exceptional child came about through a series of landmark legal decisions which affirmed that all exceptional children have the right to the following: (a) an appropriate education, (b) due process of law, (c) nondiscriminatory testing and evaluation procedures, (d) a free public education, and (e) placement in the least restrictive environment.

Two landmark cases, *Diana v. State Board of Education* and *Larry P. v. Wilson Riles*, enacted into law that discriminatory tests not be used to diagnose and place African American, Asian, or Spanish-speaking exceptional children into classes for the mentally retarded. As a result of the above cases and other litigation, a number of laws resulted, such as P.L. 94-142 and P.L. 99-457 enacted in 1975 and 1986, respectively.

PUBLIC LAW 94-142

This law referred to as the Education for All Handicapped Children Act has been responsible for mainstreaming, evaluating, and providing education for exceptional students. The major provisions of P.L. 94-142 are as follows:

1. *Zero reject*—All children with disabilities between the ages of 3 and 21 are entitled to a free and appropriate public education.

2. *Early identification and intervention*—The early identification and intervention of children with disabilities between the ages of 3 and 5 are encouraged by providing financial incentive grants to those that provide such children with special education.

3. *Individualized Education Programs (IEPs)*—A statement is drawn up so that an individually prescribed educational program is developed by a school official, the child's teacher and parents, and, where possible, the child. This plan must identify the child's strengths and weaknesses, short- and long-term goals, and the services that will be used to reach those goals. In addition, the plan must indicate the amount of time the child is to spend in the regular classroom and the manner in which the child's progress is to be assessed and monitored.

4. *Nondiscriminatory evaluation*—All tests, scales, inventories, and assessment tools used to diagnose, classify, and place exceptional children must be free from racial and cultural bias. All testing is to be done in the child's native language.

5. *Least restrictive environment*—Exceptional and nonexceptional children will be taught together as long as possible. Exceptional children will be placed in special classes only when the type or severity of the exceptionality is such that it precludes them from obtaining maximally effective instruction in the regular classroom.

6. *Prereferral and screening*—All exceptional children must be identified through preliminary screening instruments.

7. *Regular evaluation and assessment*—Each child is to be evaluated regularly in the program.

8. *Diagnostic assessment by team*—The diagnostic assessment is to be done by a team composed of school psychologists, resource specialists, administrators, and teachers—with parent participation—using a variety of techniques.

9. *Due process*—This principle refers to a system of checks and balances that seeks to ensure the fairness of educational decisions and the accountability of both the professionals and the parents who make those decisions.

10. *Parental participation*—Ensures that parents are informed of decisions made about their children and encourages parental participation.

The implementation of P.L. 94-142 must involve programmatic efforts by teachers, counselors, administrators, and parents. According to P.L. 94-142 the IEP should be written by a child study team (which includes the teacher, parents or guardian, and child). The child study team has responsibilities in the following areas: identification, individual assessment, and development of an IEP. Identification involves using aptitude and achievement test data to differentiate whether a child is a slow learner or has learning disabilities. Individual assessment involves the teacher's gathering (supposedly) reliable and valid information about the child's competencies. This assessment usually includes the evaluation of the mental, physical, language, psychomotor, adaptive, and social functioning of the child. Procedures can include informal classroom assessments and standardized tests. The last responsibility of the regular classroom teacher after data gathering is the establishment of the child's educational objectives and instructional strategies.

Public Law 94-142 mandates the identification of all children eligible for special education services. It also specifies some explicit guidelines for the use of tests, such as the following:

1. IQ tests should not outweigh other test results in making diagnostic decisions.

2. IQ tests should be viewed as *only one* piece of evidence in making diagnoses and assessments.

3. IQ tests must be translated, modified, and administered in the child's native language without undue influence from linguistic differences.

Public Law 99-457

Among the recommendations in the Education of the Handicapped Act Amendments of 1986 was the need to identify and establish programs for infants and toddlers (children from birth to age 2) with disabilities. This amendment defines infants and toddlers with disabilities as children from birth to age 2 who are experiencing developmental delays, as measured by appropriate diagnostic instruments and procedures. This increased emphasis on early intervention has resulted in the creation of new developmental tests and the revision of several older ones.

Public Law 99-457 mandates the extension of services under P.L. 94-142 downward to the 3- to 5-year-old age group. Preschoolers with disabilities became entitled to a free and appropriate public education as of the 1990–1991 school year. Additionally, a federal Handicapped Infants and Toddlers Program was initiated for children from birth to 2 years of age. These provisions are broadbased and should facilitate more appropriate screening and identification of at-risk children, who are then more thoroughly evaluated for programs by trained professionals.

In order for at-risk and African American children to receive adequate services, a comprehensive public relations effort must be conducted in the African American communities to "find" these children experiencing handicapping conditions. According to Allen (1986) an effective Child Find program depends on the following two things:

1. Widespread publicity campaigns to make African American families aware of the services available

2. Selection of suitable screening tests

In addition, when implementing Child Find procedures, African American parents must be assured that neither children nor parental rights will be violated. Therefore, their participation must be holistic and developmental throughout the assessment and programming phases of the program.

ASSESSMENT: PHILOSOPHY, PURPOSES, AND PRACTICES

Educational and psychological assessment of exceptional students is the systematic process of gathering relevant information to make legal and instructional decisions about the provision of special services (McLoughlin & Lewis, 1990). Educational assessment ought to be an interdisciplinary effort to facilitate the learning of students with exceptionalities. This information gathering should entail psychologists, physicians, speech–language clinicians, physical therapists, teachers, and parents. Unfortunately, in actual practice, parents are often left out of the assessment process. They often are not treated as stakeholders and experts about their own children. In addition, factors affecting school learning, achievement, and overall development should be evaluated through culture-sensitive lenses.

Educational assessment of exceptional students has developed considerably over the past 80 years. It appears to have been influenced by trends in education, measurement, psychology, law, and social forces. McCloughlin and Lewis (1990) contended that these trends include the following:

1. One debate centers around whether intelligence is one entity or comprises a set of factors.

2. Many people wonder if intelligence is changeable. Most professionals consider intelligence as a product of the interaction between people and their environment and, therefore, as subject to change.

3. There are many abuses of assessment. Some assessments are too narrow in nature, and some discriminate on the basis of the student's language, ethnic or cultural background, or gender.

4. A particular challenge has been creating culture-fair procedures to assess minority students suspected of having an impairment or a disability.

MOVEMENT AWAY FROM A DEFICIT MODEL TO A DIFFERENCE MODEL OF ASSESSMENT: A PRIMER

The assessment process can be biased against individuals of a certain gender, race, linguistic background, culture, religion, or disability if it includes or excludes them from a service or opportunity because of their nondominant status in society. The five main purposes for educational assessment are screening, determining eligibility, planning a program, monitoring student progress, and evaluating a program. Testing and assessment models have often viewed difference as deviance. I support the movement away from this stereotypic paradigm, and make a call for an acceptance of a cultural-different versus a cultural-deficit model of assessment.

Unfairness and discrimination can occur in many ways in the assessment process for exceptional learners. Inappropriate referrals may be made because of a student's race, age, or sex. Test administrators or interviewers may mistreat, rush, intimidate, or otherwise abuse a student. Many of the concerns about discrimination in testing revolve around the technical inadequacies of the instruments and the way the data are used. Reliability and validity should be considered. Certain tests may be better measures for specific sex, age, or racial groups, and items on some tests may penalize students from different backgrounds. Major bias is possible when professionals interpret and apply test results. Various studies have noted that professionals tend to base special education placement decisions more on the student's sex, socioeconomic status, or physical appearance than on the test data (Ysseldyke, Algozzine, & Allen, 1981).

According to Sharma (1986), a proper perspective for the assessment of African American children should entail the following:

1. Testing should focus on discovering ways to help children attain their potential and it should deemphasize classification and labeling.

2. Multipurpose and multilevel test batteries, instead of a single score or a small number of scores, can provide a more accurate picture of the range of a child's intellectual abilities. Criterion-referenced testing should supplement the normative testing to evaluate the extent to which the child has met the educational objectives.

3. Standardized tests should be supplemented with information obtained through observing, interviewing, narrative self-reports, autobiographies, actual work samples, and anecdotal information. For educational classification and placement, along with the test scores, there should be a careful consideration of a child's adaptive behavior, classroom performance, medical and family history, and cultural pattern.

4. Culture-specific tests may assist in the assessment process of understanding the abilities and psychological processes by which African American children learn.

5. The learning difficulties experienced by African American children should be viewed by teachers as a result of cultural differences rather than as indices of inherent and incorrigible intellectual deficit. For example, limited command of the English language should not be viewed as evidence of deficient cognitive functioning and as a justification for placement in special classes for the mentally retarded.

6. Efforts should be made to increase minority children's motivation and interest in testing by helping them feel comfortable and at ease. An examiner who has knowledge and understanding of African American children's culture and community would be best able to alleviate their fear of testing and encourage them to take it seriously.

7. An assessor working with African American children should (a) examine personal feelings about the ethnic minority group, (b) understand the ethnic minority group's viewpoints, and (c) accept the goal of equal opportunity for all children and help them achieve their potential.

8. For a bilingual child, it is preferable to administer intelligence tests in both languages on the assumption that the ability repertoire in the separate languages would seldom overlap completely.

9. Scholastic aptitude should be developed through educational strategies such as the following: (a) instruction in the formation of concepts, (b) coaching in the acquisition of problem-solving skills, (c) training in study habits, and (d) development of motivation for academic achievement.

Sattler (1988) and others (Samuda et al., 1991; Sharma, 1986; Williams & Mitchell, 1991) have suggested that tests, and in particular intelligence tests, are often inappropriate in assessing ethnic minority children. Sattler (1988) identified major implications for assessing African American children:

1. Intelligence tests have a cultural bias. Standardized intelligence and aptitude tests have a strong, White, Anglo-Saxon, and middle class bias.

2. National norms are inappropriate for minorities. National norms based primarily on White, middle class, and Anglo-Saxon samples are inappropriate for use with ethnically and racially different children.

3. Ethnically and racially different children are generally less privileged and sophisticated in test-taking skills. For example, African American children are handicapped in taking tests because of (a) deficiencies in motivation, test practice, and reading; (b) failure to appreciate aspects of the test situation; and (c) limited exposure to White, middle class, and Anglo-Saxon culture.

4. The fact that most examiners are White has the effect of depressing the scores of ethnically and racially different children. Rapport and communication problems exist between White examiners and ethnically and racially different children. These problems interfere with the children's ability to respond to the test items.

5. Test results lead to inadequate and inferior education. Test results are the main reason why ethnically different children are segregated into special classes. These classes have inadequate curriculum and provide inferior education. Test results also create negative expectations in teachers.

Thus, I propose a programmatic approach to enhance the exceptional learner's chances of receiving adequate assessment and educational planning with involvement of the parent, child, teacher, assessors, nonblood kin, church, social service agencies, and other vital stakeholders.

THE PROGRAMMATIC EDUCATION PLAN (PEP)

Any assessment of ethnically or racially different exceptional students must involve programmatic efforts on the part of psychologists, teachers, administrators, parents, and other community stakeholders. Nondiscriminatory assessment and evaluation must occur if African American children with exceptionalities are to be adequately served and placed (Samuda, 1985; Samuda & Wolfgang, 1985). A nondiscriminatory assessment results in similar performance distributions across cultural groups that may differ from one another in language and dialect, value systems, information, and learning strategies (Alley & Foster, 1978; Bailey & Harbin, 1980). In addition, Oakland and Laosa (1977) contended that standardized tests are biased and unfair to persons from cultural and socioeconomic minorities because most tests reflect largely White, middle class values and attitudes. Test results may present minorities as less intelligent and adaptive on standardized procedures normed on White, middle class populations. Assessors who do not appreciate or understand the value of the culture of the African American child will not be able to elicit a level of performance that accurately reflects the child's underlying competence. Typical special education has a tendency to foster expectations that may be damaging by contributing to the self-fulfilling prophecy and rigidly shaping (via the IEP and adults' behavior) school curricula, educational achievement, and development. Meaningful input is required from "actual" concerned and authentic participants to develop a Programmatic Education Plan (PEP) (Figure 1.1) rather than the traditional or so-called Individualized Education Program (IEP). Usually, the development of the IEP is professionally driven, whereas the PEP is a collaborative effort on the part of the student learner, parent, and professionals. Input and evaluation involve all concerned and authentic stakeholders. All assessment should involve the stakeholders—those influenced most by the decision-

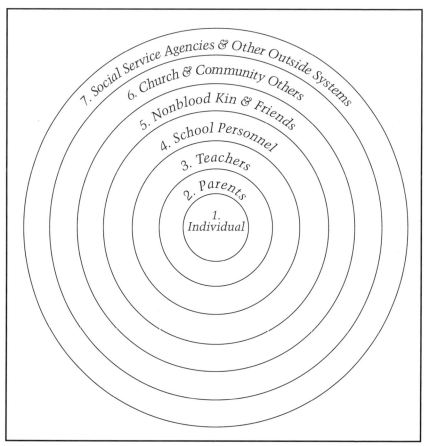

FIGURE 1.1. Programmatic Education Plan (PEP).

making process. Each level of participation is very important and interwoven to positively influence the child's PEP.

A Case for Involving Parents in the Assessment Process

Some social scientists, educators, and other evaluators have characterized African American children and families as devoid of strengths. Thus, when African American children are in transaction with schools, they often are viewed from a pathological and deficit model. Therefore, when assessing and intervening with

African American families and children, the goals for assessment and intervention with these families ought to be based on a *culturally different model*—that is, one specific to the culture(s) of this group (Boyd-Franklin, 1989; Hill, 1972; Pinderhughes, in press). Pinderhughes (1988) noted that "many African American families have been able to acquire culturally-positive structure for themselves, securing the necessary external and internal resources" (p. 217). However, it is clear that such functioning is in constant jeopardy of being undermined, because its existence is largely dependent upon successfully managing the dual position held by African American families, for which few supports exist.

Parent–Teacher Partnerships

The interdependent relationship between the school and the home in the education process underscores the importance of developing effective partnerships with parents. Parents play a critical role in laying the foundation for school learning, assessment, and instructional planning, as well as in maintaining a nurturing home environment in which it can flourish. As noted by Marion (1979), "historically and legally, the function of education in this country has been vested in state educational agencies and chiefly delegated to local districts; but in reality, the family is the primary educator" (p. 1). Consequently, when school personnel and parents fail to work together as a team, the effectiveness of the educational program is compromised (Diggs, 1974).

Attention to the task of developing effective parent–teacher partnerships is particularly critical when working with high-risk populations facing special challenges—as is true in the case of culturally diverse exceptional learners. Parents of these students not only must encounter the everyday stresses of parenting, but also must manage stresses associated with having a child identified as disabled, compounded by the stresses associated with being culturally different in a society that often views such differences as "deviant, difficult, inferior, or wrong" (Brantlinger & Guskin, 1985, p. 1). Because parents of culturally diverse exceptional learners face many unique challenges, educators seeking to develop collaborative relationships with these parents are likewise challenged.

Counterproductive Efforts

Despite the fact that parent involvement has been regarded as an integral part of planning and implementing special education services, as mandated by P.L. 94-142, a number of practices occur that are counterproductive in efforts to solicit parent participation (Baruth & Manning, 1992; Marion, 1979, 1980; Voltz, Leake, & Leake, 1992). One stifling practice is the use of a "menu-driven" approach, which attempts to force parents into predetermined roles over which they have little or no control in shaping. Marion (1979) indicated that "the parent of the disabled child generally has been expected to fulfill two roles in the educational planning process: (a) loyal supporter of the educational system, and (b) a recipient of reports concerning the child" (p. 1). In extreme versions of the menu-driven approach such as this, a prescribed set of behaviors is offered to parents as *the way* to interact with school personnel. In less extreme versions, parents are provided more options to choose from. However, there is one characteristic of these options worthy of note: They are determined by school personnel without input from parents. In this case, school professionals are dictating, unilaterally, what the nature of the relationship will be between parents and educators. If parents feel comfortable with the school's conceptualization of parent involvement, they may be inclined to abstain from any of the "menu items" made available by school personnel.

A second counterproductive practice in which school personnel sometimes engage is the "tracking" of parents (Voltz et al., 1992). This occurs when school officials decide, either consciously or subconsciously, that certain groups of parents are usually "concerned parents" (the redbirds) who want to be involved in the education of their children, while other groups of parents are usually "unconcerned parents" (the buzzards) who do not care to be involved in the education of their children. Based on these preconceived notions, interactions may occur with the redbirds that are qualitatively different from interactions that occur with the buzzards. Greater effort may be exerted to involve the redbirds, who are assumed to be concerned, than is exerted to involve the buzzards, who are assumed not to care. Likewise, the contributions, suggestions, and criticisms of the redbirds may be highly valued and taken more seriously than those of the buzzards. Consequently, some of the variance in the response of the redbirds and the buzzards to the school may be due, in part, to differences in the nature of the school's interactions with the redbirds and the buzzards from the outset. Teacher expectations can affect parent–teacher interactions in the same way that teacher expectations can affect student–teacher interactions (Baruth & Manning, 1992).

A third problematic area in promoting effective partnerships is the lack of sensitivity to cultural differences. This lack of sensitivity may be due to limited exposure to individuals whose cultural backgrounds vary from the dominant culture. In other cases, however, lack of sensitivity results from a reluctance to appreciate cultural differences, even though these differences are apparent. If the cultural differences of parents are not taken into account, however (regardless of the reason), the outlook for developing optimal partnerships with parents is grim (Baruth & Manning, 1992).

Beyond the factors in direct control of individual educators, such as those described above, are other factors not as easily manipulated, but which can nevertheless adversely affect interactions with parents. For example, parents themselves may harbor preconceived notions about schools and school personnel that are barriers to the development of successful home–school ties. This may occur for several reasons. If the parents of students with learning disabilities experienced school difficulties themselves, their attitudes toward their children's schools may be influenced by past negative experiences (Olion, 1988). Additionally, parents of culturally diverse exceptional learners may experience feelings of distrust for school personnel that result from the view that schools are merely extensions of a culture that they find oppressive and from which they feel alienated. The overinclusion of culturally diverse learners in certain categories of exceptionality serves to exacerbate these feelings. Marion (1980) stated that "the greatest reaction expressed by parents of culturally diverse disabled children has been one of anger and dismay at the policy of overinclusion of their children in classes for the mentally retarded and emotionally disturbed. The anger displayed by these parents has been a reaction against an educational system that they feel has promoted these two categories as the only appropriate depositories for their children" (p. 617).

Other socioeconomic realities over which educators have minimal control can negatively impact the development of partnerships with parents of culturally diverse exceptional learners. The fact that students from culturally diverse environments are disproportionately represented among the nation's poor is a factor that can predispose these parents to expend a greater proportion of their time, energy, and efforts in meeting basic survival needs than is the case for the average parent of the dominant culture. For example, it has been estimated that one third of African Americans live below the poverty line, in comparison to one tenth of Caucasians (Williams, 1986). Parents who find themselves economically challenged and struggling for survival may not have as much time and energy to devote to home–school relationships as would be desired, or perhaps expected (Kroth, 1985).

Building Effective Parent Involvement

Despite the special challenges associated with building partnerships with parents of culturally diverse exceptional learners, such partnerships can successfully be developed. A number of strategies have been found useful as a means to this end. Among the most important of these is building an atmosphere of respect, which is requisite to establishing the coequal relationship most conducive to effective collaboration (Shea & Bauer, 1991). The following are ways to develop an atmosphere of respect between teachers, professionals, and parents:

1. *Appropriate use of titles*—Use titles, such as Mr. or Ms., when addressing the parent, unless prompted by the parent not to do so (Baruth & Manning, 1992; Marion, 1979).

2. *Appropriate tone of voice*—Use a tone of voice that expresses courtesy and respect (Baruth & Manning, 1992; Marion, 1979).

3. *Use of understandable language*—Use language that the parent can understand, but avoid being condescending (Baruth & Manning, 1992; Marion, 1979).

4. *Authentic involvement of parents*—Listen to parents. Be mindful that there is at least as much opportunity for professionals to learn something helpful from parents as there is opportunity for the parents to learn something helpful from the professionals. Make sure to convey the message to par-

ents that their input is considered valuable (Olion, 1988). Involve parents from the very beginning in the development of assessment and instructional strategies for their children.

5. *Open and honest communication*—Communicate and respond to parents. Give parents straight answers to their questions. Act on their suggestions, when possible.

6. *Value of each parent*—Treat parents as individuals. Resist the stereotyping of parents based on race, ethnicity, socio-economic class, or any other characteristic. Recognize the diversity that occurs within cultural groups, as well as that which occurs between cultural groups (Cushner, McClelland, & Safford, 1992).

Establishing Collaborative Relationships

A second cluster of helpful strategies involves redefining parent involvement and focusing on developing relationships that are more collaborative in nature. Friend and Cook (1992) defined interpersonal collaboration as "a style for direct interaction between at least two coequal parties voluntarily engaged in shared decision-making as they work toward a common goal" (p. 5). This implies that parity must exist between members of the collaborative team. Presently, this parity is not characteristic of most parent–teacher interactions (Johnson & Pugach, 1992). The following strategies have been found effective in establishing collaborative relationships with parents:

1. *Avoid the menu-driven approach to parent involvement.*

2. *Make special efforts to establish rapport*—Parents in general, and culturally diverse parents in particular, may be intimidated by school personnel or by the institutional structure of the school (Baruth & Manning, 1992). Consequently, efforts should be made to reduce the impact of any parental anxieties associated with interaction with school personnel.

3. *Avoid crisis-driven parent–teacher relationships*—If interaction with parents occurs only when school crises do, parents may become defensive and resentful (Olion, 1988).

This practice does not facilitate the development of true partnerships, as it includes parents only when the school situation is deemed unmanageable by the educators involved.

Families, Parents, Schools, and Cultural Sensitivity

A final cluster of strategies relates to the issue of cultural sensitivity, which is requisite to the development of effective relationships with parents (Bailey & Winton, 1990; Shea & Bauer, 1991). As stated by Hilliard (1980), "respecting cultural diversity is not a benevolent act but a prerequisite for science and valid professional practice" (p. 588). The following factors should be considered in fostering cultural sensitivity:

1. *Being aware of cultural differences*—School personnel should become familiar with the cultural patterns of the students and families with whom they work in order to be responsive to ways these cultural patterns may affect the parent–teacher relationship (Shea & Bauer, 1991). Reading relevant professional literature, taking classes, and attending conferences also have been recommended (Baruth & Manning, 1992; Midgette & Meggert, 1991).

2. *Being aware of variance in family constellations*—Extended and blended families may play a significant role in the education and socialization of children from culturally diverse backgrounds (Bailey & Winton, 1990; Baruth & Manning, 1992).

3. *Being aware of the need of parental involvement in schools*—The development of effective collaborative relationships with parents of culturally diverse exceptional learners is integral to the task of planning and delivering appropriate educational services to this population of students.

4. *Being aware of negativistic depicting of African American families*—The role of education in African American families remains of paramount importance, despite negativistic depiction of African American children in the media and

low expectations held by some school personnel. As America's schools become increasingly culturally diverse, the importance of good parent–teacher collaborations is critical for effective schooling to take place. Working with culturally diverse exceptional learners will increase, and schools must develop more effective strategies to empower this segment of our student population.

Surely, African American families are extremely interested in the education of their children; however, without meaningful *invitations* to these families, parents, extended family members, and children, educators will lose another generation of valuable minds and resources. Educators must accept the notion that all students want to be affirmed as valuable, responsible, and capable of learning, and should be invited to actively participate in a meaningful and culturally relevant manner (Purkey, 1978).

The education of African American children in the 21st century requires multicultural, systemic analyses, assessments, Programmatic Education Plans versus Individualized Education Programs, interventions, and supports by parents, families, teachers, counselors, other school personnel, and communities to make a difference required in today's multicultural society (Bates, 1990; Croninger, 1990; Greenbaum, 1990; Mimms, 1990). African American families must all be invited and welcomed to schools to make a difference.

CONCLUSION

The issues of test fairness and test bias in the United States have been debated since the introduction of mental tests to the country following the pioneering work of Alfred Binet in France (Johnson, 1988). More recently, educators have been pushing for equitable educational opportunities for children from different cultures. More programmatic parent involvement is indicated for African American exceptional learners in assessment and instructional planning.

Psychological and educational assessment can serve to hinder or deter educational advancement by ethnically or racially different children (Kamin, 1974). A common source of problems with assessment of African American exceptional learners is the tendency to overlabel, overidentify, and overplace them in special education classes (Gibbs, 1988; Gibbs & Huang, 1990; Hilliard, 1976; Reed, 1988; Samuda, 1975; Samuda et al., 1991). In addition, Gay and Abrahams (1973) contended that African American children have been subjected to psychological and educational testing, diagnostic procedures, and numerous other methods of assessing educational capabilities which are ethnocentric (p. 330). Consequently, Gay and Abrahams called for significantly more reliable and valid assessment, and assessors must develop testing protocols that are culturally relevant for African American children. Clearly, to make claims of their usefulness for African American exceptional learners, tests must measure what they intend to and over repeated testings. The best solution seems to be to use test information where appropriate, change tests dramatically where needed, and discontinue use where warranted.

Educational assessment and testing must move beyond the "Testing Game" (Williams & Mitchell, 1991), in which the African American exceptional learner is a pawn. The ultimate goal is to increase the achievement of children and not limit the scope of their educational experiences. Programmatic Education Plans are suggested to truly involve the parent, teacher, community, and various significant others in the educational planning of African American exceptional children.

REFERENCES

Allen, K. E. (1986). *Mainstreaming in early childhood education.* Albany, NY: Delmar.

Alley, G., & Foster, C. (1978). Nondiscriminatory testing of minority and exceptional children. *Focus on Exceptional Children, 9,* 1–14.

Bailey, D. B., & Harbin, G. L. (1980). Nondiscriminatory evaluation. *Exceptional Children, 46,* 590–596.

Bailey, D. B., & Winton, P. J. (1990). Families of exceptional children. In N. G. Haring & L. McCormick (Eds.), *Exceptional children and youth* (pp. 491–514). Columbus, OH: Merrill.

Baruth, L. G., & Manning, M. L. (1992). *Multicultural education of children and adolescents.* Boston: Allyn & Bacon.

Bates, P. (1990, Spring). Parents and schools: Partners for equity. *Equity Coalition, 1,* 1–2.

Boyd-Franklin, N. (1989). *Black families in therapy: A multisystems approach.* New York: Guilford Press.

Brantlinger, E. A., & Guskin, S. L. (1985). Implications of social and cultural differences for special education with specific recommendations. *Focus on Exceptional Children, 18,* 1–12.

Croninger, B. (1990, Spring). African American parents. Seeing them as colleagues, neighbors and friends? *Equity Coalition, 1,* 8–9.

Cushner, K., McClelland, A., & Safford, P. (1992). *Human diversity in education.* New York: McGraw-Hill.

Diggs, R. W. (1974). Education across cultures. *Exceptional Children, 40,* 578–584.

Friend, M., & Cook, L. (1992). *Interactions: Collaboration skills for school professionals.* New York: Longman.

Gay, G., & Abrahams, R. D. (1973). Does the pot melt, boil, or brew? Black children and White assessment procedures. *Journal of School Psychology, 4*(11), 330–340.

Gibbs, J. T. (1988). *Young, Black and male in America: An endangered species.* Dover, MA: Auburn House.

Gibbs, J. T., & Huang, L. V. (1990). *Children of color: Psychological interventions.* San Francisco: Jossey-Bass.

Greenbaum, J. L. (1990, Spring). The parent involvement checklist. *Equity Coalition, 1,* 12–13.

Hill, R. B. (1972). *The strengths of Black families.* New York: Emerson Press.

Hilliard, A. G. (1976). *Alternatives to IQ testing: An approach to the identification of the gifted in minority children* (Report No. 75175). San Francisco: San Francisco State University.

Hilliard, A. G. (1980). Cultural diversity and special education. *Exceptional Children, 46,* 584–589.

Johnson, L. J., & Pugach, M. C. (1992). Continuing the dialogue: Embracing a more expansive understanding of collaborative relationships. In W. Stainback & S. Stainback (Eds.), *Controversial issues confronting special education: Divergent perspectives* (pp. 213–222). Boston: Allyn & Bacon.

Johnson, S. (1988). Test fairness and bias: Measuring academic achievement among Black youth. *The Urban League Review, 11,* 76–92.

Kamin, L. J. (1974). *The science and politics of IQ.* Potomac, MD: Erlbaum.

Kroth, R. L. (1985). *Communicating with parents of exceptional children.* Denver, CO: Love.

Marion, R. L. (1979). A systematic model approach: Focus on assessment. *Exceptional Children, 10,* 1–15.

Marion, R. L. (1980). Communicating with parents of culturally diverse–exceptional children. *Exceptional Children, 46,* 616–623.

McLoughlin, J. A., & Lewis, R. B. (1990). *Assessing special abilities* (3rd ed.). New York: Merrill.

Mehrens, W. A., & Lehmann, I. J. (1991). *Measurement and evaluation in education and psychology* (4th ed.). New York: Holt, Rinehart and Winston.

Midgette, T. E., & Meggert, S. (1991). Multicultural counseling instruction: A challenge for faculties in the 21st century. *Journal of Counseling and Development, 70*, 136–141.

Mimms, E. M. (1990, Spring). Welcoming parents into the schools. *Equity Coalition, 1*, 19–20.

Oakland, T., & Laosa, L. M. (1977). Professional, legislative, and judicial influences on psychoeducational assessment practices in schools. In T. Oakland (Ed.), *Psychological and educational assessment of minority children* (pp. 21–51). New York: Bruner/Mazel.

Olion, L. (1988). Enhancing the involvement of Black parents of adolescents with handicaps. In A. A. Ortiz & B. A. Ramirez (Eds.), *Schools and the culturally diverse exceptional student: Promising practices and future directions* (pp. 96–103). Reston, VA: Council for Exceptional Children.

Phi Delta Kappa National Study Committee on Evaluation (1971). *Educational evaluation in decision-making.* Ithasca, IL: F. E. Peacock.

Pinderhughes, E. B. (1988). Treatment with middle class families: A systemic perspective. In A. F. Coner-Edwards & J. Spurlock (Eds.), *Black families in crisis: The middle class* (pp. 215–226). New York: Bruner/Mazel.

Pinderhughes, E. B. (in press). *Teaching cultural sensitivity: Ethnicity, race, and power at the cross-cultural treatment interface.* New York: Free Press.

Purkey, W. W. (1978). *Inviting school success.* Belmont, CA: Wadsworth.

Reed, R. J. (1988). Education and achievement of young Black males. In J. T. Gibbs (Ed.), *Young, Black and male in America: An endangered species.* Dover, MA: Auburn House.

Samuda, R. J. (1975). *Psychological testing of American minorities: Issues and consequences.* New York: Dodd, Mead.

Samuda, R. J. (1985). Current methods in the assessment of minorities: A critique. In R. J. Samuda & A. Wolfgang (Eds.), *Intercultural counseling and assessment: Global perspectives* (pp. 127–140). Toronto: Hogrefe.

Samuda, R. J., Kong, S. L., Cummins, J., Pascual-Leone, J., & Lewis, J. (1991). *Assessment and placement of minority students.* Toronto: Hogrefe.

Samuda, R. J., & Wolfgang, A. (Eds.). (1985). *Intercultural counseling and assessment: Global perspectives.* Toronto: Hogrefe.

Sattler, J. M. (1988). *Assessment of children.* San Diego: Author.

Sharma, A. (1986). Assessment strategies for minority groups. *Journal of Black Studies, 17*, 11–124.

Shea, T. M., & Bauer, A. M. (1991). *Parents and teachers of children with exceptionalities.* Boston: Allyn & Bacon.

Voltz, D. L., Leake, D., & Leake, B. (1992, February). *Family profiles of high-performing vs. low-performing African American students.* Paper presented at the meeting of the Association of Teacher Educators, Orlando, FL.

Walsh, W. B., & Betz, N. E. (1990). *Tests and assessment* (2nd ed.). Englewood Cliffs, NJ: Prentice-Hall.

Williams, R. (1986). *White America, they stole it. Black America, you must return it.* New York: HEMA Publishing.

Williams, R. L., & Mitchell, H. (1991). The testing game. In R. L. Jones (Ed.), *Black psychology.* Berkeley, CA: Cobb and Henry.

Ysseldyke, J. E., Algozzine, B., & Allen, D. (1981). Participation of regular education teachers in special education team decision making: A naturalistic investigation. *Elementary School Journal, 82,* 160–165.

CHAPTER TWO

Identifying and Transforming the Potential of Young, Gifted African Americans: A Clarion Call for Action

James M. Patton and Joy L. Baytops

A cursory review of the literature in the field of gifted education reveals a voluminous collection of research articles, books, and manuscripts that contain a plethora of theory, speculation, and basic and applied research results related to the education of learners with gifts and talents. With a few exceptions, however, only recently have the unique needs and concerns of young (ages 4 to 14), gifted African Americans been addressed seriously by those writing about exceptionally gifted and talented people (Baldwin, 1984, 1987; Frasier, 1979; Hilliard, 1976; Jenkins, 1936; Renzulli, 1973; Torrance, 1969). Of this limited culturally focused research and practice, most have been centered on assessment and identification issues, to the exclusion of philosophical and conceptual issues related to the race, culture, and ethos of African American children and youth with gifts. In too many instances, policies and practices in gifted education appear to manifest a belief system that suggests that young, African American learners do not possess the abilities, aptitudes, or personality characteristics usually ascribed to the gifted label. These cultural-deficit merchants believe that the disproportionately small percentage of giftedness identified in African American populations (Zappia, 1989) is a result of the limited capacity of these learners to demonstrate behaviors associated with giftedness.

Still other contemporary researchers, thinkers, and writers of the gifted experience generally plead with their readers to accept the hypothesis that young, gifted African Americans exist and can be found if only a certain procedure, test, or the like is used. Apart from a few exceptions offered in this chapter, most current assessment and measurement theory evolves from a paradigm that esteems cognitive traits of upper and middle income European Americans (Ford, Winborne, & Harris, 1991; Gould, 1981; Hilliard, 1976; Patton, 1992), while eschewing and denigrating manifestations of giftedness in various African American cultural contexts. Thus, remnants of the still silent presumption held by too many practitioners and theoreticians in gifted education persist: that gifted and talented African Americans represent an anomaly that rarely exists. Accordingly, we believe that this continuing fixation with a host of activities associated with identification typifies, in part, a ruse by some educators to deny the existence of the multiple and complex gifts and talents possessed by African Americans and to avoid the need to nurture their development once identified. According to Zappia (1989), although African Americans comprise approximately 16.5% of the population of public school–age children, they make up only 8.4% of those identified as gifted.

In this chapter, we wish to communicate three messages. First, this society, and relatedly gifted education, must accept the reality that young, gifted African Americans exist well beyond current levels of identification and remain unserved by programs designed for gifted learners. Second, building upon the work of African American scholars such as Hilliard (1976), Rashid (1981), and others, the education of African American youth, especially those with special gifts and talents, cannot be fully realized without using their culture as a bridge to enhance gifts and talents. Third, we provide information to make teachers, administrators, parents, families, the African American community, and the general populace more knowledgeable of and involved with certain assessment, identification, and curriculum and instruction interventions and processes designed to transform the educational, social, psychological, and subsequent economic power of gifted African American learners.

FINDING THEM: TOWARD A HOLISTIC MODEL

Efforts aimed at identifying and serving the needs of young, highly gifted and talented African Americans would be enhanced if identification were conducted within the context of a comprehensive and dynamic giftedness construct that includes (a) assessment and identification, (b) authentic and comprehensive curriculum and instruction based on assessment results, (c) professional development and empowerment programs, and (d) parent and extended-family empowerment efforts (Ford & Harris, 1991; Frasier, 1991; Kitano, 1991; Patton, 1992; Richert, 1985).

Also important to this model is the development and sustenance of efforts that link elements within each component with one another. Isolated, disconnected, and piecemeal identification and service delivery approaches, no matter how well intentioned, do not result in the development of African Americans with gifts and talents. Furthermore, each of these components must advance along with several important overlays. Specifically, each must carry historical and contemporary considerations of race, culture, oppression, power, and socioeconomic factors. The subsequent narrative contains a discussion of the components identified as essential to this holistic approach and should provide helpful insights into developing and transforming the potential of young, gifted and talented African American learners.

The Search: Shaping Belief Systems

Traditional practice in schools regarding gifted programs places teachers in the role of initial identifiers of giftedness among students. However, parents and extended family members should also play important roles in the processes involved in identifying gifts and talents among young African American learners. In fact, a recent study by Ward, Ward, and Patton (1992) found that African American students identified as gifted and talented by their parents were the strongest and most eligible candidates for a federally funded gifted and talented program, Project Mandala (Patton, Prillaman, McLaughlin, & VanTassel-Baska, 1989). This finding is generally supported in the literature. Identification of individuals for programs for the gifted and talented usually involves a sequence of activities that include nomination, screening, assessment, identification, and at times intervention planning. Parents, equipped with certain knowledge, skills, and attitudes, can bring balance to this power equation.

Although most often parents of African American learners want their children's gifts and talents to be identified and nurtured, some have mixed emotions about certain school-based gifted and talented programs. For example, some African American parents reject having their child considered for a particular gifted program because (a) most include a disproportionately high number of non–African American students (even in locales with predominant African American student enrollment in public schools), and thus are less likely to incorporate values and processes that complement African American culture; (b) many programs are perceived to be "elitist" in their orientation, function, and presentation; (c) some professionals associated with these programs are too often perceived to be "smug," indifferent, and noninvitational; and (d) these programs often utilize homogeneous ability grouping.

To many of these parents and students, considerations of admittance to a gifted program often entail choosing between (a) self and one's African American values and culture and (b) the European-centered values, ethos, and conventions that provide the foundations of most gifted programs in the United States. This choice, even today, illustrates what DuBois (1961) referred to as the duality of the "two warring souls" of African Americans. On the one hand, African Americans generally grow and develop within an African American cultural context, yet, on the other hand, they must meet the requirements, norms, and conventions of a larger society mainly defined, governed, and controlled by European Americans.

Contrariwise, given the fact that African Americans are a heterogeneous population, some African American parents may advocate for their children to be in gifted and talented programs for some of the same reasons above, albeit given an opposite interpretation. Some African Americans believe that the underrepresentation of African Americans in gifted programs provides legitimacy to these programs. Accordingly, they relish that their son or daughter would be in a predominately all-White gifted class environment. Thus, the preference for exposing their children to what many consider a more suitable preparatory environment to meeting the demands, norms, and standards of mainstream culture outweighs considerations related to racial identity and group membership. Thus, African American parents often bring to the assessment, identification, and intervention processes this "mixed baggage" that has been shaped by their culture, race, degree of mainstream, societal assimilation, and experiences with schools and other institutions in U.S. society.

Teachers, both Black and White, also bring some baggage to these processes. Some have a great deal of understanding, knowledge, respect, and positive belief systems concerning African Americans, their race, culture, and ethos. Often, these individual teachers go beyond their expected role definitions and responsibilities and impose even higher standards and expectations upon themselves and their students. Such expectations allow these teachers to work actively and forcefully toward identifying and nurturing the development of exceptionally gifted and talented African Americans. It is from these types of teachers that one finds real and devoted advocates for gifted and talented African Americans.

On the other hand, some teachers bring negative baggage with them to the identification and intervention processes. Such individuals tend to bring narrow, ethnocentric beliefs, attitudes, and predispositions, or xenophobic attitudes to the identification and intervention processes that will inhibit or prevent them from recognizing and validating gifts and talents in populations of young African Americans, even if such talents were obvious. Unfortunately, too many teachers in this latter category do not wish to believe in the existence of gifted and talented African Americans, let alone the existence of these learners in numbers beyond the level documented by this nation's schools. To them the notion of gifted and talented African Americans is largely an oxymoron. Furthermore, in too many instances, it is these same types of teachers who view their role or responsibility as that of maintaining the extreme racial inequities that exist in gifted and talented programs across this nation.

Not all teachers and parents fit so neatly into either one of these categories. Given the large amount of within-group differences, teacher and parent behaviors often occur at all points along a continuum, with one end reflecting a culturally complementary power-enhancing orientation, the other a power-negating assimilationist orientation. Both teachers and parents of African American youth are challenged to wrestle with beliefs, attitudes, behaviors, and the lack of knowledge that inhibit appropriate identification and nurturance of gifts and talents existing in these youth.

So how do teachers and parents unite to meet this most important societal challenge—the identification and development of gifts and talents among young African Americans? Where is the common ground? Several guideposts have been advanced that claim to have met this challenge.

The Search: Nominating and Screening

The search for overlooked populations of young, gifted and talented African Americans must be conducted within the context of an understanding of the uniquely complicated culture, values, and worldview of African Americans. Frasier (1990), Gardner (1983), Patton (1992), and Sternberg (1991) reminded professionals that the use of nontraditional screening and assessment instruments and procedures provides an alternative avenue in the search for larger numbers of gifted African Americans. Specifically, the work of these individuals and Baldwin (1984, 1987), Harris and Ford (1991), Hilliard (1976), Renzulli (1973), and Torrance (1977) suggests the need to develop assessment and identification systems, instruments, and practices that involve multimodal approaches to assessment and identification and are contextually and culturally based. The observation about one's belief system cannot be overemphasized. As noted, before teachers or parents can identify an African American as being gifted, they must believe that this reality is possible and most probable. For a host of reasons, some African American parents have not formed belief systems that allow them to recognize the unique gifts and talents of their son or daughter, to advocate for their appropriate identification, and to insist on proper, appropriate, challenging, and nurturing programming once the child has been identified. The same can be said of some teachers. On the other hand, some parents and teachers who internalize positive belief systems are forming groups and coalitions for the purpose of sharing these affirming beliefs and experiences with others.

As an example, the Project Mandala parent checklist provided in Appendix 2A allows "affirming" parents to nominate their children to gifted programs. This represents one of the first steps in the identification process.

Likewise, the *Renzulli Hartman Scales (Ren*zulli, Hartman, & Callahan, 1971) have been helpful in the nomination and screening phase of the gifted and talented identification process. Further work by Renzulli (1978) led to the development of the "three-ring" conception of giftedness, based on the belief that giftedness represents an interaction of multiple, dynamic traits displayed within the context of one's environment. Specifically, above-average ability, task commitment, and creativity were identified by Renzulli as characteristic of gifted individuals regardless of background or ethnicity. This triad model has been used as the basis for the development of nomination and screening tools within local districts across the country.

Hilliard (1976) and Torrance (1977) have developed and advocated the use of teacher screening checklists and rating scales based upon assessing the distinct social and psychological indicators of giftedness within the normative structure of African American culture. Inclusion of these rating scales and checklists at the nomination stage of the assessment process is likely to increase the number of African Americans subsequently identified as gifted (Frasier, 1989).

At the request of the San Francisco Unified School District, Hilliard (1976) devised prescreening devices that would recognize the "basic African American cultural contributions to patterns of human behavior" (p. 14). Accordingly, his resulting checklists, the "Who" and "O," are based upon the uniqueness and commonalities in the deep-structure culture of African Americans. These checklists emphasize synthetic–personal stylistic characteristics of African American learners, including such behaviors as creative improvisation, divergent experimentation, inferential reasoning, and harmonious relationships with nature and one's environment.

Using a curriculum-based assessment approach in his creativity workshops, Torrance (1969) identified a set of behaviors of African Americans that provided the basis for the *Checklist of Creative Positives* (CCP) (Torrance, 1977). Torrance identified a "set of characteristics that helped to guide the search for strengths of culturally different students for giftedness among such students"

(p. 25). The subsequent 18 characteristics became known as "creative positives." Torrance argued that indicators of these creative positives, such as verbal fluency and spontaneity in role-playing situations, creative type of parables and story telling, use of expressive speech, responsiveness to the kinesthetic, and originality of ideas in problem solving, to name a few, could best be assessed through observational techniques with results recorded on a checklist. The CCP has enjoyed wide use and represents another pre-screening instrument that would increase the number of African Americans considered for gifted and talented programs (see Frasier, 1989; VanTassel-Baska, 1989; VanTassel-Baska, Patton, & Prillaman, 1989).

It is important that teachers and parents who recognize the gifts and talents of African American learners come together with like-minded individuals uniting to actualizing these beliefs and values through concerted, prolonged, and focused actions. Thus, as teachers engage in the nominating and screening process, it has been found that the number of African American children identified as gifted and talented increases if a teacher-nomination procedure is augmented during the screening phase with nominations from multiple data sources from within and outside the school setting (Blackshear, 1979; Davis, 1978; Kitano & Kirby, 1986; VanTassel-Baska et al., 1989). These additional data sources should include nominations from community leaders, the individual student, and peers.

More aggressive and focused early efforts to find gifted children would include the following:

1. Establishing contact with African American spiritual leaders and ministers, African American–owned major print and nonprint media, boy's and girl's clubs, YWCAs, and the like. These efforts should be used to build the candidate pool and provide information related to nurturance once students are identified.

2. In urban and suburban areas, establishing broad and continuous contact with African American Greek-letter fraternities and sororities, educational organizations, Masonic organizations, social and professional organizations, political organizations, and self-help organizations. All African American

Greek-letter fraternities and sororities and social organizations require their members to pursue very active individual and collective social action agendas. Therefore, these organizations are always looking for an education "project" that will enhance the development of young African Americans, especially those who have gifts and talents.

3. Casting this identification and nurturing net in the rural communities poses additional challenges. The rural communities in the South provide the roots of African adaptations to American culture. The traditional values of family, community, religion, and hard work are readily apparent in these African American communities. In addition to making the type of contacts previously discussed, educators should build relationships with the leadership and members of Ruritan Clubs, 4-H Clubs, NAACP groups, the Agriculture Extension Service, and the formal and informal communication networks in existing rural African American communities.

Baytops (1994) found that the African American community, particularly the Black church and extended family members, has historically provided substantial support to African American families in the educational and socialization processes. This finding is supported by Clark (1983), Hale-Benson (1986), Kitano (1991), and others who have determined that the role of grandparents and other significant adult role models has been very important in enabling gifted learners from socioeconomically disadvantaged and culturally diverse backgrounds to achieve their educational goals. Therefore, it would be wise for educational practitioners to tap the resources of the total African American community in the search for gifted students.

The creation of carefully focused and financed school–business partnerships that center on talent identification and development of young African Americans, especially males, would benefit schools, businesses and industry, and ultimately the collective economy and power of African Americans and this nation. African American entrepreneurs and community leaders have an opportunity to lead the way in developing coalitions among businesses, schools, institutions, and organizations in the African American communities and social organizations for the express purpose of identifying and empowering the gifts and talents of young African American students.

Identification: Expanding and Demystifying the Process

Not only can teachers and parents play significant roles in the advocacy and nominating phases of assessment, they also have critical roles to play in later assessment phases designed to gather and evaluate data, products, and other representations of the potential gifts and talents of African Americans. Until recently, the use of traditional norm-referenced intelligence tests has not yielded the numbers of identified gifted and talented African American learners thought to exist in the nation's schools. Furthermore, the conventional and routine use of these tests often results in their serving as the single and/or most potent criterion used in the identification process in most of this nation's school systems. Data from current research suggest, however, that the combined use of certain test results can be a valid and reliable source of data for identifying giftedness in culturally diverse learners (Ward, Ward, Landrum, & Patton, 1992). Alternative processes and instruments do exist. If used collectively, they have been proven superior to the sole use of traditional intelligence tests.

Most recently, profile approaches have been used in attempts to increase the quality and quantity of identified gifted and talented African Americans. These approaches have their origins in the earlier matrices approach advocated and used by Baldwin (1984) and Dabney (1983). The work of Frasier (1990) has placed the profile approach at the center of attempts to identify gifted and talented African Americans.

A major assumption of any profile approach embraces a pluralistic view of giftedness, which recognizes the existence of multiple domains for the manifestation of gifts and talents (aptitude, achievement, creativity, leadership, etc.). Seemingly, this approach requires the use of multiple quantitative and qualitative measures to obtain relevant data in the various domains of giftedness. A profile system allows for and recognizes the possibility of manifestations of giftedness in one specific domain of intelligence while allowing for average or above-average performance in other domains.

The *Frasier Talent Assessment Profile* (F-TAP) (Frasier, 1990) allows the user to collect quantitative and qualitative data on individual students that provide an array of information from multiple sources. The resultant individual "biography," or profile, includes information from which identification and selection decisions can be made. Judgment is based, then, upon multiple and broad areas of indicators of giftedness or potential giftedness (Frasier, 1990).

A recent study designed to determine the reliability of a profile identification approach, similar to that proposed by Frasier, has successfully established such reliability (Ward, Ward, Landrum, & Patton, 1992). Furthermore, this research, conducted as part of Project Mandala, also found that a profile approach was not influenced by race or culture. The use of the profile system in Project Mandala resulted in identifying large numbers of gifted, young African Americans (children aged 4 to 8 and 11 to 14) who exhibited disparate gifts and talents across the previously cited domains of intelligence. Much work remains to be done to design appropriate and effective measures of aptitude, achievement, and creativity that can be used for identifying giftedness among African Americans. However, the alternative use of certain existing measures represents improvements to the use of cutoff scores in traditional intelligence tests.

As previously stated, the use of traditional, norm-referenced intelligence tests has not yielded the numbers of gifted African American students that are known to exist in this nation's schools. Nonassimilated African Americans are especially missed by conventional instruments and approaches used in the identification process. However, some intelligence tests, as a result of their conceptual, technical, and cultural sensitivity attempts, show some promise. For example, according to a recent national study by VanTassel-Baska et al. (1989), as well as the work of Baska (1986) and Frasier (1989), the *Standard, Advanced,* and *Coloured Progressive Matrices* (Raven, 1938, 1947a, 1947b) are nonverbal intelligence tests used by local school systems nationwide in attempts to increase the number of African American learners in gifted programs. Although the use of these tests alone for identification purposes is insufficient to recommend their use, they are appealing when used with African American learners for the following reasons: their high to moderate positive correlations with other intelligence and achievement tests; their high concurrent validity of use with African Americans (Court & Raven, 1982; Sattler, 1982;

Valencia, 1979); and their predominantly nonverbal administration and content. Other attractive features of these tests are their quick and simple administration, which is untimed, and the option of individual or group administration. These tests have been faulted because of the unidimensional definition of intelligence upon which they have been built.

Another recent aptitude measure, the *Matrix Analogies Test*, both the expanded and short forms (MAT-EF and MAT-SF) (Naglieri, 1985), is purported to be normed on a large and representative national sample of individuals with regard to gender, race, ethnicity, socioeconomic status, and geographic region. This test has been reported to have a high degree of internal reliability and evidence of validity (Naglieri & Prewett, 1990). It measures nonverbal ability through the use of figural matrices and appears to be useful with individuals whose scores may be influenced by speed (Naglieri & Prewett, 1990). The MAT-EF has been employed recently as a part of an assessment protocol used in a federally funded project designed to identify gifted African American learners. Studies conducted by Ward, Ward, and Patton (1992) found that large numbers of previously unidentified gifted African American learners (aged 4 to 13) were identified by the MAT-EF. In fact, the MAT-EF provided a higher estimate of general intellectual ability for a substantial portion of African Americans than any other aptitude measure employed in the assessment protocol. Furthermore, the MAT-EF correlated with the *Wechsler Intelligence Scale for Children–Revised* and the *Peabody Individual Achievement Test–Revised*, resulting in validating the instrument as a nonverbal measure of general intellectual ability (Ward, Ward, & Patton, 1992).

Frasier (1989) reported that considerable evidence suggests that the *Kaufman Assessment Battery for Children* (K-ABC) (Kaufman & Kaufman, 1983) "is fair to minorities" (p. 281). As a group, African Americans have generally scored higher on the K-ABC than on other more traditional intelligence tests. The developers attribute these higher scores to the test's emphasis on a multidimensional concept of intelligence and "de-emphasis of applied skills and verbal expression" (Kaufman & Harrison, 1986, p. 151). Although these tests have yielded higher scores for African Americans, they have been faulted for their low ceiling for gifted populations (Sattler, 1982) and their lack of validity (Salvia & Ysseldyke, 1978).

In the area of creativity, the *Torrance Test of Creative Thinking* (TTCT) has proven useful for identifying gifted African American learners (Torrance, 1987). Not only does this test measure an important dimension of giftedness and creativity, it has also been found to be culturally fair, particularly the figural form of the test. This test enjoys moderate levels of reliability based on recent data obtained from longitudinal studies attesting to its ability to "predict quantity and quality of public personal creative achievements" (Torrance, in press). Although the time-consuming and complex nature of the scoring may restrain use of the TTCT, its quick and easy administration (30 minutes) and wide application (individual or group; grades kindergarten through graduate school) make it very appealing, particularly in light of the paucity of tests measuring the creativity domain.

A series of self-report inventories of creativity known as *The Group Inventory for Finding Talent* (GIFT) (Rimm, 1976; Rimm & Davis, 1976, 1980) and *The Group Inventory for Finding Interest* (GIFFI I and GIFFI II) (Davis & Rimm, 1983) were developed for use with individuals from preschool to senior high school. According to Torrance (in press), these inventories are technically sound and contain a breadth of psychometric design that should allow their use with learners from diverse cultural groups and socioeconomic levels. Some of the traits purportedly measured by these inventories include independence, flexibility, curiosity, and perseverance. Empirical evidence about the validity and reliability ·of these inventories when applied to African American learners has not been reported.

In addition to the profile approach and instruments believed to be valid and effective in the search for gifted African Americans, several alternative assessment approaches deserve mention. For example, Archambault (1992) reported that portfolio assessment techniques that include review of actual student products or presentations represent viable and effective alternatives to paper-and-pencil tests. Berger (1992) found that many of the recently federally funded Jacob K. Javits projects use student products in the assessment and identification process for underrepresented gifted learners.[1] This finding signals the

---

[1] In 1988 Congress passed legislation to promote the interests of gifted and talented students. The Jacob K. Javits Gifted and Talented Students Education Program was authorized under Title IV, Part B, of the Hawkins–Stafford Elementary and Secondary Amendments of 1988. The enabling legislation calls for the U.S. Department of Education, through the Javits Program, to provide grants to assist state and local education agencies, institutions of higher education, and other public and private agencies and organizations to meet the needs of gifted and talented students.

potential for significant progress and should be further explored. The use of student products should move the field of gifted education toward creating an assessment system that represents a closer fit between student task performance and the mental, social, and emotional demands of adult life.

No matter what instruments or approaches are used, it is important that assessment and identification lead to appropriate and effective intervention planning. In the field of gifted education, several curriculum-based assessment models have been reported to be effective in increasing the number and kind of African American learners included in programs for the gifted and talented. Based primarily upon "dynamic assessment" models advocated by Haywood (1988) and popularized previously by Feuerstein (1968, 1977), "an identification-through-teaching" approach (a test, teach, retest approach) is used as the basis for assessment, identification, selection, and instruction. As discussed by Johnson, Starnes, Gregory, and Blaylock (1985), this approach allows students being considered for gifted programs to develop and display cognitive and affective abilities over extended periods of time, thus enabling them to further refine these skills while project staff withhold their decision on program inclusion. Students selected will be those who have responded most favorably to curriculum exposure. Responsiveness to differentiated classroom curricula, then, becomes a part of the gifted program assessment and identification paradigm, thereby allowing for an appropriate linking of identification and curriculum (Johnson et al., 1985).

The Program of Assessment, Diagnosis, and Instruction (PADI) and the Potentially Gifted Minority Student Project, described by Alamprese, Erlanger, and Brigham (1988), represent examples of the effectiveness of a curriculum-based approach in the identification of gifted and talented, or potentially gifted, African American learners. In addition to the identification-through-teaching approach, both programs employ several features that reflect practices found to result in increased numbers of African Americans being identified as gifted and talented.

First, the philosophical orientation undergirding the selection of diagnostic and identification instruments and procedures reflects an attempt to select those diagnostic instruments that have the potential to tap reasoning and creative abilities of African

American learners (Johnson et al., 1985). As a result, the ability of a given instrument or procedure to identify and diagnose the strengths, skills, and needs of potentially gifted African American learners becomes a major criterion for project personnel. Second, both programs employ multidimensional diagnostic batteries composed of assessment instruments and procedures that obtain objective and subjective information from multiple data sources, and therefore reflect an expanded vision of the giftedness construct. Third, both programs emphasize early identification and intervention approaches that exemplify an inclusive and developmental philosophical view. Finally, the curriculum-based measurement emphasis of both programs allows teachers to use assessment data to teach students rather than rank them.

COMPREHENSIVE PROGRAMMING IMPERATIVES FOR YOUNG, GIFTED AFRICAN AMERICAN LEARNERS

In attempts to solve the myriad educational, social, and economic problems, many educators and social critics are calling for all sorts of "paradigm" shifts. This collective call for radical changes in education and society reflects a recognition of the enormity of many of our problems and an expression of a resolve that historical, piecemeal, and disconnected solutions to problems have not met with mass success, especially in relation to the education of African Americans. In the case of identifying and educating young, gifted African Americans, most psychoeducational identification and programming paradigms have not resulted in thinking patterns and programming that can transform the education and lives of the individual and collective gifted and talented African American learner.

In follow-up to the suggestion earlier in this chapter of major rethinking of the way young, gifted African American learners are assessed and identified, a new paradigm is also needed to guide programming for these learners once identified. In particular, such a model should be (a) reflective of and complementary to African American culture, (b) multicultural and global, (c) cognitively and creatively challenging, (d) active and interactional, (e) reflective of formative and summative evaluation efforts, and (f) power enhancing.

The following sections describe characteristics of a model designed to transform the education and psychosocial power of young, gifted African American learners. While the major attention is on the necessity of considering cultural factors in program design and including exemplary programming for gifted and talented, an additional focus is on providing insights into enhancing the psychosocial, emotional attributes of these young gifted learners.

Culturally and Multiculturally Complementary

All programmatic efforts must incorporate activities and experiences focused on the development and liberation of the total African American gifted learner, including the cognitive, affective, psychomotor, and spiritual sides. These efforts are facilitated if they are based on assessment data and include exemplary curriculum theory, design, and practice for curriculum in general, and exemplary curriculum elements for gifted and talented learners in particular (Feuerstein, 1977; Gallagher, 1985; McLaughlin, Baytops, & Sims, 1993). Furthermore, certain African American social scientists (Anderson, 1988; Hilliard, 1976; Nobles, 1987; Ogbu, 1988) have emphasized the need to consider cultural factors unique to African American learners in the curriculum development and delivery process. Thus, these and other researchers point to the unique and historical needs, characteristics, and attributes of learners of African descent in America, as reflecting an African-centered heritage, culture, worldviews, and ethics. Such attributes, it is argued, should be embraced and integrated into a more comprehensive and empowering curriculum development and delivery system for these learners.

We acknowledge that within the African American population, a diversity of identifiable individual and group characteristics may be found. Consequently, the recommendations presented here reflect the work of a number of scholars, including psychologists, sociologists,. multicultural theory specialists, and gifted education specialists, whose research and study have identified some distinct features of African American learners. Learner academic, cognitive, affective, and psychomotor strengths, as identified by Hilliard

TABLE 2.1. Methods of Accentuating Selective Strengths and Learning Modes of African American Gifted Learners

Selective Strengths and Learning Modes	Responsive Teaching– Learning Methodologies
Verbal fluency; stylistic, charismatic use of language	Emphasize creative writing, poetry, public speaking, oral discussion, debating, drama, literature
Expressive movement, advanced kinesthetic ability	Emphasize hands-on learning strategies and allow flexible classroom organization
Advanced aesthetic sensibilities	Integration of arts with core instruction
Resourcefulness, inventiveness, advanced creative abilities	Utilize problem-based learning: opportunities for experimentation with ideas, and seeking solutions to real problems
Preference for person-to-person (over person-to-object) interaction	Emphasize development of social interaction and leadership skills, attention to world affairs, and current issues
Sensitivity for the interconnectedness of humankind with nature	Focus on science, ecology, outdoor field experience, anthropology, and social sciences
Expressed spirituality related to sense of power of external forces of nature, existence of a supreme being, and a heightened sense of responsibility for others within primary reference group	Use of moral, affective overarching themes as base for instructional experiences: study use of parables and proverbs of varying cultures; examine life experiences of selected leaders (those characterized by intense spirituality, individuation, and moral responsibility)

Note: This table represents selective strengths and learning modes most often noted by scholars as characteristic of African American gifted/high-ability learners (Baytops, Sims, & Patton, 1993; Hale-Benson, 1986; Hilliard, 1976; Shade, 1990; Torrance, 1977). The concomitant methodologies were developed from work of Baytops et al. (1993).

(1976), Torrance (1977), and Shade (1990), and further supported by the work of Hale-Benson (1986) and Baytops, Sims, and Patton (1993), form the basis on which culturally complementary program design begins. Table 2.1 provides a summation of certain academic and creative strengths of African American gifted learners, their preferred modes of learning, and related curriculum implications as identified by these researchers. These findings can be used as a framework for program development matched to the specific characteristics of African American gifted learners.

Such an approach to curriculum development would enable practitioners to use culture as a mediator in program development, while infusing design elements into the curriculum aimed at those having exceptional gifts and talents. Therefore, a paradigm is being advanced that uses African American culture as a mediator in curriculum and program development for young, gifted African Americans, thereby advancing the dichotomy put forth by Kitano (1991). According to her analysis, there are two separate frameworks from which curriculum may be developed and implemented: the "assimilationist" and the "cultural pluralistic." Kitano asserted that "assimilationism and cultural pluralism constitute two competing philosophical views affecting educational practices for culturally diverse gifted students" (1991, p. 14). Using the former perspective, the purpose of curriculum and program development is to develop in learners the knowledge, skills, and attitudes required for mainstream European society. By contrast, the "cultural pluralist" view drives curriculum and program development efforts from a multiculturalist foundation. That is, activities and programs prepare learners to survive and thrive in a multicultural setting, thereby respecting, appreciating, and affirming diverse cultures, not merely one centered exclusively on European culture.

We suggest that neither of these opposing views offers the proper foundation and direction for program development for African American learners. Instead, the two perspectives should be viewed along a continuum, not as dichotomous variables. If indeed the assimilationist view represents education and development that result in relinquishing one's "Blackness" in order to become assimilated into mainstream European American culture, whereas the pluralist view represents advocates of curriculum and programming efforts that result in teaching content and processes through a multicultural lens, we argue that at no point does this cultural pluralist foundation for curriculum development allow for learners to be grounded in their own culture. Instead, therefore, we suggest that program and curriculum development for gifted African American learners consist of experiences and activities that ground or immerse them in their own "Blackness" first.

The research of several prominent African American psychologists is particularly instructive in this regard. For example, Cross (1971, 1978), Cross, Parham, and Helms (1991), and Helms (1986) explored the stages in the development of Black or African American identity. The pioneering work of Cross and his colleagues offers us progressive direction here. Specifically, these researchers found that one cannot reach the culturally pluralistic perspective, or transcendent stage (Cross, 1971), without previously experiencing several successive stages of one's own racial identity to include the immersion–emersion stage that totally grounds African Americans in their Blackness. Mastery of this immersion–emersion stage serves as a necessary antecedent to the later stage of racial transcendence, or pluralism, whereby "a person loses his/her 'hang ups' about race, sex, social class and sees himself or herself as a part of humanity in all its flavors" (Hall, Cross, & Freedle, 1970, p. 158). Once grounded in their own race and culture, it is believed that African American learners can develop knowledge and appreciation of other culture's values, norms, symbols, belief systems, epistemologies, and modes of learning. In this manner, curriculum and programs are developed that add to the potency of these learners, thereby allowing and affirming their "Africanism," while preparing them to function, operate, and even thrive in more global, multicultural, and multiracial environments.

The approach presented here, then, is neither a pure assimilationist nor a pure cultural pluralist perspective. In fact, we believe that the failure to include this missing immersion–emersion curriculum development stage as a precursor to the pluralist perspective has resulted in a lack of depth and substance in many well-intentioned multicultural programs designed to challenge, nurture, and transform the potentials of African American gifted learners. The outcomes of the proposed form of transformation suggest that these learners would be better able to actualize their own potential and function within the boundaries of their cultural communities, as well as cope, survive, and thrive in the larger context of American and global societies.

Challenging for Gifted Learners

Early intervention and nurturance can have the most significant and sustained impact on individual learner growth and development. Therefore, program interventions that begin as early as preschool are recommended. In the design of program services for the gifted, current practice recommends that exemplary programming for all gifted learners provide:

- Opportunities for exploring of topics of significance and interest to individual learners.

- Clearly defined purposes, goals, and objectives that are tailored to the learner's individual and cultural needs.

- Opportunities for problem solving at higher levels of cognitive processing.

- Opportunities for creative and productive thinking and idea production in response to real-world problems and issues.

- Opportunities for advanced instruction in core content areas of mathematics, science, social studies, language arts, and foreign languages.

- Instruction that is interdisciplinary in nature, providing for a thematic approach to delivery of curriculum across content areas.

These service delivery options should also provide opportunities for acceleration of regular content experiences, independent study with mentors or professionals who have expertise in areas of interest to the learners, and enrichment classes in foreign languages, liberal arts, philosophy, creative arts, humanities, and technology (Feldhusen, 1985; VanTassel-Baska, 1992). All curriculum experiences should be appropriately matched to the previously identified cognitive strengths and learning preferences of African American gifted learners, resulting in their complete and absolute empowerment.

Interactive and Reflective of Evaluation Efforts

This comprehensive programming model is thought to be dynamic and interactional. Input in the design and delivery of all programming must be sought and obtained, not only from educational experts, but also from learners themselves, their families, and significant others in the larger community. As mentioned, the increased involvement from the African American community in the development, implementation, and evaluation of programmatic elements is important. Equally important is the inclusion of some flexibility and dynamism in the design and implementation of the curriculum. To accomplish this, constant and continuous evaluation is required.

The importance of collecting formative and summative evaluation data on every aspect of program development and implementation cannot be overemphasized. Although a qualitative approach is helpful, we suggest evaluation efforts that triangulate qualitative, quantitative, and observational data. Furthermore, while it is important to identify process variables, the need to use authentic performance measurement systems that are outcome based and results driven should not go unheeded. The evaluation modes selected should reflect the outcome goals for the gifted program and for each learner in each class or experience. The use of both qualitative and quantitative evaluation systems enables educators to (a) reflect on current practice, (b) feed results back to ongoing programmatic efforts, and (c) make programmatic changes based upon learner outcomes.

Power Enhancing

Gubbins (1982) observed that exceptionally high ability and aptitude may be necessary but not sufficient conditions for high-level performance. A host of other personality, temperament, and motivation-enhancing variables also are needed for truly high levels of productivity. It becomes necessary, then, to identify, nurture, and challenge yet another side of gifted African American learners—a side that has traditionally been called the affective or psychosocial. Erikson (1950) long ago noted that at about age 5 the child enters a socioemotional stage where the primary challenge becomes one of establishing a sense of competence, or personal mastery. This stage is followed by an adolescent period, when the development of a sense of identity becomes paramount. Given the U.S. society's historical treatment of African Americans, the development of a sense of competence as well as self and racial identity requires an additional programmatic overlay. Not only must these learners deal with Dubois's "two warring souls" duality (1961), they must also deal with the status and role of being defined as gifted or talented. These are burdens that weigh heavily on the socioemotional psyche of young and gifted African American learners.

Recent studies, news reports, and experiences in programs for gifted African American learners tell us that one of the emotional challenges facing gifted African Americans, especially those who live in low-resource environments, involves coping with and overcoming the contradictions often experienced in varying degrees by gifted and talented African American learners enrolled in gifted courses or programs. Many are forced to endure and make sense of the never-ending series of isolation, frustrations, and ridicule experienced in many gifted classes where they are usually in the "minority." Furthermore, they are expected to act and behave consistent with the normalized values of the usual middle class school setting. Yet, at the same time, it is not unusual for relatives, friends, and acquaintances to poke fun of, ridicule, generally "mess with," or denigrate that same gifted learner for exhibiting "school" behavior at home. In a recent *Virginia Pilot and Ledger Star* (Staunton, 1993) article, the comments of Charlise Lyles, a highly gifted journalist, epitomize these contradictory influences:

> A sophomore year of C's bruised my ego, and I struggled to regain confidence won at my old public school, where an "A" was a mere matter of memorization. *Back home in the projects,* my friends despised my good grammar and babbling about Sylvia Plath and T. S. Elliot. "You sound like a white girl, using those big words," they teased. "Think she better than everybody else since she went out to that school." (p. C1)

Programmatic efforts nationwide that focus on addressing the socioemotional aspects of young African American learners' development are generally spotty at best. However, a study by Alamprese et al. (1988) found that empowerment and socioemotional support were critical elements in the success of "disadvantaged" learners enrolled in exemplary gifted education programs.

Researchers and commentators of the African American and gifted education experience have variously conceptualized, defined, and categorized this line of inquiry as "psychosocial-emotional" or "intrapersonal" relationship development (Gardner, 1983), affective development (Ascher, 1991; Dabney, 1976; Howells, 1992), and developmental potential theory (Piechowski, 1986). Other writers in the area of gifted education have discussed efforts aimed at identifying, challenging, and nurturing the temperaments and personality characteristics of these learners as counseling factors (VanTassel-Baska, 1992) and psychosocial support factors (Alamprese et al., 1988). Furthermore, a number of programs that address the myriad psychosocial–emotional needs of African American learners have been developed by African Americans under such labels as African American male or female socialization and bonding programs (Ascher, 1991; Baye, 1989), rites-of-passage programs for African American males and females (Akbar, 1991; Coppock, 1990; Hare & Hare, 1985), and programs based on the Nguzo Saba, or African American value system (Karenga, 1977).

Common to all of these efforts is an attempt to identify and build upon those psychosocial–emotional aspects of temperament and personality variables that enhance these learners' total development and have the potential to transform them into self-actualized, integrated human beings. Although Wilson (1992) observed that little "empirical" research exists to inform about several of these categories of activities purported to enhance these learners' total development, insights, approaches, and strategies are known and provide some potential direction for this aspect of these students' total development. The scope of this chapter does not permit a detailed discussion of the psychosocial and power-enhancing needs of young, gifted African American learners and corresponding programmatic responses. However, some needs in this category, along with suggested programmatic responses, are noted in Table 2.2.

These psychosocial–emotional vectors of development must be recognized and responded to in all programming elements. Infused, therefore, in all curriculum programming options for African American gifted youth should be efforts that move them psychically from a past that is reflective of the pre-colonial African experience through the Americanization experience, which for many began with slavery, oppression, and poverty, to a present that emphasizes sensitivity to the valued traditions of African and African Americans and onward to the visualization of a positive

TABLE 2.2. Psychosocial Power-Enhancing Needs of Young, Gifted African Americans and Suggested Programmatic Responses

Power-Enhancing Needs	Suggested Programmatic Responses
To develop a sense of competence, self and group identity, and cross-cultural competence	Construct and infuse the total curriculum with experiences that help the learner *internalize* a "sense of self-competence," strong self and collective knowledge, consciousness, identity, and cross-cultural competence. Programs and activities should focus on developing a sense of efficacy, confidence, and personal mastery. Schools should establish or connect with existing African American male and female rites-of-passage programs within the community. Inculcate within these learners a deep knowledge of African and African American history and culture.
To counteract the effects of isolation, alienation, and powerlessness[a]	Develop a keen sense of love of self and others; develop prosocial, cooperative interaction skills. Develop programs and experiences that assist these learners to deal with anger and frustration through self-control techniques and nonviolent conflict-resolution techniques. Develop a deep understanding of and ability to actualize the concepts of power, authority, control, leadership, and followership. Offer experiences that allow African American learners to "connect with" each other to learn, share, bond, and further develop the "power" within their selves and their communities.
To counteract the effects of racism and oppression	Process real and/or create simulation experiences that help these learners become aware of the origins, perpetuation, and psychology of racism and oppression. Their feelings related to these forces must be processed, and problem-solving strategies to cope with and mitigate the effects of racism and oppression should be developed.
To develop a sense of self-actualization and super-ego development	Construct programs that include activities that focus on moral development, self-perception, and self-evaluation. Offer opportunities for these learners to understand, process, and deal with the various "forms of overexcitabilities" (Dabrowski, 1972; Piechowski, 1986) they may experience in day-to-day interactions or specific situations.

[a]Some information regarding isolation, alienation, and powerlessness is drawn from the conceptual work of Wilson (1992).

future. Simultaneously, many of these learners, particularly those from low socioeconomic circumstances, are regularly challenged by peers, family, community, and schools to deny their own unique gifts and talents. The outcome of such transmission and transformation would be that these learners would become better able to actualize their own potential; function within the boundaries of their cultural communities; and cope, survive, and thrive within the larger context of American and global societies.

STAFF DEVELOPMENT: EMPOWERING AND LIBERATING

The traditional role of teacher in U.S. education has been that of a transmitter of knowledge. However, for teachers of the gifted, the primary role is to encourage learners to become "producers" of knowledge, not merely consumers of transmitted knowledge. In this role, the teacher becomes a power broker, one who has the capacity and the mandate to liberate students by providing them with methods and strategies to enhance their ability to access information for themselves. Such a "high calling" requires that teachers of the gifted possess certain sensibilities and personality traits, be firmly grounded in an extensive content knowledge, and possess a rich interdisciplinary experience base. Combining these personality and experience traits of teachers of the gifted with an enhanced receptivity to the notion that gifted individuals can be found among all population groups without regard to class, gender, or ethnicity creates a monumental challenge for staff development specialists.

The literature is replete with references to the impact of teacher attitudes and expectations on student achievement. Rarely discussed in open forum, however, are those silent presumptions that gifted youth are those who are endowed with external advantages seldom available, accessible, or provided in culturally and racially diverse populations. Such labels as "educationally disadvantaged," "at risk," "culturally deprived," "economically disadvantaged," and "underprivileged" reflect the continuing deficit view that overshadows efforts made by educators to deal effectively and positively with

African American learners. These labels and subsequent overemphasis on the perceived academic and social deficits of African American youth have contributed greatly to their overrepresentation in special education programs designed for learners with deficient academic and psychosocial skills (Ford, 1992).

Nonetheless, mislabeling, misidentification, and the subsequent mismatch between true potential and service provision are not the only problems that plague service professionals. A more foreboding issue is professionals' identity and development in terms of their own ethnicity, environment, and cultural ethos. Increasingly, classroom teachers, counselors, and other educational professionals originate from European American backgrounds. As the 21st century approaches, their racial and ethnic backgrounds will differ significantly from an increasingly culturally diverse student population (Hodgkinson, 1993). Among this increased population of culturally diverse learners will be a significant number of gifted African American children and youth.

The challenge for educators and those who train them will be first to deal with and resolve their own presumptions, beliefs, and baggage regarding the giftedness construct as it relates to African Americans, their race and culture. New staff development efforts must aim at helping these individuals to develop skills that will enable them to recognize the diversity of gifts and talents in African American children and youth and, once identified, to respect, challenge, and nurture the total development of these learners. Several additional major features of more liberating, empowering staff development efforts are suggested in Table 2.3. Behaviors and attitudes of teachers and other professionals can make the difference between the creation of stimulating, nurturing environments and environments that are restrictive and nonflexible and that provide little support for the diverse expressions of the gifted African American learner.

Professional educators who have internalized and operationalized a belief system that is grounded in these staff development concepts will be more likely to accelerate the growth and development of African American gifted learners than those whose training is confined to a more traditional approach. Such education and training, however, must be connected to traditional and contemporary educational support practices valued by the learners' families and communities.

TABLE 2.3.   Features of Liberating, Empowering Staff Development Efforts

Avoidance of Traditional Practices that:	*Encouragement of Practices that:*
Provide specific training for select group of teachers of the gifted only	Provide training to regular classroom teachers, counselors, administrators, specialists, and other support staff
Provide for developing of individual teacher proficiency to work with gifted learners	Develop collaborative teaming skills of all professionals who impact lives of the gifted (counselors, teachers, administrators, parents, support staff, and community members)
Allow teachers to use extant curriculum modules designed by external experts and identified as appropriate for teaching the gifted	Train teachers and others to become developers of innovative curriculum appropriate to meet the needs of a more diverse population of students
Support recruitment of primarily European American teachers to enroll in preservice training programs relative to the education of the gifted	Broaden the recruitment pool to include liberally educated African Americans to encourage their interest in becoming educators of our gifted African Americans
Support a narrow, unidimensional view of giftedness	Acknowledge and value a multidimensional view of the manifestations of giftedness as expressed by African American gifted learners
Provide training of staff to involve parents of the gifted in a limited advisory capacity	Provide staff training to involve African American parents, extended family members, and community as partners in roles of nurturer, supporter, and advocates for gifted learners
Provide training focused on deficit views of traits of African American learners (e.g., use of terms such as "culturally disadvantaged," "deprived," "at risk," "underprivileged," etc.)	Focus on inherent strengths of African American learners regardless of socioeconomic backgrounds (accentuating the positive)
Provide limited training concerning the impact of culture on learning–teaching styles, and preferences	Provide research-based training relative to the impact of race and culture on learning styles, preferences, and strengths of African Americans
Provide training only to teachers related to meeting the intellectual needs of gifted	Provide training to include counselors, social workers, and administrators concerning the affective, cognitive, and psychosocial needs of these gifted learners

DRAWING ON THE STRENGTHS OF THE VALUED TRADITIONS OF FAMILIES: A NEW DISCOURSE

Parents and other family members may have the greatest impact upon the life of a child during the early developmental years. Family background, past experiences with the educational system, and students' perceptions of and attitudes toward education influence school performance. Positive and consistent responses of parents are valued by children; thus the child's psyche is impacted by such responses or the loss thereof.

A recent study (Baytops, 1994) revealed several trends in the research literature relevant to family and community nurturance of gifted youth. Although families and communities have traditionally provided educational, social, and economic support for the development of talent in children who later became eminent adults (Clark, 1983; Comer, 1988; Kulieke & Olszewski-Kubilius, 1989), collaboration and cooperation between educational institutions and African American families and their communities appear to be lacking. Baytops (1994) discussed trends related to (a) support provided by the extended family, (b) the role of the Black church as a support system for African Americans, and (c) traditional values held by the collective African American community.

Family configurations in the African American community vary in background, economic level, and membership. Wilson and Tolson (1990) estimated a 25% to 85% incidence rate of extended families within the African American community. Additional resources provided by the extended family to the gifted learner can serve as an important survival mechanism for the African American community at large. The gifted child for whom resources are pooled is expected to reciprocate. This tradition of giving back some of what one has received was described by Wilson and Tolson (1990) in their definition of a family "as a functional group situation in which opportunities exist for at least economic and instrumental cooperation, informal communication and reciprocated social and emotional obligations among family members" (p. 347).

An additional socialization responsibility of the extended family and fictive family support network is to teach African American children how to cope with racism. The need to combat racism has made it necessary that African American communities emphasize achievement, motivation, self-confidence, and high self-esteem. The emphasis on these values and the encouragement of a strong extended family network provide a cushion of support and a filter from some of the negative effects of racism that African American students may experience in mainstream society. Allen and Majidi-Ahi (1989) provided empirical research suggesting that homogeneous African American communities can provide cohesive environments that shelter African American children from a hostile outside world. Slaughter and Epps (1987) also discussed studies by psychologists and educators on the African American experience, which characterize families of high-achieving, low-income youth as those who consistently, openly, and realistically socialize these youth regarding racism and oppression in mainstream society. These same families model behaviors that their children can emulate to cope with racial barriers. Optimism, persistence, and tenacity are other characteristics of families of successful students from poor backgrounds. The perceptions of families of high-achieving youth regarding the benefits of education differ from those of families of low-achieving students in that the family socialization process makes it clear to high achievers that education is "the way out" from current circumstances *and* the most certain route to success for themselves and normative others.

Relatedly, in an extensive study of the African American church, Lincoln and Mamiya (1990) pointed out how the church became an extension of the African American family support system in the early days of its establishment as an institution. Billingsley and Caldwell (1991) contended that all three aggregates—church, family, and schools—operate as socializing agents within the domains of the larger society. Out of necessity, Black churches have always been more intimately involved with their communities than have White churches. For many successful gifted African American adults, the church has served as a bulwark of safety, support, and nurturance in their developing years. The challenge for families with gifted learners, therefore, is to connect with the Black churches in ways that will be mutually rewarding.

Developing a value system and set of practices that build upon the strengths of the families of gifted learners requires a new definition of "family." One need only study the contributions of African American scientists, inventors, scholars, artists, civic leaders, and the like to realize that giftedness among African Americans is not new. Therefore, one can presume that many African American gifted learners have a background comprised of bright, creative, intuitive, and rationally superior parents, grandparents, friends, siblings, and other ancestors. We suggest, therefore, a new discourse and interaction pattern with these families that begins with recognizing, valuing, affirming, and respecting their gifts, their intelligences, and their desire to be involved with their gifted children's educational program.

Table 2.4 provides suggestions for enhancing family involvement by utilizing approaches that empower and liberate the families of African American gifted learners. Use of these suggestions will result in improved relationships between the African American community at large and the educational system. Opening the doors of schools so that their services are extended into communities, while increasing school personnel's understanding of the diverse strengths, resources, and needs of the African American community, will result in more successful outcomes for all.

CONCLUSION

Summary

Several principles or propositions have been advanced in this chapter. Principles needed to establish proper assessment, identification, and development of the gifts and talents of young African American learners are intertwined with a host of challenges related to needed reforms in psychoeducational assessment in general, effective school and curriculum reforms, and family empowerment, as well as to larger societal issues of equity, cultural and cross-cultural competence, and the distribution of social, political, and economic power. The following are summary and concluding statements concerning these principles:

1. The call for paradigm shifts related to theorizing and defining the giftedness construct as it relates to young, gifted African Americans represents a part of a larger shift in defining the giftedness construct. A conceptual shift has taken place in the field of gifted education, away from defining the gifted construct as a manifestation of innate, immutable cognitive abili-

TABLE 2.4. Approaches to Involving Families in the Education of Their Gifted Children

Traditional Approach	Empowering, Liberating Approach
Initial contact with parents is primarily to obtain permission to test the child.	Initial contact with family and community leaders should be at level of referral to obtain data for referral and description of gifted behaviors as expressed in home and/or community.
Letter is sent to notify parent(s) of child's eligibility to participate in program.	Educators should share results of assessment with family members and clarify the meaning of test results and their implications for the child's future.
Parent sessions are held to provide information about program offerings and to solicit support for advocacy with policymakers.	Family sessions are held to: 1. Provide training regarding characteristics of giftedness and concomitant behaviors to expect in home and school. 2. Provide information regarding socioemotional needs of gifted African American learners; ways that families can help counteract negative pressures, plan effectively for future; and so forth. 3. Train African American families to develop advocacy skills and understand the educational policymaking process. 4. Solicit input and share expertise relative to program offerings.
Individualized Education Program is developed that focuses only on the child's academic needs.	Individualized Family Service Plan is developed to document learner and family strengths, resources, areas needing enhancement, and support needs of family (e.g., psychosocial, economic, educational).
Parent education services are provided only to *parents* of gifted learners.	Services are provided to parents, extended family members, church, community leaders, and agency personnel using a collaborative support model to enhance services for African American gifted learners.

Note: Table adapted from work of Damiani and Baytops (1993) and Baytops (1994).

ty to emphasizing developmental potential in multiple areas of extraordinary human ability and intelligences.

2. Programs for African American gifted learners should be designed that (a) are holistic in their overall structure, (b) focus on the individual and collective needs of these

learners, (c) are complementary to their culture, (d) are inter-disciplinary, and (e) are challenging in content and process. It is important that programs be designed and delivered that enhance the development of the "whole" learner. Accordingly, the affective, moral, ethical, and psychomotor requirements of these learners must be addressed, along with their cognitive or academic development. As a part of these efforts, students must be allowed to deal with their feelings, their dualities, and the myriad other factors associated with being young, gifted, and African American. A culturally affirming, interdisciplinary curriculum focus, in our view, offers the greatest possibility for connecting with these learners and transforming their potential.

3. Professional staff development reform should simultaneously personalize and broaden the roles of teachers, counselors, administrators, and others involved with educating African American gifted learners. Changing emphases in preservice and inservice education are recommended, focusing on enhancing educators' sensitivity to the impact of environment, context, and culture on knowledge acquisition and transmission.

4. The value of including parents and family members in assessment, identification, and programmatic efforts has been emphasized consistently in this chapter. To accomplish this involvement, a "new discourse" must be developed between parents and professionals, based on knowledge from systems theory, extended family organizational development, community development, and the like.

Needed Research and Practice

Over the years many terms have been used to describe and label those high-ability learners that we generally refer to as gifted and talented. In the United States, only recently have constructs of intelligences emerged that have the potential of affirming the individual and collective culture of African Americans. Viewing giftedness from expansive, holistic, developmental, and culturally specific perspectives offers opportunities for more clearly identifying definitional constructs in consonance with the cultural and learning styles of African Americans. With this in mind, there is a need to engage in both quantitative and qualitative research aimed at studying the predictive and construct validity of the constructs of giftedness offered most recently by Gardner (1983), Sternberg (1985), and others. Research that examines the mediating effects of culture, race, and class on these new and more expanded definitions of giftedness should provide a solid foundation for future development and research.

The validity, reliability, and general value of research and practice in the area of gifted African American learners would be enhanced by the involvement of African American researchers from various disciplines telling their own stories. More African American sociologists, political scientists, economists, psychologists, historians, educators, and the like must speak not only to definitional constructs of giftedness from their narrow disciplinary perspective, but also address empirically and qualitatively the myriad issues related to the kinds of education and socialization efforts needed to identify, actualize, and accelerate the various potentials of young African American learners. After establishing such knowledge bases, efforts should be made to share results, insights, and ideas through collaborative, interdisciplinary modes of dissemination.

Furthermore, additional research is needed on the effects of the gifted label on young, gifted African American learners. In particular, research is needed that identifies the stresses, strains, and challenges imposed on young African American learners who must simultaneously deal with their Blackness, giftedness, socioeconomic status, gender, oppression, and issues related to mainstream assimilation. Such research should also probe the perception of the giftedness label held by young African Americans, their families and communities, and the general public, and the effect of these perceptions on these learners' motivation to assume the status, role, and label of being gifted.

Obtaining the best mix of curriculum and programming elements for these learners remains a challenge. Research and development efforts targeted at what Passow (1986) described as the "kinds of educational experiences and opportunities that result in optimal development and utilization of potential" (p. 124) continue to be needed. Such curriculum research and development efforts must include an analysis of the hidden curriculum in the home and community, as well as the various forms of parallel curricula employed in noneducational settings. Accompanying this research and development effort should be a focus on the identification and resolution of policy issues related to identification and nurturance of gifts and talents of young African Americans.

Related to this subject is the need to produce effective research that identifies the most appropriate organizational arrangements for delivering the best instruction. Determining the most appropriate delivery systems, or combination of delivery modes, such as pull-out programs, acceleration, enrichment, curriculum compacting, cooperative groups, and so forth, for these learners must be a major part of this line of research.

It is important that research be undertaken that focuses on the personality traits and appropriate experiential base needed by staff in order to work with this distinct learner population. Those personality variables needed by teachers, counselors, administrators, and others that nurture and accelerate the talent of young, gifted African Americans must be identified and utilized in the staff selection process. It has been recommended that staff development efforts employ an experiential–interactive approach to training (Richert, 1987).

Efforts must also be made to evaluate systematically the effectiveness of staff development. Factors in all training efforts that sustain and propel the learning of these students and that carry over into the daily teaching, counseling, and administrative routines of school staff members must also be studied and identified.

The central role played by parents, extended family members, and significant others is being increasingly recognized. More research is needed that focuses on the roles played by African American family members and significant others; the drives, motivations, pleasures, and forces that enhance the gifts and talents of their children; and the forces that impede those talents. Case study research techniques provide a good match for this type of research.

Research and evaluation are also needed that provide formative and summative data related to total program functioning and effectiveness. Process-oriented evaluation along with results-driven performance evaluation should guide these efforts, with a focus on both program and individual learner outcomes. The ability of individuals to achieve predetermined outcomes is an important element of this research agenda.

In closing, we recommend that society invest resources in research and practice that provide educators and the larger society with an understanding of the synthesis of conditions required to identify, develop, and actualize the potentials of highly gifted and talented, young African American learners. Accomplishing this task will increase not only the potency of the entire community of African American learners, but also the power, future, and potential of the collective U.S. society. A loud and clear clarion call to do so is offered here.

REFERENCES

Akbar, N. (1991). *Visions for Black men.* Nashville, TN: Winston-Derek.

Alamprese, J. A., Erlanger, W. J., & Brigham, N. (1988). *No gift wasted: Effective strategies for educating highly able, disadvantaged students in mathematics and science. Vol. I: Findings.* Washington, DC: Cosmos Corporation.

Allen, L., & Majidi-Ahi, S. (1989). Black American children. In J. T. Gibbs & L. N. Huang (Eds.), *Children of color* (pp. 140–178). San Francisco: Jossey-Bass.

Anderson, J. A. (1988). Cognitive styles and multicultural populations. *Journal of Teacher Education, 39*(1), 2–9.

Archambault, F. X. (1992). *Alternative assessment and the evaluation of programs for the gifted and talented.* Unpublished manuscript, University of Connecticut, National Research Center on the Gifted and Talented.

Ascher, C. (1991). *School programs for African-American male students.* Trends and Issues No. 15. New York: ERIC Clearinghouse on Urban Education, Institute for Urban and Minority Education.

Baldwin, A. Y. (1984). *The Baldwin Identification Matrix 2 for the identification of the gifted and talented: A handbook for its use.* New York: Trillium Press.

Baldwin, A. Y. (1987). I'm Black but look at me, I am also gifted. *Gifted Child Quarterly, 31,* 180–185.

Baska, L. (1986). The use of the Raven Advanced Progressive Matrices for the selection of magnet junior high school students. *Roeper Review, 8*(3), 181–184.

Baye, B. W. (1989, November). Fighting back. *Essence,* pp. 59, 118–120.

Baytops, J. L. (1994). At-risk African American gifted learners: Enhancing their education. In J. S. Stanfield (Ed.), *Research in social policy* (Vol. 3, pp. 1–32). Greenwich, CT: JAI Press.

Baytops, J. L., Sims, S. J., & Patton, J. M. (1993). *Project Mandala: A comprehensive program. Implementation guide to serve the needs of special population of gifted learners.* Unpublished manuscript, The College of William and Mary, Williamsburg, VA.

Berger, S. L. (1992). *Programs and practices in gifted education.* Reston, VA: The Council for Exceptional Children.

Billingsley, A., & Caldwell, C. H. (1991). The church, the family and the school in the African-American community. *Journal of Negro Education, 60*(3), 427–440.

Blackshear, P. (1979). *A comparison of peer nomination and nomination of the academically gifted Black, primary level student.* Unpublished doctoral dissertation, University of Maryland, College Park.

Clark, R. (1983). *Family life and school achievement: Why poor Black children succeed or fail.* Chicago: University of Chicago Press.

Comer, J. P. (1988). Educating poor minority children. *Scientific American, 259*(5), 42–48.

Coppock, N. (1990). *Afrocentric theory and applications: Adolescent rites of passage* (Vol. 1). Washington, DC: Baobab Associates.

Court, J. H., & Raven, J. (1982). *Research and references: 1982 update.* London: H. K. Lewis.

Cross, W. E. (1971, July). The Negro-to-Black conversion experience. *Black World*, pp. 13–27.

Cross, W. E. (1978). The Thomas and Cross models of psychological nigrescence: A review. *Journal of Black Psychology, 5*(1), 13–31.

Cross, W. E., Jr., Parham, T. A., & Helms, J. E. (1991). The stages of Black identity development: Nigrescence models. In R. L. Jones (Ed.), *Black psychology* (3rd ed., pp. 319–338). Berkeley, CA: Cobbs & Henry.

Dabney, M. (1976). Curriculum building and implementation in mainstream settings: Some concepts and propositions. In R. L. Jones (Ed.), *Mainstreaming and the minority child* (pp. 109–131). Washington, DC: Department of Health, Education and Welfare.

Dabney, M. (1983). *Perspectives and directions in assessment of the Black child.* Paper presented at the meeting of the Council for Exceptional Children, Atlanta.

Dabrowski, K. (1972). *Psychoneurosis is not an illness.* London: Gryf.

Damiani, V., & Baytops, J. L. (1993). *Family involvement resource guide for special population of gifted learners.* Unpublished manuscript, The College of William and Mary, Williamsburg, VA.

Davis, G. A., & Rimm, S. (1983). Group Inventory for Finding Interest (GIFFI) I and II: Instruments for identifying creative potential in the junior and senior high school. *Journal of Creative Behavior, 6*, 50–57.

Davis, P. (1978). *Community efforts to increase the identification of the number of gifted minority children.* Ypsilanti: Eastern Michigan College of Education.

DuBois, W. E. (1961). *The souls of Black folk.* Greenwich, CT: Fawcett.

Erikson, E. (1950). *Childhood and society.* New York: Norton.

Feldhusen, J. (1985). *Toward excellence in gifted education.* Denver, CO: Love.

Feuerstein, R. (1968). *The learning potential of assessment device: A new method for assessing modifiability of the cognitive functioning of socioculturally disadvantaged adolescents.* Unpublished manuscript, Israel Foundation Trustees, Tel Aviv.

Feuerstein, R. (1977). Mediated learning experience: A theoretical basis for cognitive human modifiability during adolescence. *Research to practice in mental retardation: Proceedings of the 4th Congress of IASMD. Vol. 2. Education and training* (pp. 105–116). Baltimore: University Park Press.

Ford, B. A. (1992). Multicultural education training for special educators working with African-American youth. *Exceptional Children, 52*(2), 107–114.

Ford, D. Y., & Harris III, J. J. (1991). On discovering the hidden treasure of gifted and talented African-American children. *Roeper Review, 13*(1), 27–33.

Ford, D. Y., Winborne, D. G., & Harris III, J. J. (1991). Determinants of underachievement among gifted Black students: Learning to underachieve. *Journal of Social and Behavioral Sciences, 35*(3), 145–162.

Frasier, M. M. (1979). Rethinking the issue regarding the culturally disadvantaged gifted. *Exceptional Children, 45*(7), 538–542.

Frasier, M. (1989). Identification of gifted Black students: Developing new perspectives. In C. J. Maker & S. W. Schiever (Eds.), *Critical issues in gifted education: Defensible programs for cultural and ethnic minorities* (Vol. 2, pp. 213–225). Austin, TX: PRO-ED.

Frasier, M. (1990, April). *The equitable identification of gifted and talented children.* Paper presented at the annual meeting of the American Educational Research Association, Boston.

Frasier, M. (1991). Response to Kitano: The Sharing of Giftedness Between Culturally Diverse and Non-Diverse Gifted Students. *Journal for the Education of the Gifted, 15*(1), 20–30.

Gallagher, J. J. (1985). *Teaching the gifted child.* Boston: Allyn & Bacon.

Gardner, H. (1983). *Frames of mind.* New York: Basic Books.

Gould, S. J. (1981). *The mismeasure of man.* New York: Norton.

Gubbins, J. (1982). *Revolving door identification model: Characteristics of gifted students.* Unpublished doctoral dissertation, University of Connecticut, Storrs.

Hale-Benson, J. (1986). *Black children: Their roots, culture and learning styles.* Baltimore: Johns Hopkins University Press.

Hall, W. S., Cross, W. E., & Freedle, R. (1970). Stages in the development of Black awareness: An exploratory investigation. In R. L. Jones (Ed.), *Black psychology* (1st ed., pp.156–165). Berkeley, CA: Cobb & Henry.

Hare, J., & Hare, N. (1985). *Bringing the Black boy to manhood: The passage.* San Francisco: The Black Think Tank.

Harris, J. J., & Ford, D. Y. (1991). Identifying and nurturing the promise of gifted Black American children. *Journal of Negro Education, 60*(1), 3–18.

Haywood, H. C. (1988). Dynamic assessment: The learning potential assessment device. In R. L. Jones (Ed.), *Psychoeducational assessment of minority group children: A casebook* (pp. 39–63). Berkeley, CA: Cobb & Henry.

Helms, J. (1986). Expanding racial identity theory to cover counseling process. *Journal of Counseling Psychology, 33*(1), 62–64.

Hilliard, A. (1976). *Alternative to IQ testing: An approach to the identification of the gifted in minority children* (Report No. 75175). San Francisco: San Francisco State University.

Hodgkinson, H. (1993). American education: The good, the bad and the task. *Phi Delta Kappan, 74*(8), 619–623.

Howells, R. F. (1992). Thinking in the morning, thinking in the evening, thinking at suppertime. *Phi Delta Kappan, 74*(3), 223–225.

Jenkins, M. D. (1936). A socio-psychological study of Negro children of superior intelligence. *Journal of Negro Education, 5*(2), 175–190.

Johnson, S. T., Starnes, W. T., Gregory, D., & Blaylock, A. (1985). Program of assessment, diagnosis, and instruction (PADI): Identifying and nurturing potentially gifted and talented minority students. *The Journal of Negro Education, 54*(3), 416–430.

Karenga, R. (1977). *Kwanzaa: Origin, concepts, practice.* Los Angeles: Kawaida Publications.

Kaufman, A. S., & Harrison, P. L. (1986). Intelligence tests and gifted assessment: What are the positives? *Roeper Review, 8*(3), 154–159.

Kaufman, A. S., & Kaufman, N. L. (1983). *Kaufman Assessment Battery for Children (K-ABC).* Circle Pines, MN: American Guidance Service.

Kitano, M. K. (1991). A multicultural educational perspective on serving the culturally diverse gifted. *Journal for the Education of the Gifted, 15*(1), 4–19.

Kitano, M. K., & Kirby, D. F. (1986). *Gifted education: A comprehensive view.* Boston: Little, Brown.

Kulieke, M. J., & Olszewski-Kubilius, P. (1989). The influence of family values and climate on the development of talent. In J. VanTassel-Baska & P. Olszewski-Kubilius (Eds.), *Patterns of influence on gifted learners: The home, the self and the school* (pp. 40–59). New York: Teachers College Press.

Lincoln, C. E., & Mamiya, L. H. (1990). *The Black church in the African-American experience.* Durham, NC: Duke University Press.

McKensie, J. A. (1986). The influence of identification practices, race, and SES on the identification of gifted students. *Gifted Child Quarterly, 30*(2), 93–95.

McLaughlin, V., Baytops, J. L., & Sims, S. (1993). *Curriculum development resource guide: A guide to developing curriculum for special populations of gifted learners* (Contract No. PR-RZ06-A00165). Washington, DC: United States Department of Education.

Naglieri, J. A. (1985). *Matrix Analogies Test, Short Form and Expanded Form.* San Antonio, TX: Psychological Corp.

Naglieri, J. A., & Prewett, P. N. (1990). Nonverbal intelligence measure: A selected review of instruments and their use. In C. R. Reynolds & R. W. Kamphaurs (Eds.), *Handbook of psychological and educational assessment of children: Intelligence and achievement* (pp. 348–370). New York: Guilford Press.

Nobles, W. W. (1987). Psychometrics and African-American reality: A question of cultural antimony. *The Negro Educational Review, 38,* 45–55.

Ogbu, J. (1988). Human intelligence testing: A cultural-ecological perspective. *National Forum, 68*(2), 23–29.

Passow, H. (1986). Educational programs for minority, disadvantaged gifted students. In F. Kanevsky (Ed.), *Issues in gifted education: A collection of readings* (pp. 119–148). San Diego: San Diego City Schools.

Patton, J. (1992). Assessment and identification of African-American learners with gifts and talents. *Exceptional Children, 59*(2), 150–159.

Patton, J. M., Prillaman, D., McLaughlin, V., & VanTassel-Baska, J. (1989). *A research and demonstration project for culturally diverse, low income, and handicapped gifted and talented learners.* Washington, DC: U.S. Department of Education, Office of Educational Research and Improvement.

Piechowski, M. M. (1986). The concept of developmental potential. *Roeper Review, 8*(3), 190–197.

Rashid, H. M. (1981). Early childhood education as a cultural transition for African-American children. *Educational Research Quarterly, 6,* 55–63.

Raven, J. C. (1938). *Standard Progressive Matrices.* London: H. K. Lewis.

Raven, J. C. (1947a). *Advanced Progressive Matrices.* London: H. K. Lewis.

Raven, J. C. (1947b). *Coloured Progressive Matrices.* London: H. K. Lewis.

Renzulli, J. S. (1973). Talent potential in minority group students. *Exceptional Children, 39,* 437–444.

Renzulli, J. S. (1978). What makes giftedness: Re-examining a definition. *Phi Delta Kappan, 60*(3), 180–184.

Renzulli, J. S., Hartman, R. K., & Callahan, C. M. (1971). Teacher identification of superior students. *Exceptional Children, 38*(3), 211–214.

Richert, E. S. (1985). Identification of gifted children in the United States: The need for pluralistic assessment. *Roeper Review, 13*(2), 68–72.

Richert, E. S. (1987). Rampant problems and promising practices in the identification of disadvantaged gifted students. *Gifted Child Quarterly, 31*(4), 149–154.

Rimm, S. (1976). *GIFT: Group Inventory for Finding Talent.* Watertown, WI: Educational Assessment Service.

Rimm, S., & Davis, G. A. (1976). GIFT: An instrument for the identification of creativity. *Journal of Creative Behavior, 10,* 178-182.

Rimm, S., & Davis, G. A. (1980). Five years of international research with GIFT: An instrument for the identification of creativity. *Journal of Creative Behavior, 14,* 35–46.

Salvia, J., & Ysseldyke, J. E. (1978). *Assessment in special and remedial education.* Boston: Houghton Mifflin.

Sattler, J. M. (1982). *Assessment of children's intelligence and special abilities.* Boston: Allyn & Bacon.

Shade, B. (1990). *Engaging the battle for African-American minds* (commissioned paper). National Alliance of Black School Educators.

Slaughter, D. T., & Epps, E. G. (1987). The home environment and academic achievement of Black American children and youth: An overview. *Journal of Negro Education, 56*(1), 3–20.

Staunton, V. (1993, June 20). Giftedness in black and white. *Virginian Pilot and Ledger Star,* p. C1.

Sternberg, R. (1985). *Beyond I.Q.* Cambridge, England: Cambridge University Press.

Sternberg, R. (1991). Giftedness according to the triarchic theory of human intelligence. In N. Colangelo & G. A. Davis (Eds.), *Handbook of gifted education* (pp. 45–53). Boston: Allyn & Bacon.

Torrance, E. P. (1969). Creative positives of disadvantaged children and youth. *Gifted Child Quarterly, 13,* 71–81.

Torrance, E. P. (1977). *Discovery and nurturance of giftedness in the culturally different.* Reston, VA: The Council for Exceptional Children.

Torrance, E. P. (1987). *Using tests of creative thinking to guide the teaching of creative behavior.* Bensenville, IL: Scholastic Testing Service.

Torrance, E. P. (in press). *The blazing drive: The creative personality.* Buffalo, NY: Bearly.

Valencia, R. R. (1979). Comparison of intellectual performance of Chicano and Anglo third grade school boys on the Raven's Coloured Progressive Matrices. *Psychology in the Schools, 16*(3), 448–453.

VanTassel-Baska, J. (1989). The role of the family in the success of disadvantaged gifted learners. In J. VanTassel-Baska & P. Olszewski-Kubilius (Eds.), *Patterns of influence on gifted learners: The home, the self and the school* (pp. 68–80). New York: Teachers College Press.

VanTassel-Baska, J. (1992). *Planning effective curriculum for gifted learners.* Denver: Love.

VanTassel-Baska, J., Patton, J., & Prillaman, D. (1989). A national survey of programs and practices for at-risk learners. *Focus on Exceptional Children, 22*(3), 1–15.

Ward, T., Ward, S., Landrum, M., & Patton, J. (1992). *Examination of a new protocol for the identification of at-risk gifted learners.* Paper presented at the annual meeting of the American Educational Research Association, San Francisco.

Ward, T., Ward, S., & Patton, J. (1992). *An analysis of the utility of the Matrix Analogies Test with at-risk gifted learners.* Paper presented at the annual meeting of the American Educational Research Association, San Francisco.

Wilson, A. N. (1992). *Understanding Black adolescent male violence: Its remediation and prevention.* New York: Afrikan World Infosystems.

Wilson, M. N., & Tolson, T. F. (1990). Familial support in the Black community. *Journal of Clinical Child Psychology, 19*(4), 347–355.

Zappia, I. A. (1989). Identification of gifted Hispanic students: A multidimensional view. In C. J. Maker & S. W. Schiever (Eds.), *Critical issues in gifted education* (pp. 19–26). Austin, TX: PRO-ED.

APPENDIX 2A

Project Mandala
Parent (Nomination) Checklist

Please respond to the following items My child . . .	Some of the time	Most of the time	Always
1. is alert, and observant.	____	____	____
2. asks many questions, wants to know how and why.	____	____	____
3. seems to "know about" ideas, issues that other children his/her age are not aware of.	____	____	____
4. likes to pretend, has an active imagination.	____	____	____
5. is aware of problems, offers solutions that are different and unique.	____	____	____
6. is very expressive in conversation, tells many detailed stories.	____	____	____
7. enjoys "acting out" characters, becomes absorbed in role playing.	____	____	____
8. sets high standards, is quick to point out "right or wrong."	____	____	____
9. enjoys the company of older children and adults, talks easily with them.	____	____	____
10. expresses a sensitivity to nature, animals, seasons, etc.	____	____	____
11. is a "leader," easily gets other children to listen to him/her.	____	____	____

12. has the following hobbies and special interests (drawing, collecting, singing, reading, writing, making models, etc.):

_____

_____

13. likes the following kinds of books: _____

_____

14. belongs to the following community or church organizations (Scouts, Boys Club, youth groups, teams, etc.):

_____

_____

_____

Child's Name	Age

Parent/Guardian Signature	Date

PART II
Antecedent Factors Surrounding Complementary School Learning Environments

CHAPTER THREE

Self-Concept Model for African American Students in Special Education Settings

Festus E. Obiakor

African American students confront a myriad of problems in school programs and the mainstream society. The response to their multidimensional problems has been in the way of reports and studies that have tended to blame them and their families for society's ills (Algozzine & Obiakor, 1995; Hamburg, 1992). These reports have stressed excellence and quality in education with little response to equity and inclusiveness. In the midst of this confusion are cries and yearnings for practical programs tailored to meet the needs of African American students in special education settings. Although successes have not been very apparent, schools are beginning to offer nontraditional identification, assessment, and instructional programs. Old misguided ideas are continuously challenged, and new ideas are modified (Obiakor, 1994). Self-concept is one construct that cuts across old and new instructional programs. It is an important educational variable, yet there are disagreements on its definition, assessment, interpretation, and utility. In working with African American students, the contemporary definition that conceptualizes self-concept as an individual's repertoire of self-descriptive behavior appears to be most beneficial. In this chapter, I use the contemporary model in discussing the self-concepts of African American students.

ISSUE CLARIFICATION

Historically, education has been called to effectively respond to social, economic, cultural, and political problems (Carnegie Forum on Education and the Economy, 1986; Committee for Economic Development, 1985; Holmes Group, 1988; National Commission on Excellence in Education, 1983). Unfortunately, schools have not responded to the needs of African American students to the greatest possible extent. It is no wonder that reforms and reports repeatedly come in different ways without respect for circumstances and "real" solutions. Many questions are beginning to surface. For instance, Cuban (1990) questioned, "Are we attacking the right problem? Have the policies we adopted fit the problem? Have practitioners implemented the policies intended? . . . Right problems, wrong solutions? or vice versa? Are we dealing with the problem or the policies of the problem?" (pp. 5–6).

It has been argued, and rightly so, that educational reports and studies that flourished in the 1980s were motivated by political conservatives to respond to educational prospects, constraints, and challenges. Authors of these reports and studies apparently failed to address serious and inescapable issues of equity and inclusiveness, especially with regard to African American students. Public education, both general and special education, has been Eurocentric, and has incessantly stressed European and Anglo concepts, values, and histories. This historical reality shows that public education has not addresssed the needs of African American students and those students who do not quite fit into the traditional categories of exceptionality (e.g., at-risk students). According to Davis and McCaul (1990) and Pallas, Natriello, and McDill (1989), indicators for at-risk students include (a) a minority racial/ethnic group identity; (b) a poverty household; (c) a single-parent family; (d) a poorly educated mother, father, or guardian; and (e) a non-English language background. It appears that many African American students have these indicators. Earlier, Clark (1988) had observed that "the bulk of young people who are at risk are subjected to psychological genocide" and "robbed of self esteem and the capacity to achieve" (p. iii). In fact, most at-risk students "fall into the mode of learned helplessness" (Lovitt, 1991, p. 387) when programs are inappropriately designed to address their special needs. Baer (1991) reiterated,

We need to understand who these kids are. They have potential; however, they don't know it. They need what we all have to offer, but they won't believe it. In a way, they may want to fail because there is a kind of comfort in that. After all, it's what they know best. Failure is a restful place to be. Nobody bothers them much because they can't be expected to give or participate . . . The crucial point to remember is that in spite of these obstacles, these kids have all the potential that other kids have. (p. 25)

Baer's (1991) comment demonstrates that African American students who are perceived as being at risk are not well understood by professionals who work with them. It implies that effective hybrid identification, assessment, and instructional strategies are needed to ameliorate their multidimensional problems. In addition, it implies that unwarranted suppositions about these students by professionals infringe on their self-concepts and do not assist them in becoming productive members of the society.

CONSTRUCT CLARIFICATION

As indicated earlier, self-concept is an important educational phenomenon that has traditionally and consistently cut across identification, assessment, and instructional programs for African American students. This importance notwithstanding, divergent viewpoints have been generated to make assessment and pedagogy very intriguing (Obiakor, 1994). In working with African American students, the contemporary and operational view of self-concept as an individual's repertoire of self-descriptive behavior has proven to be more productive, especially in designing Individualized Education Programs (IEPs). Like any self-descriptive behavior, self-concept can be measured, observed, and broken into identifiable subareas.

Although self-concept has continued to be the primary focus of programs for African American at-risk, disadvantaged, and atypical students, the term means different things to different people. The variability in the definition, assessment, and interpretation of self-concept has, to a large extent, led to the proliferation of measurement tools. Two particular models (perceptual and operational models) have dominated recent debates on the self-concept construct. In the following sections, I provide detailed discussions on these important models and the nature of their influence on instructional programming.

Perceptual Model of Self-Concept

The traditional or classical definition of self-concept has been based on the interrelated self. This view, which has come to be known as the perceptual or global model of self-concept, simply describes how one sees or perceives oneself. This conceptualization assumes that one's self-perceptions are fully developed before entering the classroom for the first time. As Canfield and Wells (1976) pointed out, "By the time a child reaches school age his self-concept is well formed and his reactions to learning, to school failure and success and to physical, social and emotional climate of the classroom will be determined by the beliefs and attitudes he has about himself" (p. 3).

This model's definition implies that a change in self-concept is likely to affect a wide range of student behaviors. It also assumes that when one aspect of the child's self-concept is affected, there is a "ripple" effect on his or her entire self-concept. These suppositions tend to defeat the purpose of early identification and intervention in special education. On the one hand, it is advantageous to know the antecedent "baggages" that children bring to programs. On the other hand, knowledge of these baggages forces educators to prejudge students. If the perceptual model of self-concept is applied in the classroom, it will require the involvement of the teacher with the school *and* home aspects of the African American student's life, and thus will lead to errors in judgment. Apparently, such a practice will place the teacher in a rather precarious position of encouraging classroom discussion on aspects of the child's life that are outside the primary domain of the school's delegated responsibility (Muller, Chambliss, & Muller, 1982, 1983). Moreover, errors in judgment encourage student labeling or categorization and hamper classroom learning and/or functional learning outcomes. It becomes educationally unproductive to use the perceptual conceptualization of self-concept in regular, special, or mainstreamed classrooms, especially in designing IEPs for African American students.

It is important to note, therefore, that traditional instruments used to measure self-concept have sometimes produced consistent results, but have failed to measure what they purport to measure. Issues of validity and reliability have continued to haunt popular standardized instruments. In fact, some instruments have failed to define self-concept, the construct they are supposed to measure. The pertinent questions, then, are as follows: How can an instrument measure the construct that it failed to define? How can strengths and weaknesses of African American students be identified when the interpretation of results is globally based on the "positive" or "negative" and "high" or "low" perspectives? How can effective individualized programs be designed to enhance self-concepts of an African American student when his or her specific area of weakness is undelineated?

Operational Model of Self-Concept

The operational model of self-concept is the contemporary approach of viewing the self. This alternative view conceptualizes self-concept as an individual's repertoire of self-descriptive behavior (Muller, 1978). Helper (1955), Marsh, Parker, and Barnes (1985), Marsh and Smith (1986), Obiakor and Stile (1989, 1990, 1993), Obiakor, Stile, and Muller (1993), and Shavelson, Bolus, and Keasling (1980) are among researchers who have attempted to approach self-concept from a similar theoretical perspective. From this framework, a student's self-descriptions can be accurate or inaccurate, consistent or contradictory, extensive or limited, covert or overt, and sometimes changeable as the context changes. Over a decade ago, Muller et al. (1982) argued that "self-descriptive behaviors quantified in terms of positiveness should, when factor analyzed, yield a number of discrete, internally consistent factors" (p. 7). Operationally, self-concept has three subsets—self-knowledge, self-esteem, and self-ideal—that can be measured in the areas of physical maturity, peer relations, academic success, and school adaptiveness (Muller, 1978; Muller et al., 1982, 1983; Obiakor & Stile, 1989, 1990, 1993). The following descriptions are based on Muller's (1978) and Muller, Chambliss, and Muller's (1982, 1983) work:

- *Self-knowledge*—A subset of self-descriptive behaviors that describe the individual's characteristics or qualities. This includes descriptions of physical appearance, behavior, abilities, and cognitive patterns. Self-knowledge includes self-descriptions that indicate an evaluation of characteristics but does not include statements that indicate self-valuations. A sample statement is "I have problems succeeding in school."

- *Self-esteem*—The subset of self-descriptive behaviors that indicate self-valuations. In this instance, the individual evaluates certain self-characteristics relative to how he or she values those characteristics. A sample statement is "I like myself for who I am."

- *Self-ideal*—The subset of self-descriptive behaviors that indicate self-qualities that the student desires to achieve or maintain through the expenditure of personal efforts. A sample statement is "I will endeavor to work hard in spite of my problems or who I am."

It appears that dividing the self-concept of the student into discrete construct areas has important educational implications (Muller et al., 1982; Obiakor, 1990a; Obiakor & Alawiye, 1990; Obiakor & Fowler, 1991; Obiakor, Muller, & Stile, 1987; Obiakor & Stile, 1993; Obiakor, Stile, & Muller, 1988, 1993; Princes & Obiakor, 1990). For example, as Muller et al. (1982) explained, "Instructional strategies designed to alter self-concept can be focused on those aspects of self-concept directly related to school. This eliminates the need to intrude into the personal or family aspects of the student's life. A related implication is that programs designed to impact on self-concept in one area (e.g. peer relations) are not likely to impact on self-concept in other areas (e.g. academics). Our own work convinced us that for the majority of students, effective classroom management of self-concept can be accomplished by limiting our efforts to the school life of the child" (p. 9).

IMPLICATIONS FOR AFRICAN AMERICAN STUDENTS IN SPECIAL EDUCATION SETTINGS

The above discussions highlight three major educational implications for African American students in special education settings. First, self-concept is an important construct that special educators and service providers working with these students should take seriously. Second, self-concept has been a misunderstood and misused construct which, when interpreted operationally, can yield fruitful dividends for African American students. Third (and probably most important), the self-concept of African American students can be measured and enhanced to assist them in making functional goal-directed decisions. As a consequence, special educators need to be aware that most standardized instruments that utilize self-description quantify the observed self-descriptions in terms of positiveness or negativeness. Those self-descriptions that reflect the social ideal of the dominant society are scored as positive and those that are at odds are scored as negative. Furthermore, self-concept scores that reflect simple positiveness have interpretive difficulties and do not provide adequate information for proper use of self-concept test results. The utility of an instrument should be the primary concern of special education practitioners. The emphasis should be on the identification of school-related and non–school-related behaviors that could facilitate or impede functional and critical goal-directed decisions of African American students. There are apparent disadvantages in globalizing behaviors that students exhibit and in wrongfully interpreting students' capabilities. These misinterpretations by professionals and/or parents might be internalized by African American at-risk and disadvantaged students very early in life. As a result, the self-fulfilling behavior is ingrained in the student.

On the whole, special educators and service providers need to understand the area-specific, situation-specific, and multidimensional nature of self-concept of African American students. For example, a student might be "low" in his or her self-knowledge but "high" in his or her self-esteem, or vice versa. The same student might be "low" in self-esteem but "high" in self-ideal, or vice versa. Self-concept is not a static phenomenon that is genetically handed down. It can be changed and enhanced. In other words, it is counterproductive to stigmatize an African American student in special education programs based on his or her self-concept results from instruments that not only lack validity and reliability but also fail to define the construct that they are supposed to measure. The student's self-concept cannot be based on service providers' perceptions. It should be viewed as a self-descriptive behavior that can be observed, described, measured, and developed.

I have used this model in many educational programs, including Project Self-Responsibility, a program that resulted from a public service to many inner-city schools. In this project, *The 24 Open-Form Self-Concept Questions* (Obiakor, 1990b) were used to assess and enhance self-concepts of at-risk students (in this case, predominantly African American males placed in self-contained classrooms because of their perceived learning and behavioral problems). These 24 questions reflect self-knowledge, self-esteem, and self-ideal. Table 3.1 lists the questions contained in this instrument. The open-form questions have been found to encourage students to take charge because no response is viewed as wrong no matter how inappropriate. Borg and Gall (1989) disclosed that in open-form questions "subjects make any response they wish in their own words" (p. 428).

Positive results of Project Self-Responsibility include the following:

1. No student involved in the project dropped out of school. One of the students in the elementary school progressed and moved into a mainstreamed regular classroom from his self-contained special education classroom.

2. Students involved in the project started developing decision-making skills and began to take control of their problems.

3. Students involved in the project began to rely on their capabilities while acknowledging their weaknesses.

4. Students involved in the project understood that they were responsible for their own feelings and actions.

5. Students involved in the project began to realistically appreciate themselves, as well as their classmates, teachers, and parents.

SELF-CONCEPT ENHANCEMENT STRATEGIES

Self-concept of at-risk, disadvantaged, or atypical students (e.g., African American students) can be enhanced. To enhance their

TABLE 3.1. The 24 Open-Form Self-Concept Questions

A. *Self-Knowledge Questions*

1. What is your name? Do you have other names?
2. What can you tell me about yourself, your classmates, your teachers, and your parents?
3. How are you similar with your classmates?
4. How are you different from your classmates?
5. How "good" a student are you?
6. How "bad" a student are you?
7. How "happy" a student are you?
8. How well do you understand yourself?

B. *Self-Esteem Questions*

1. Which names do you prefer to be called?
2. What are the things that you like best about yourself, your classmates, your teachers, and your parents?
3. Why do you like yourself for being who you are?
4. Why do you not like yourself for being who you are?
5. How do you like yourself for being similar with your classmates?
6. How do you like yourself for being different from your classmates?
7. Why do you think you are proud of who you are?
8. Why are you happy (or maybe unhappy) because you love (or maybe hate) yourself for who you are?

C. *Self-Ideal Questions*

1. How did your understanding of yourself influence your school work?
2. How did your love for yourself influence your adjustment in school or how you relate to your peers?
3. How did your love for yourself influence your hard work?
4. How has your understanding of your classmates, teachers, and parents influenced your academic success in school?
5. How have your similarities with your classmates affected your efforts?
6. How have your differences with your classmates affected your efforts?
7. What is your daily schedule? Do you know that "time is money"? What exciting or unexciting thing have you done today?
8. What was your high point this week? What was your low point this week? What have you learned about yourself that you are willing to change this week? What do you plan to change or accomplish next week?

From *The 24 Open-Form Self-Concept Questions* by F. E. Obiakor, 1990, Chattanooga: The University of Tennessee.

self-concepts, five major human development activities should be practiced by special educators and service providers. These activities are (a) caring for students, (b) having reasonable expectations, (c) listening to students, (d) providing rewarding environments, and (e) involving the student.

Caring for Students

One of the problems in special education today is that educators and service providers are so concerned with the "end" that they ignore the "means" to that end. Feelings are as important as intellect. There is nothing wrong with appealing to the senses of African American students. DeBlassie and Jones (1976) explained that "when a person's self-concept is threatened his perceptual field is narrowed and distorted" (p. 69). Bandura (1977) indicated that children are more prone to imitate the behavior of adults who appeal to them. Because children learn what they live, it is important that special educators working with African American students realistically care for these students. This caring spirit should be reflected in the adequate identification, assessment, and instructional procedure for African American "special" students.

Caring special educators spend time trying to know their African American students. Caring helps these students to accurately assess their capabilities as they relate to self-knowledge, self-esteem, and self-ideal. Caring should entail understanding of students' strengths, and using these strengths to work on their weaknesses. Students who are not *appropriately* challenged are not well cared for. Caring for African American students involves a combination of many variables, such as commitment to quality and equity, positive teacher attitudes, culturally relevant curriculum content and pedagogy, culturally relevant behavioral systems, and positive interpersonal communication with students and their families (Obiakor, Algozzine, & Ford, 1993).

Having Reasonable Expectations

Educators' expectations usually influence their students' self-concepts. These expectations lead to competency, and sometimes to frustration. It is important that special educators respect their

African American students' learning styles and communication patterns. These students are different interindividually and intra-individually, and their expectations sometimes differ. African American students need to be taught very early the importance of self-determination, self-respect, and self-responsibility. As Wilson (1991) pointed out, "these students have low academic expectations of themselves, and the schools have low expectations of them: thus self-fulfilling prophecy of low achievement is hardly surprising" (p. B1).

African American students in special education settings deserve realistic expectations. Dedrick and Froyen (1980) stated that "our current motivation problem in schools stems from a lack of consensus among adults about the ends of education and the evidence we will accept that these ends have been achieved" (p. 297). Self-knowledge, self-valuation, and self-responsibility are basic ingredients of intrinsic motivation and internal focus of control. Special educators should challenge African American students in their programs, and desist from the assumption that "poverty" correlates with "poor" intelligence or self-concept. According to Dedrick and Froyen, "it is never enough to act as if one is motivated. Motivation should sustain behaviors that produce quality results" (p. 301). Special educators and service providers should motivate African American students with reasonable expectations. More than a decade ago, Goodfried (1983) wrote, "Encountering discrepant challenging, or novel stimuli and experiences may not only produce cognitive intrusive motivation, but may allow for the child's experience of mastery and competence through developing understanding of unfamiliar materials" (p. 68).

Listening to Students

Active listening skills are useful tools for special educators. It is easy to discover present expectations and levels of functioning of African American students by listening to them. Active listening skills prevent self-hatred and enhance self-esteem. Cultural and family pride of African American students cannot take place without good teaching and good listening. Good teaching does not entail punishing the child indiscriminately under the umbrella of discipline—such a discipline can lead to alienation and deception.

Active listening brings together teachers, parents, and students. If listening is appropriately and consistently done, it will be easy to observe personality changes in African American students. Supported children are inspired to be self-confident in whatever they set out to do. "Blind" support for the African American student is as dangerous as "no" support at all.

As a consequence, special educators and service providers should make listening a priority when working with African American students. There are situational variables that constantly impinge upon their learning experiences. African American students constantly reveal their individual characteristics and personalities. Somehow, practitioners fail to listen. Unfortunately, when they do listen, they see these students from their jaundiced views. Minton and Schneider (1980) remarked that "situational variables appear to be especially pertinent to the prediction of school achievement when they are interacting with individual difference characteristics" (p. 153). Using his personal experience as a student of a White teacher, Steele (1990) confirmed how individuals carry oppressional memories that overshadow their sense of identity. Steele wrote,

> The condition of being Black in America means that one will likely endure more wounds to one's self esteem than others and that the capacity for self-doubt born of these wounds will be compounded and expanded by the Black race's reputation for inferiority. . . . Black skin has more dehumanizing stereotypes associated with it than any other skin color in America, if not the world. When a Black presents himself in an integrated situation, he knows that his skin alone may bring these stereotypes to life in the minds of those he meets and that he, as an individual, may be diminished by his race before he has a chance to reveal a single aspect of his personality. (p. 36)

Providing Rewarding Environments

The environments in which students grow up are an integral part of their social and emotional growth. The classroom environment provides another element that can influence students' growth and self-concept. Special educators and service providers can help African American students to realistically evaluate their environment. Goodfried (1983) asserted that "if the environment provides feedback to children about their competence, both mastery and attributions of mastery should be enhanced" (p. 68). Special educators should provide an environment that recognizes the symbols, values, history, and culture that African American exceptional students bring to school programs. Teachers from the dominant culture should not teach and evaluate African American students on the bases of their own values and personal idiosyncracies.

The learning environment cannot be downplayed. The best environment should be that which provides African American students with accurate self-understanding, self-knowledge, self-esteem, and self-ideal. Put another way, the best environment should produce the best experience for African American students. Therefore, the best experience should lead to a constant renewal and self-improvement of the student, his or her behavior, and capabilities to maximize his or her potential. As Minton and Schneider (1980) pointed out,

> We cannot limit ourselves to the identification of trait dimensions or topological classification across individuals without also considering the characteristics of the environment within which the individuals function. Nor can we limit ourselves to analysis of the environment determinants. . . . We have to ask ourselves what kind of society is most desirable for the expression of human diversity—for the opportunity for each of us to grow as individuals and at the same time not infringe on the rights of others to develop their own individuality. (p. 489)

Involving the Student

In all situations, African American students should be involved in making rules concerning their behaviors. Teachers always like to take charge without involving students that they are supposed to help. Responsibility should come not only from teachers and other professionals, but also from the students themselves. Self-concept cannot be enhanced without the personal involvement of the African American student in question. Very often, African American students judged as inferior based on the old theory of biological determinism (Gould, 1981; Minton & Schneider, 1980) are inappropriately classified, categorized, and placed in special education

(Hilliard, 1989; Samuda, 1975). These students experience few realistic African American role models (American Association of Colleges for Teacher Education, 1987; Ogbu, 1990) and frequently are presumed to have low or negative self-concepts and inferior self-perceptions (Lawrence & Winchell, 1973; Obiakor, 1990a, 1991; Obiakor & Alawiye, 1990). These problems are interrelated because they all affect the self-identity, self-pride, and self-involvement of African American students. Unfortunately, special educators, even those with good intentions, often sympathize with African American learners rather than honestly involving them in their growth and uplift. By not involving African American students, these educators help to perpetuate negative attributes of self-pity. As Mahoney (1990) observed, "Self-pity, when practiced over a period of time, can become a deadly habit. That habit becomes like a chain, heavy enough to enslave us. The result of such enslavement can be physical illness, depression, anger, frustration, and bitterness" (p. A7).

PERSPECTIVES

African American students confront divergent problems that include poor school performance, negative attitudes and low expectations toward them by school personnel, and uncertainty about their future. These problems continually challenge special educators and service providers to search for new ways to enhance the self-love, self-understanding, and self-concept of African American students. Even with this effort, the definition, assessment, and interpretation of self-concept remains difficult. The perceptual definition of self-concept and its application to assessment, interpretation, and enhancement of self-concepts of African American students present numerous problems, which include the following:

1. Instruments that are traditionally used to measure self-concepts of African American students (e.g., the *Piers-Harris Self-Concept Scale*) have failed to define self-concept.

2. Interpretations based on the traditional perceptual model are global and fail to identify specific areas of strengths and weaknesses of African American students.

3. Some self-concept instruments have standardized norms, and it is counterproductive educationally to compare African American students' specific self-descriptive behaviors with those of students of different cultures and socioeconomic backgrounds.

4. The typical high and low or positive and negative interpretations of self-concept are not useful for designing Individualized Education Programs for African American students.

5. Errors in interpretations may affect student behavior. When an African American student is misperceived or misjudged as having a low or negative self-concept, he or she might unconsciously develop a behavior pattern that leads to a self-fulfilling prophecy. There is a stigma that goes along with a wrong label or categorization.

CONCLUSION

African American students are capable of learning and making goal-directed decisions when they have accurate self-understanding, self-love, and self-empowerment. Special educators and service providers should look at self-concept as a self-descriptive behavior that can change as situations change. They need to minimize the conscious and unconscious categorization of African American students, especially those in special education settings. Coming from disadvantaged environments does not signal disadvantaged self-concepts. Poverty does not indicate poor intelligence or poor self-concept. Special educators must be willing to invest the time and energy needed to understand, test, teach, retest, and reteach African American students so that they will be self-motivated, self-responsible, and self-productive citizens in today's changing world.

REFERENCES

Algozzine, B., & Obiakor, F. E. (1995, Spring). African American quandaries in school programs. *Scholar and Educator, 17*(2), 75–88.

American Association of Colleges for Teacher Education. (1987). *Minority teacher recruitment and retention: A public policy issue.* Washington, DC: Author.

Baer, G. L. (1991). *Turning our at-risk kids around.* Moravia, NY: Chronicle Guidance Publications.

Bandura, A. (1977). *Social learning theory.* Englewood Cliffs, NJ: Prentice-Hall.

Borg, W. R., & Gall, M. D. (1989). *Educational research: An introduction* (5th ed.). New York: Longman.

Canfield, J., & Wells, H. C. (1976). *100 ways to enhance self-concept in the classroom.* Englewood Cliffs, NJ: Prentice-Hall.

Carnegie Forum on Education and the Economy. (1986). *A nation prepared: Teachers for the 21st century.* New York: Carnegie Foundation.

Clark, K. B. (1988). Foreward. *America's shame, America's hope: Twelve million youth at risk.* Chapel Hill, NC: MDC.

Committee for Economic Development. (1985). *Investing in our children: Business and the public schools.* New York: Author.

Cuban, L. (1990, January–Febuary). Reforming again, again, and again. *Educational Researcher, 19*(1), 3–13.

Davis, W. E., & McCaul, E. P. (1990). *At-risk children and youth: A crisis in our schools and society.* Orono, ME: Institute for the Study of At-Risk Students, University of Maine.

DeBlassie, R. R., & Jones, W. P. (1976). *Educational psychology: The teaching–learning process.* Monterey, CA: Brooks/Cole.

Dedrick, C., & Froyen, L. (1980, March). Motivation maxims: Why they fail to motivate. *The Education Forum,* pp. 295–304.

Goodfried, A. A. (1983). Intrinsic motivation in young children. *Young Children, 39*(1), 64–73.

Gould, S. J. (1981). *The mismeasure of man.* New York: Norton.

Hamburg, D. A. (1992). *The family crucible and healthy child development.* New York: Carnegie Corporation.

Helper, N. M. (1955). Learning theory and self-concept. *Journal of Abnormal and Social Psychology, 5,* 184–194.

Hilliard, A. G. (1989, December). Cultural style in teaching and learning. *The Education Digest,* pp. 21–23.

Holmes Group. (1988). From tomorrow's teachers. In K. Ryan & J. M. Cooper (Eds.), *Kaleidoscope: Readings in education* (5th ed., pp. 484–493). Boston: Houghton Mifflin.

Lawrence, E. A., & Winchell, J. (1973). Self-concept and the retarded: Research and issues. *Journal of Exceptional Children, 39,* 310–319.

Lovitt, T. C. (1991). *Preventing school drop-outs: Tactics for at-risk, remedial, and mildly handicapped adolescents.* Austin, TX: PRO-ED.

Mahoney, N. W. (1990, August 1). Self-pity can be a deadly habit. *Chattanooga News Free Press Plus,* p. A7.

Marsh, H. W., Parker, J., & Barnes, J. (1985). Multidimensional adolescent self-concepts: Their relationship to age, sex, and academic measures. *American Educational Research Journal, 22*(3), 422–444.

Marsh, H. W., & Smith, I. D. (1986). Cross-national study of the structure and level of multidimensional self-concepts: An application of confirmatory factor analysis. *Resources in Education, 21*(9), 192 (ERIC Document Reproduction Service No. ED 269 429).

Minton, H. L., & Schneider, F. W. (1980). *Differential psychology.* Prospect Heights, IL: Waveland Press.

Muller, D. (1978). Self-concept: A new alternative for education. In *The College of Education Dialogue Series Monograph* (ERIC Document Reproduction Service No. ED 165 067). Las Cruces: New Mexico State University.

Muller, D., Chambliss, J., & Muller, A. (1982, October). *Enhancing self-concept in the classroom.* Paper presented at the Annual Conference of the National Education Association of New Mexico, Las Cruces.

Muller, D., Chambliss, J., & Muller, A. (1983, March). *Making self-concept a relevant education concern.* Paper presented at the Annual Conference of the Association for Supervision and Curriculum Development, Houston.

National Commission on Excellence in Education. (1983). *A nation at risk: The imperative for educational reform.* Washington, DC: Author.

Obiakor, F. E. (1990a, Spring). Development of self-concept: Impact on students' learning. *SAEOPP Journal: The Journal of the Southeastern Association of Educational Opportunity Program Personnel, 9*(1), 16–23.

Obiakor, F. E. (1990b). *The 24 Open-Form Self-Concept Questions.* Chattanooga: The University of Tennessee.

Obiakor, F. E. (1991, Spring). Self-concept: Impact on Black students' learning. *SENGA, 1*(2), 48–53.

Obiakor, F. E. (1994). *The eight-step multicultural approach: Learning and teaching with a smile.* Dubuque, IA: Kendall/Hunt.

Obiakor, F. E., & Alawiye, O. (1990, October). *Development of accurate self-concept in Black children.* Paper presented at the Council for Exceptional Children (CEC) Symposia on Cultural Diverse Exceptional Children, Albuquerque, NM.

Obiakor, F. E., Algozzine, B., & Ford, B. A. (1993, October). Urban education, general education initiative, and service delivery to African American students. *Urban Education, 28*(3), 313–327.

Obiakor, F. E., & Fowler, W. R. (1991, November). *African-American males experiencing school failure: Alternative self-concept model for special educators.* Paper presented at the Council for Exceptional Children Topical Conference on At-Risk Children and Youth, New Orleans.

Obiakor, F. E., Muller, D., & Stile, S. (1987, July). *The development of self-concept in visually impaired persons.* Paper presented at the Regional Conference for the Education and Rehabilitation of the Blind and Handicapped, New Mexico School for the Visually Handicapped, Alamogordo.

Obiakor, F. E., & Stile, S. W. (1989). Enhancing self-concept in students with visual handicaps. *The Journal of Visual Impairment and Blindness, 83*(5), 255–257.

Obiakor, F. E., & Stile, S. W. (1990, March). The self-concepts of visually impaired and normally sighted middle school children. *The Journal of Psychology, 12*(2), 199–206.

Obiakor, F. E., & Stile, S. W. (1993). *Self-concept of exceptional learners: Current perspectives for educators.* Dubuque, IA: Kendall/Hunt.

Obiakor, F. E., Stile, S. W., & Muller, D. (1988, March). *The self-concept of the visually impaired: An area-specific model.* Paper presented at the 66th Annual National Convention of the Council for Exceptional Children, Washington, DC.

Obiakor, F. E., Stile, S. W., & Muller, D. (1993). Self concept in school programs: Conceptual and research foundations. In F. E. Obiakor & S. W. Stile (Eds.), *Self-concept of exceptional learners: Current perspectives for educators* (pp. 1–17). Dubuque, IA: Kendall/Hunt.

Ogbu, J. U. (1990, August). Understanding diversity: Summary statements. *Education and Urban Society, 22,* 425–429.

Pallas, A. M., Natriello, G., & McDill, E. L. (1989). The changing nature of the disadvantaged population: Current dimensions and future trends. *Educational Researcher, 18*(5), 16–22.

Princes, C. W., & Obiakor, F. E. (1990). Disabled students: An area-specific model of self concept. In J. J. Vander Putten (Ed.), *Researching new heights: Proceedings of the 1989 AHSSPPE conference* (pp. 35–50). Madison, WI: Omni Press.

Samuda, R. J. (1975). *Psychological testing of American minorities: Issues and consequences.* New York: Harper & Row.

Shavelson, R., Bolus, R., & Keasling, J. (1980). Self-concept: Recent developments in theory and methods. *New Directions for Testing and Measurement,* pp. 23–43.

Steele, S. (1990, October 3). The "unseen agent" of low self-esteem. *Education Week,* p. 36.

Wilson, R. (1991, August). Intellectually and philosophically, we must divorce educational achievement from cultural affirmation. *The Chronicle of Higher Education,* pp. B1–B3.

CHAPTER FOUR

The Language of African American Learners: Effective Assessment and Instructional Programming for Children with Special Needs

Harry N. Seymour, Tempii Champion, and Janice Jackson

The need for educators to provide appropriate attention for African American children is a major thesis throughout this book. Several of the contributing authors of this text express concern about the widespread academic failure of African American children, particularly males. In addressing this concern, the contributors attempt to identify causes for poor performance and to make recommendations for educational reform. Much of the discussion focuses on the normal classroom learner; however, in many ways the issues raised about children without disabilities are just as important to and applicable for the child with "special needs." Within the context of this larger and more general educational problem involving all African American children, we address in this chapter the child with special needs.

To properly treat African American children with special needs, the teacher and speech–language pathologist (SLP) must have an understanding of and an explanation for the poor academic performance of African American children in general. The reasons for such widespread failure cannot be ignored when treating the particular problems of children with special needs. Although by definition there can be many differences between the child with special needs and children without disabilities, there are nevertheless important similarities with respect to the context in which their learning takes place as well as the curriculum demands they both must face. Indeed, the curriculum demands determine the academic preparation and skills required of both children without disabilities and children with special needs. For this reason, factors affecting children without disabilities will also affect children with special needs, but to an even greater degree. Professionals must gain an understanding of what these factors are in order to adapt and create appropriate educational strategies and methods. Thus, treatment strategies must relate to expectations of the academic program.

Factors often cited as major explanations for poor academic success among African American children are social, economic, political, and cultural. These factors converge in creating a climate of racism, poverty, and inadequate educational opportunities for a majority of African American children. The Committee on the Status of Black Americans analyzed data concerning the education of African Americans in the United States since World War II and concluded that separation and differential treatment continue to be widespread in the elementary schools (cited in Jaynes & Williams, 1989). The committee also reported that, to reduce impediments to children's advancement, four areas of national life need improvement: (a) access to education and health care, (b) economic growth, (c) reduction of all forms of racism, and (d) development and reform of social welfare programs that avoid long-term poverty.

Similar issues were raised by Hilliard (1980), who stated the following three principles as requisite for special education to succeed with African American children:

1. We must accept the reality of culture.

2. We must accept the reality of oppression.

3. We must accept the meaninglessness of *minority* as a term for a group.

In discussing the first principle, Hilliard defined culture as "the distinctive creativity of a particular group of people" (p. 585), and he included language, worldview, values, and style as important components of one's culture. He insisted that African retentions have had an important impact on American culture, particularly within the African American culture, and continue to play a major role today. Thus, when working with African American children, it is important to realize that they have a culture that did not begin with slavery in the United States.

The reality of oppression, Hilliard's second principle, refers to the fact that many of today's conditions were prevalent when the Emancipation Proclamation, legally freeing African Americans from slavery, was signed by President Lincoln in 1863. African Americans in the United States have fought racism and oppression for as long as they have been in this country. Throughout these years of struggle, the public education system has remained a formidable and somewhat immutable form of oppression. Although this system was founded on the principle of a free and equitable education for all children, it has failed in this primary principle.

Smitherman (1977) insisted that, for education to be meaningful and successful for African American children, changes are needed not only in educational policy, but also in social and economic policy. Simply meeting the educational needs of African American children does not address the conditions in which they live. The Children's Defense Fund (1991) reported that infant mortality is greater for African American infants born only 5 miles from the White House than in many third-world countries such as Trinidad. This outrageous statistic is only one of many indicators of how African American children continue to be placed at the bottom of public policy, which supports and maintains conditions of poverty and disenfranchisement.

The lives of children of color are marginalized within U.S. society. Even the way in which society refers to these children is a source of derogation. Hilliard (1980) made the point, with respect to his third principle, that the term *minority*, used to describe groups of people, is meaningless. It has a numerical referent designating minority status for those whose population count is less than the majority group made up of White Americans. However, this concept distorts and misrepresents the people to whom the term refers. Moreover, the minority-versus-majority distinction is becoming less clear in the 1990s given that so-called minorities make up a majority of the top 25 of our largest cities (U.S. Department of Commerce, 1990). Indeed, by the middle of the next century, people of color will approach majority status nationwide. More important, relegating any group to a minority status homogenizes such groups and ignores their individual contributions, as well as their heritage and culture.

According to Hilliard (1980), the three principles just discussed should be important considerations in conducting assessments, interpretation, communication, and establishing rapport with African American children. Otherwise, he contended, diagnosis and interpretations could be incomplete and/or misleading. We agree with Hilliard and also recognize the importance of social, economic, and political factors to children's educational welfare. Although these factors are of critical importance and must be addressed, their scope is so broad that adequate coverage is not possible in a single chapter. Thus, our comments about these factors constitute a brief and incomplete overview, focusing on the cultural factor as it pertains to communicative behavior and cognitive learning style.

As speech–language pathologists, our primary emphasis is communication via speech and language. However, we recognize an important link between speech and language behavior and cognition. In many respects cognition forms a "scaffold" and a framework for speech and language development and function. This relationship between cognition and language is particularly important within the context of academic success. The relevance of communication skills to reading, speaking, and writing is obvious. So too is the relevance of cognition, in that the material children are able to read and understand, the subject matter of their conversations, and the text of their writing are very much dependent on what the children have learned and are capable of learning.

Thus, learning, as it pertains to cognition, cannot be ignored when discussing communicative behavior within the context of curriculum demands. Because cognition and learning style are so pervasive, touching upon almost every facet of education, it is discussed in several ways throughout this text. However, we confine our discussion in this chapter to language behavior and cognition relative to assessing and treating language disorders among children with special needs. We begin this discussion by describing the aspects of language and cognition that concern us most.

LANGUAGE AND COGNITION

Language

Perhaps the most controversial language variety in the United States is that spoken by many African Americans. The controversy arises from a misunderstanding about language variation in general and the language of African Americans in particular. This controversy is not simply one of "White folks" not understanding "Black folks." Even among African Americans there is much contention over such basic issues as how the language of African Americans should be described and what it should be called. For example, the term *dialect* is objectionable to some when applied to African American speech and language patterns. Those objecting to this term contend that African Americans have retained essential language elements that have their roots in African languages, and thus, they argue, any description that relegates speech and language of African Americans to a dialect of English erases its history as a derivative of African languages and diminishes its status. Similar objections are raised for Black English, Black English Vernacular, Black Speech, Black Dialect, and more recently African American English. It is further argued that the "language" of African American people should bear a label that reflects its status as a language and its distinctiveness from English. According to these proponents, a more acceptable term to represent the grammatical, syntactic, and semantic dimensions of this language is *Ebonics*, a term that combines black and phonics and has no reference to English, comparatively or descriptively.

Currently this controversy is ongoing and cannot possibly be settled within the scope of this chapter. Nevertheless, we do not believe the use of the term African American English or dialect in any way denigrates or demeans the language status or integrity of the legitimate and rule-governed language system of African Americans. The position taken here is the more conventional one—that the speech and language of African Americans is considered a variety of English and, as such, a dialect. We refer to this dialect as African American English (AAE) throughout the remainder of this chapter.

Despite what we call this language system, it remains stigmatized in the larger mainstream community. This is so even though most dialects of English carry no particular stigma. Because of historical and current socio- and political dynamics within the United States, AAE is considered a nonstandard variety of English. The basis for this characterization and a further explication of the nature of language variation in this country follow.

Nonstandard English refers to dialects that differ from English patterns considered "standard." The term *Standard English* (SE) is used to describe that variety of English spoken by the most educated of a speech community (Wolfram & Fasold, 1974). Although linguists make the standard-versus-nonstandard distinction, they nevertheless recognize that both are dialects of English. As such, their position is that no dialect is inherently better than another. Indeed, linguists argue for the equivalency among dialects for much the same reasons they view languages as equal. They take the position that there is no objective basis for viewing one language as better than another. French, English, Russian, Hebrew, Swahili, and so on, are equally capable of serving the communicative needs of their respective speech communities.

The same properties that exist for languages also exist for dialects. Most particularly, what may be described as an adaptability property allows one language to serve the culture of another via the borrowing of vocabulary and imbedding of that vocabulary into a language's syntactic structure. Thus, a dialect has the capacity to adapt to practically any circumstance that requires different language lexicon, jargon, and concepts. There is nothing about Appalachian English, for example, that prevents West Virginians from talking about intricate musical arrangements of Beethoven or the complexity of Newton's law. Indeed, it may be rare to hear AAE speakers discussing the migratory pattern of the hummingbird, but there is nothing about the linguistic properties of the dialect to prevent such a discussion.

To understand these linguistic properties and their rule-governed nature, one should become familiar with the linguistic features of AAE. Ideally, this requires a more detailed linguistic description than is possible within this chapter. However, an abbreviated summary of the most prominent features is presented in Table 4.1. This summary should be viewed as an abbreviated listing of the features that differentiate AAE from other dialects of English. Also, it should be noted that such a description is not exclusive to AAE, and that several of the identified features overlap with other dialects, particularly several "nonstandard" and southern varieties of English.

The reasons for designating certain dialects as standard and others as nonstandard are more or less sociological rather than linguistic. However, there are consequences for such distinctions in that advantages accrue to those who speak the standard dialect. For this reason, there is a vested interest in maintaining the standard

TABLE 4.1. An Abbreviated List of African American English (AAE) Features

AAE Features	Examples
Phonology	
1. Reduction of final consonant of a consonant cluster	
a. When both consonants of a cluster belong to the same word (usually applies when both members of the cluster are either voiced or voiceless).	a. best → bes; band → ban
b. When past tense {-ed} is added to a word.	b. robbed → rob; kissed → kis
c. When a word beginning with a vowel follows a word with a final consonant cluster.	c. best apple → bes apple
2. Production of / ð / and /θ/	
a. The voiced interdental fricative /ð/ may be pronounced as [d] when in the initial word position.	a. this → dis
b. The voiceless interdental fricative (/θ/) may be produced as a [t].	b. thin → tin
3. Production of /r/ and /l/	
a. The /r/ and /l/ may be substituted by an unstressed schwa.	a. sister → sistuh; steal → steauh
b. The /r/ and /l/ may be omitted when they precede a consonant in a word.	b. horse → ho's
c. The /r/ and /l/ may be omitted when they follow an /o/ or /u/.	c. carol → ca'ol
4. Devoicing of final /b/, /d/, and /g/. In word-final positions /b/, /d/, and /k/ may be produced as [p], [t], and [k].	pig → p::ik; lid l::it; lab → l::ap
5. Vowel glide production. Vowels that precede a voiceless consonant may be produced with a glide.	kite → k::ite; flight → fl::ight
6. Nasalization. The final nasal consonant in the word-final position may be deleted, but the preceding vowel sounds may have a nasalized quality.	nasalization of vowels preceding nasals produce homophones in words such as *rum, run,* and *rung*
Syntax	
1. Deletion of {-ed} suffix. Because of the consonant rule discussed under phonology, the {-ed} marking for past tense, past participial forms, and derived adjectives is affected.	They talked yesterday → They talk yesterday. He has finished the job → He has finish the job. She is a blue-eyed baby → She is a blue-eye baby.
2. The regularization of irregular verbs. The {-ed} marker may be added to the present tense form of verbs that should have an irregular past tense.	He ran home → He runned home.
3. Deletion of forms of *have*. The auxiliary *have* may be contracted to form 've and 's; however, in AAE these contractions may be deleted in the present tense.	She's done well → She done well. They've gotten together → They gotten together.

(continues)

TABLE 4.1. *Continued*

4. **Deletion of {-s} suffix in third person subject–verb agreement.** The {-s} suffix marker may be deleted in the present tense of verbs when the subject of those verbs is in the third person singular.	He bakes a cake → He bake a cake.
5. **Deletion of third person singular forms of *have* and *do*.** In standard English *have* and *do* become *has* and *does* in third person singular subject constructions. This change may not take place in AAE.	He has two coins → He have two coins. She does many tricks → She do many tricks.
6. **Deletion of {-s} suffix plural marker.** When nouns are classified by a plural quantifier, the {-s} plural marker may be deleted.	The boy has five apples → The boy has five apple.
7. **Deletion of {-s} suffix possessive marker.** The {-s} marker may be deleted in possessive-word relations.	Bill's hat → Bill hat.
8. **Deletion of *is* and *are* when *gonna* is used.** *Is* and *are* may be deleted when they are followed by *gonna*.	He is gonna go fishing → He gonna go fishing.
9. **Forms of *gonna* vary.** *Gonna* takes on different forms.	I am going soon → I'mana going soon, I'mon going soon, I'ma going soon.
10. **Deletion of contracted form of *will*.** There are two conditions under which the future indicator *will* may be deleted:	
a. When it is contracted.	a. I'll follow the train → I follow the train.
b. When it precedes a word that begins with a labial consonant.	b. I will be quick about it → I be quick about it.
11. **Invariant *be* form of the verb *to be*.** The form *be* may be used as a main verb and can refer to either habitual or intermittent action as opposed to a single event.	He is writing → He be writing.
12. **Deletion of contracted *is* and *are*.** Whenever *is* and *are* can be contracted in standard English, they may be deleted in AAE.	She's pretty → She pretty. They're bold → They bold.
13. **Multiple negation.** Negation is expressed in several ways in AAE:	
a. The addition of two negatives to an auxiliary.	a. I can't go → I can't never go.
b. Two negatives added in converting an indefinite to a negative form.	b. I am somebody → I am not nobody (I ain't nobody).
c. Two negatives added to *did*.	c. I did not do anything → I ain't did nothing.
14. **Questions.** Speakers of AAE may	
a. Delete the auxiliary in yes–no questions.	a. Can he run fast? → He run fast?
b. Not invert the subject and verb in wh-questions.	b. What can we eat? → What we can eat?
c. Invert the subject and verb in embedded questions where there is no such inversion.	c. I want to know if he can sing → I want to know if can he sing.

Adapted from *The Study of Social Dialects* by W. Wolfram and R. W. Fasold, 1974, Englewood Cliffs, NJ: Prentice-Hall.

by those who speak it, even though those standards are arbitrarily derived and may be rooted in linguistic prejudice. In fact, the reasons for choosing one dialect over another as the standard have to do with people's preferences, which in turn pertains to those who are influential and powerful within society. Leaders of a society will hardly select to be prestigious any language forms that they themselves do not speak. Moreover, dialects take on the status of those who speak them. In the case of AAE, African Americans have been held in low esteem in the United States, and therefore their dialect has been held in low esteem as well. As a consequence, African American English would hardly be considered a variety of standard English, even though its linguistic properties are just as legitimate.

The implication of linguistic prejudice is that one group of language users is treated differently from another. An often-cited justification for this differential treatment is that there must be a standard for purposes of education and trade, and the most reasonable standard is that which is spoken by the most educated of the society. Hence, the "doctrine of correctness," which specifies what is correct English, serves this end (Labov, 1969). Because of the doctrine of correctness and contrary to attestations of linguistic equivalency, many nonstandard varieties of English are stigmatized and regrettably viewed to be substandard. This is unfortunately true of AAE.

The stigma carried by AAE is an indication of how greatly misunderstood it is by the general public. The nature of this misunderstanding stems from the misperception that there is something wrong with the way so many African Americans speak, and for this reason it is viewed to be substandard. Although many people confuse nonstandard with substandard, there is a distinct difference. Nonstandard implies a difference from the agreed-upon standard of a speech community, but it is not viewed to be a problem requiring a fix. This distinction is important in order to both educate the public and dispel deficit claims about AAE. Linguists do not equivocate on this issue. Linguistic scholarship exists that affirms the legitimacy and linguistic integrity of AAE and rejects the notion of substandardness.

The question of whether something is wrong with AAE dominated discussion among educators during the 1960s and 1970s. This debate centered around the deficit-versus-difference argument in which some argued that AAE was merely a different linguistic grammar from SE, whereas others asserted a deficiency. Among linguists and educators in the "ivory tower" of academia, this debate was considered won by the proponents of the difference position. Indeed, few if any linguists today argue that AAE is in any way deficient as a dialect. Moreover, the position of the American Speech-Language-Hearing Association (ASHA) (1983), the professional accreditation association for SLPs, is clear about treating AAE as a legitimate dialect of English. Nevertheless, in practice, ample evidence exists that AAE is held in low esteem and is devalued throughout the educational establishment. Consequently, the deficit position has never quite gone away and continues to be reflected in education programs and in the ways teachers and SLPs view and interact with African American children.

There is no question that within the schools a preference is demonstrated for the standard English speech patterns of middle class children. Dandy (1991) described teacher attitudes about child AAE speakers in the following ways: (a) they equated lack of school vocabulary with an overall lack of vocabulary; (b) they characterized children as not speaking in sentences or in complete thoughts and as using strange grammatical constructions; (c) they complained that children's mispronunciations resulted from failure to use their tongue, teeth, and lips; and (d) they thought children did not know the correct English sounds.

These teacher attitudes are deficit views about African American children's capacity, which cannot be attributed solely to how they talk, but also are influenced by poor educational performance across several domains of education. The children's more general educational performance and the results of standardized tests raise questions about African American children's cognitive–intellectual capacity. Deficit proponents contended that not only was there a language deficit among African American children, but that it either was caused by or reflected a cognitive deficiency. In the 1960s, several scientists (Coon, 1962; Ingle, 1964; Jensen, 1969; Shockley, 1968, cited in Marable, 1983) proposed that African Americans were not advanced intellectually and socially. Shockley (1968) stated, "the major deficit in Negro intellectual performance must be primarily of hereditary origin" (cited in Marable, 1983, p. 252). During the same time period, African American children were entering into desegregated classrooms and failing at a disproportionate rate compared with White middle class children. Whether this failure is attributed to socioeconomic factors or, as deficit proponents would have it, to cognitive–intellectual inade-quacies, it has grave implications. The subject of cognition is directly pertinent to the study of children's capacity to learn and function competently with language.

Cognition

As with language, there have been several observations that aspects of cognition may be different or at least reflected differently in African American child behavior. Assertions that African American children have different learning styles from other groups of children have been proposed by several African American educators (Hale-Benson, 1982; Hilliard, 1980). These educators contend that much of the failure of African American children can be attributed to a mismatch between the children's learning styles and the teaching style of schools. Before more is said about the nature of this mismatch, we shall explore the likely origin of this cognitive difference.

The argument is made that cognitive behavior of African American children reflects various cultural and socialization patterns that derive from an African origin. Holloway (1991) claimed that the enforced isolation of slaves contributed to the retention of Africanisms. Many of today's customs, within the African American community, including soul food, music (jazz, blues, gospel), religious customs, and expressions of the arts, may be traced back to either Africa, slavery, or both. Herskovits (1958) described Africanisms in African American's funeral practices, folklore, motor habits, ways of dressing, hair wearing of headkerchiefs, etiquette, concept of time, cooperation and sharing, and child rearing practices. These Africanisms in the behavior of today's African Americans are evidence of an African influence from preslavery to the present.

Because segregation and isolation of the African American was so dominant for much of the United States's history, the survival of Africanisms was inevitable. Yet, until the writing of Herskovitz (1958), much of what was considered stereotypical behavior of the American Negro was thought to be a product of the American experience, with African influences being eradicated during slavery. Contrary to this view and because the African American community continues to be isolated in sociological, psychological, and physical ways, a distinctive African American culture has survived and indeed flourishes.

Even the most casual observation of a group of African American children will show behaviors not shared with the broader American community. An important question is the extent to which these behaviors are a cultural phenomenon. Undoubtedly, much that is described as African American culture is strongly influenced by the American experience and general popular culture, representing an amalgamation between Africa and America. Also, that which is African in origin is not easily identified or easily separated from the larger context of the American experience. A challenge for educators and researchers is the identification and description of behavioral characteristics (verbal and nonverbal communication, cognitive skills, and learning styles) that are indigenously and validly representative of African Americans.

In an attempt to describe cognition in African American children, Cohen (1969) suggested that cognitive style is shaped by socialization patterns within the child's environment. Some socialization patterns that may differ in African American children from the larger mainstream community are affective orientation, nonverbal communication, and physical precocity and movement. Within the area of affect, African American children may be more feeling oriented and people oriented than other ethnic groups. Socialization toward distinctive kinds of affect occurs from birth in that children are held and almost never left alone (Heath, 1983; Young, 1970). They are passed from one lap to another and very seldom are left in a crib, which differs from common practices in European American middle class families.

Young (1970) stated that there is an interactive rhythm within the socialization patterns of the African American community. "There is a kind of rhythm found between eating and napping with short periods of each activity found with frequent repetition. This rhythm is very different from the disciplined long span of attention cultivated in middle class child rearing and expected in schools" (p. 276). Because African American children are socialized from an early age to be feeling oriented and people oriented, emphasis is not placed on verbal exchange between parents and children. Heath (1983) reported that "when infants begin to utter sounds which can be interpreted as referring to items or events in the environment, these sounds receive no special attention. Trackton adults believe babies 'comes up' as a talker; adults cannot make babies talk: 'When a baby have sump'n to say, he'll say it'" (p. 75).

Although there was little verbal exchange between adults and children in Heath's (1983) study, she reported that there was considerable verbal exchange between children. African American mothers constantly held their babies, which is believed to stimulate physical precocity and movement at a higher rate than children not exposed to these child rearing practices. Authors of several studies (Ainsworth, 1967; Brazelton, Koslowski, & Tronic, 1967) reported that African American infants have a higher rate of physical precocity and movement in their first year of life than European American children.

If indeed African American children in the first year of life demonstrate unique cognitive patterns, there is every likelihood that these patterns persist in one form or another into the school years. How these patterns manifest themselves in cognitive capacity for memory, attending, stimulus identification, discrimination, and meaning associations is an important question, for these are fundamental and necessary cognitive skills important not only to the teaching of math, reading, and other content subjects, but also to the special educator who must teach and improve children's language skills. Thus, special educators and SLPs must be concerned about children's cognitive styles and capacity to learn.

Cohen (1969) defined two cognitive styles: the *analytic style* and the *relational style*. The analytic style is "characterized by a formal or analytic mode of abstracting salient information from a stimulus or situation by a stimulus centered orientation to reality" (pp. 829–830), whereas the relational style "requires a descriptive mode of abstraction and is self centered in its orientation to reality; only the global characteristics of a stimulus have meaning to its users, and these only in reference to some total context" (p. 830). Cohen reported that the analytic style is the style preferred in the education system. She also stated that the two styles are not only different but mutually incompatible. If these two styles are mutually incompatible, children who prefer the relational style may experience difficulty in the school setting. For a more detailed account of these cognitive style differences, we refer readers to Cohen (1969) and Hale-Benson (1982).

Clearly, claims of cognitive differences for African Americans can have serious and adverse consequences in a society with a history of racism. The likelihood of a stereotypically negative characterization of the African American is as strong today as ever before. This is in part due to the widespread and persistent incidence of crime, drugs, and poverty within African American communities. These negative forces produce behaviors that have little to do with African American culture. The culture described by Hilliard (1980) is positive in attributes and must not be confused with behavioral outcomes of despair and degradation. However, history shows that, in the absence of valid description of cultural norms, it is easy to relegate behaviors that differ from mainstream patterns to be somehow aberrant.

In a recent McNeil and Lehrer News interview, the noted African American philosopher and scholar Dr. Cornell West (1993) described observations of hyperactivity and inattentiveness among African American children as paralleling what was found in children during World Wars I and II. The inability of African American children to attend and focus in the classroom may be attributed to a form of "combat zone" distractibility, according to West. On the other hand, it is very possible for the physical precocity of African American children to be confused for distractibility and lack of attending.

History is replete with examples of misguided educational programs designed to help African American children. Among the more classic was a compensatory education program for African American children developed by Bereiter and Englemann (1966). This program focused on changing language patterns of African American English. These psychologists claimed that African American children who spoke AAE were "verbally deprived" and entered school with little or no language. Proponents of the compensatory program advocated that if African American children were taught the vocabulary, grammar, and syntax of White America, they would succeed scholastically in school (Bereiter & Englemann, 1966). This conclusion reflects the false assumption that "standard English" is somehow endowed with special powers not available in some other dialects, such as AAE.

Bereiter and Englemann's assertions were widely held in the 1960s, and these views are still around today, as evidenced in the disproportionate number of African American and Latino children enrolled in special education classes around the country. African American children in urban areas are referred for speech and language problems at a higher rate than White middle class children (Seymour & Bland, 1991). African American children are three times more likely to be placed in classes for the educable mentally retarded (Sanford, 1993). Indeed, if it were not for the work of sociolinguists, the 1960s programs such as Bereiter and Englemann's might have gained a stronger foothold on educational policy and practice, to the detriment of African American children.

EDUCATIONAL VERSUS CLINICAL ISSUES

The educational and clinical issues surrounding AAE are very much interdependent even though educators and clinicians have somewhat different missions. With respect to English, educators have the basic responsibility of teaching children to read, write, and speak English. This seems to be a reasonable and practical goal even though that variety (dialect) of English is standard English. The clinician, however, may be concerned less about a child's standard English skills and more about the skills necessary to communicate intentionally and meaningfully. The child with a language disorder first and foremost should be helped to communicate effectively, which is most likely to occur first in his or her native and most natural dialect. Hence, the clinician's role is not to focus on the English of the educated, but instead to emphasize the nurturing of foundational communicative skills. One might interpret this to mean that the educator prepares the child to function in the world, and the clinician, at least in the short term, prepares the child to be able to function in school.

Unfortunately, neither the educator nor the clinician has performed his or her role very well when applied to the child who speaks AAE. Unless a child first arrived at school with a standard English background and had reasonably good standard English skills, it is unlikely that he or she would acquire them in school. Attempts to teach standard English to speakers of AAE have failed dismally in our public schools, as evidenced by the written, spoken, and reading performance of urban African American children. Moreover, many AAE speaking children erroneously have been considered to be using "substandard" English, and as noted earlier, formal testing often resulted in large numbers of children being designated as disabled. As a consequence, there have been several court action suits brought on behalf of African American and other children of color (*Diana v. State Board of Education*, 1970; *Larry P. v. Riles*, 1972; *Martin Luther King Junior Elementary School Children et al. v. Ann Arbor School District Board*, 1979). Although the topic of this chapter deals with clinical problems in the speech and language of African American children, broader educational issues must be considered because it is through education that the notion of a "correct" English is most widely propagated. In fact, a considerable degree of attention has been given to AAE in the educational arena. The educational establishment views itself as the body responsible for projecting the standards of the educated class of society. Indeed, the very notion of nonstandard behavior runs counter to much of the philosophical framework of the educational system. It is unlikely that the educational establishment will abandon its goal of teaching children to speak, read, and write in standard English; this would be inconsistent with one of its primary objectives—that of maximizing the educational opportunities of all children by teaching them to function with the variety of English that is consonant with educated people of the land.

As stated above, however, SLPs have a different mission, which in some respects conflicts with the educational objective. The SLP must not label as pathological or in need of their services those who speak, read, and write in nonstandard English. The SLP also should not insist that those being seen for treatment have standard English as the target dialect. Clearly, there is a clinical issue and an educational issue, and the two should not be confused. Nevertheless, the educational–clinical issue has been a source of controversy within the profession of speech–language pathology for the past two decades. Only since 1985 has the American Speech-Language-Hearing Association (ASHA) adopted a position on this issue. The following is an abbreviated summary of ASHA's (1983) position paper on social dialects:

1. No dialectal variety of English is a disorder or a pathological form of speech or language.

2. Clinicians m...
   from disorders.

3. Clinicians must trea...
   and not attributable to ...

4. Because standard English is ...
   archetype, the clinician may im...
   teaching for those who wish it.

5. Clinicians may serve in a consultative ...
   tors in utilizing the features of nonstanda...
   tate the learning of reading and writing.

A CLINICAL-EDUCATIONAL PROGRAM

We have identified two related factors—AAE and cognitive learning style—that are unique to the African American child with special needs. In addition, a case has been made for implementing treatment plans within a context of the child's overall educational program. With these issues in mind, we think that a nonbiased and effective treatment plan should aim for and assure the following four outcomes: (a) that AAE is not the target for remediation; (b) that AAE not be an impediment to learning to read, write, and speak English; (c) that the child's cultural background and experiences be reflected in educational themes for both language intervention and general curriculum; and (d) that the child's cognitive learning style be considered in treatment and educational plans. For these treatment outcomes to occur in meeting the special and educational needs of African American children, we strongly advocate two philosophical positions as underlying principles for educational planning and clinical treatment. The first is that there be collaboration between teacher and SLP in all aspects of a child's Individualized Education Program (IEP). The second is for language treatment to draw upon whole language methods.

In the following section, we discuss how collaboration and whole language apply and relate in the education and treatment of African American children. A general discussion of collaboration these

ıe needs
roblems.
ımes full
ɔrks with
nmunica-
l to as the
classroom
nd curricu-
e most sig-
nd intellec-
s.
ch attention
he *Merriam-*
) defines *col-*

Webster *laboration* as "to work ,...), which cap-
tures the essence of this approach and chat... vhat should go
on between teacher and SLP. Such a partnership maximizes the
flow of essential information about the child. The SLP should provide the teacher with details of the treatment plan and ways in
which they might collaborate in implementing this plan within the
classroom setting. The teacher can provide information regarding
the child's academic and classroom performance relative to objectives of the treatment plan. As improvements or lack thereof are
made in the child's specific communicative skills, and carryover
and generalization to academic work occur, both teacher and SLP
are fully aware of the child's status.

The flow of information may derive from both formal and
informal interaction, but must be carried out in such a way and be
frequent enough to assure that both collaborators are aware of the
child's status with respect to areas of weakness and progress. The
child's IEP keeps educators informed about ongoing treatment
objectives. However, it is often the subtle behavioral changes that
occur that must be observed, recorded, and shared between professionals. This should take place in daily interactions. Ideally, these

interactions would emanate from the SLP's presence in the classroom, which, if effective, would be natural and unobtrusive.

In many respects the classroom setting is a dynamic social milieu in which highly personal and interactive exchanges take place between and among adults and children. At the same time, this setting is a place of learning, excitement, intimidation, fear, accomplishment, and embarrassment. In such an environment, an effective teacher is capable of orchestrating classroom dynamics to maximize positive experiences and feelings among students. Add to this classroom context children with special needs and the integration of treatment goals into typical classroom activities, and the entire educational process becomes much more complex.

In recent years there has been a strong movement in education toward inclusiveness. Children with mild to moderate and even severe deficits are integrated into the regular classroom through mainstreaming programs. The inclusion of these students in the regular classroom greatly complicates the teacher's role. To handle this added complexity and to achieve an effective and balanced classroom environment, the teachers and the SLP must have sufficient understanding and knowledge of each other's professional terrain. It is through collaboration that each expands knowledge about the other's specialty and is able to learn the important principles and methods about each other's discipline. For example, an SLP could be helpful in familiarizing a teacher with the most common AAE features while also explaining the difference between a child's dialect patterns and possible disorders of language. This shared knowledge would heighten the classroom teacher's awareness of the difference–deficit distinction, resulting in a more accepting posture toward children whose dialect patterns differ from school expectations. Clearly, with knowledge gained from each other's perspective, implementation of treatment is facilitated and the classroom becomes a richer learning environment.

Whole Language Method

According to Goodman, Bird, and Goodman (1991), whole language integrates educational knowledge (scientific knowledge of teaching, learning, language, and curriculum) with a positive and humanistic philosophy, which provide the foundation for teacher decision making and methods of teaching. Whole language is a philosophy of teaching rather than a system of specific techniques. It is process oriented as opposed to method oriented. In many respects, it constitutes a paradigm shift in education. Having its origin in the area of literacy, the paradigm shift has gone from a basal skills approach to a literature-based language approach (Westby, 1992). A parallel shift has occurred in the field of communication disorders wherein language assessment and treatment has shifted from focusing on structural components of language to functionally based levels of analysis, such as pragmatic and discourse analysis (Norris & Damico, 1990).

Whole language has particular merit for working with African American children because it does not focus on specific components of language but instead on the overall effectiveness of communication. Consider AAE speaking children who delete the possessive /s/ in "John's book" ("John book") or the plural /s/ in "fifty cents" ("fifty cent"). It should be recognized that possession is being marked by word order and that "fifty" designates quantity (plurality). Thus, functionally, the meaning of these utterances is preserved even though the standard English forms are not used. With a whole language approach, one could focus on the meaning expressed without regard for structural linguistic contrasts with standard English.

Freeman and Freeman (1992) discussed certain whole language principles that they apply to the bilingual learner. Their principles have been adapted here for working with AAE children with special needs. In addition, whole language principles can be incorporated by any school personnel working with African American learners. We discuss these principles in the following paragraphs.

1. *Facilitate language from whole to part.* Cohen (1969) proposed that children who use relational learning styles have a sensitivity to global characteristics rather than to parts. Thus, children who use this style of learning would benefit from a whole language learning approach, which emphasizes a global-to-specific paradigm. Children are first presented with general concepts and are later asked to handle specific details of the language. For example, children who demonstrate difficulty using prepositions in talking about spatial relationships would first be exposed to relationships among concrete objects. Only after they have a cognitive founda-

tion for positional proximity (in front of, behind, on top, in, on, etc.) would the specific language terms be targeted.

2. *Language facilitation should be child centered.* According to Freeman and Freeman (1992), "Lessons should be learner centered because learning is the active construction of knowledge by students" (p. 8). Because the African American child's cultural and experiential reference often differs from that of mainstream America, curriculum lessons should be geared to the child's background. These lessons would incorporate the child's language, worldview, style, and values (Hilliard, 1980). When language begins from the child's perspective, interests, capacity, relevance, and so forth, the acquisition of information becomes actively sought rather than simply passed along from teacher to student.

3. *Language facilitation should be meaningful and currently relevant in the child's life.* Lessons should be valid and functional to the child's current life situation. Activities are developed and utilized not only to enhance language function but to provide children with applicable choices and solutions to everyday needs and situations. The subject content of speech and language treatment can focus on daily activities and routines with which the child can easily draw upon. Also, the integration of treatment objectives with curriculum subject matter can form a reality bridge between effective communication on the one hand and academic success on the other.

4. *Language facilitation should involve group social interaction.* Typically, children first entering school find that discourse style requirements of the school differ from those to which they have been exposed in their homes. This is particularly so of children who come from culturally diverse linguistic backgrounds. Consequently, children are often more reticent in large group settings than in smaller and more intimate groups. The small group model encourages social and conversational interaction, which is much more conducive to learning pragmatic and discourse skills. A skilled SLP can orchestrate role shifts between the listener and speaker so that certain conversational skills (turn-taking, information sharing, topic initiation and maintenance, etc.) are practiced and mastered. By engaging in whole language activities, children can be given ample opportunities to develop both home and school discourse styles because all linguistic styles are appreciated for their communicative function.

5. *Language facilitation should incorporate both oral and written language.* Whole language encourages the development of communicative effectiveness no matter whether it is speaking, writing, or reading. Depending on the age and grade level of the child, treatment need not focus on one of these areas of communication to the exclusion of another. There can be an important generalization effect wherein success in oral communication affects positively written and literacy skills. Simply because AAE does not match the SE of reading materials, there need not be an impediment to developing reading and writing skills. Indeed, this is a fundamental principle of the whole language philosophy—that is, that meaning takes precedence over structural form.

6. *Language facilitation should accommodate the child's dialect.* The child should be allowed to use AAE without admonishment or retribution. In fact, it is important for teachers to show acceptance of the child and the child's form of verbal expression. To do otherwise will undermine the child's confidence and willingness to freely communicate and participate in academic activities. This acceptance and support provides a trusting relationship upon which the teaching of standard English skills may be possible. More important, treatment goals must recognize language patterns of AAE. SLPs would not choose as treatment targets language that violates the child's dialect.

7. *Language facilitation should project faith in the child's potential.* Unfortunately, African American children often have been provided with negative feedback about their linguistic and academic capabilities. For too many African American children, these perceptions become a self-fulfilling prophecy. Teachers must avoid these negative signals and use positive projections to demonstrate their faith in the learner's abilities. When using the whole language paradigm, teachers are to exude confidence in their students' abilities to carry out tasks successfully.

Whole language has gained considerable attention in recent years. Its promise for children whose language backgrounds differ from mainstream English appears great. However, much remains unknown about how best to apply the whole language philosophy, and empirical evidence of its effectiveness with children of color is limited. In fact, Delpit (1988) and de la Reyes (1991) are critical of how the whole language approach has been used with African

American and Hispanic students. These concerns notwithstanding, the extent to which whole language lives up to its promise rests with the ability of educators to foster throughout the educational enterprise respect for all children's language and assure that there exists no area of academic pursuit in which a child's language is devalued. Such a commitment requires collaboration and a willingness to adopt a program, such as whole language, that emphasizes functional similarities among diverse dialects as opposed to superficial differences embodied in structural linguistic forms.

The collaborative model and the whole language approach can be quite compatible in implementing a clinical program for children with special needs. This clinical process comprises an assessment phase and a treatment phase. In the assessment phase, the extent of collaboration between teacher and SLP is not as great as for treatment because the primary responsibility must rest with the SLP. However, it is critically important that the teacher provide necessary background information to the SLP and that the teacher be kept abreast of assessment progress and results. It is during treatment that teachers can play a more significant role in planning and implementing a treatment plan utilizing whole language. In the following sections on assessment and treatment, we discuss the clinical process and describe how collaboration and whole language may be implemented.

ASSESSMENT AND TREATMENT

Assessment

To effectively assess speech and language disorders among AAE speaking children, the SLP and the classroom teacher are faced with a far greater challenge than when assessing children of standard English backgrounds. The complexity of the problem deals with such factors as conflicts in cultures between SLPs and the children; an inadequate norm-based reference for speakers of AAE; the absence of standardized test instruments; and the impact of various outcomes of poverty. Some of these factors can be altered through conscientious effort on the part of the clinician, but others remain immutable.

Despite these formidable clinical problems and regardless of the client's dialect, three important clinical questions must be answered in the assessment process:

1. Is there a problem?

2. What is the nature of the problem?

3. What should be the intervention goals?

How SLPs should address these questions for the AAE speaking child within the classroom context is addressed below.

Is There a Problem?

Typically SLPs rely on standardized tests for determining whether a child has a problem. However, to the best of our knowledge, no test of speech and language could withstand close scrutiny with respect to the issue of bias. These tests have been normed, for the most part, on White children and have standard English as the "normal" referent. Some professionals advocate modifying existing tests or normalizing such tests on African American children to make them more suitable (Evard & Sabers, 1979); however, such efforts violate validity criteria of tests normed on and standardized for a different population, and therefore are not recommended (Seymour, 1986; Vaughn-Cooke, 1983).

Information obtained from referral sources, such as parents, teachers, and others familiar with the child, can be extremely useful when standardized tests are not used. These referral sources represent those who are most familiar with the child and who are in the best position to reveal whether a child is noticeably different from siblings and peers. Questions should be posed to these referral sources about the child's general health, the child's developmental and educational history, and family history of speech and language problems. This information, along with teacher insights and the SLP's formal test results, is often sufficient to admit a child into therapy without relying on standardized test scores.

To be complete, the assessment process should include nonlanguage factors, such as hearing, cognitive–intellectual status, fine and gross motor behavior, peripheral oral mechanism, and perceptual skills. Standardized tests will undoubtedly be used in assessing cognitive–intellectual status; however, it is important to consider many of the same concerns raised about tests of speech and language. Because language is often an important component of many intelligence tests, in the form of administrative instructions and test content, it becomes a confounding variable in interpreting scores for children whose language differs from that of the test protocol. It is quite possible that a low score on such tests by an African American child is attributable to conflicts between the child's language and the language of the test. One might avoid this language bias by selecting nonverbal tests of IQ. However, even nonverbal tests can have elements of cultural and cognitive bias that are difficult to identify. Consequently, the entire domain of intelligence testing with African American children should be viewed with a healthy dosage of skepticism.

Hilliard (1983) identified IQ testing as one area in which African American children's language patterns have an adverse effect. He argued that the measurement of intellect is greatly biased when tests are based on norms and culture of middle class European Americans. Bogatz, Hisama, Manni, and Wurtz (1986) also stated the effects of the misdiagnosis of children of color. They contended that the mere labeling of children as different is stigmatizing and causes rejection by other children and adults. Opportunities that are necessary for healthy development are often unavailable to such children. The misdiagnosis of children as mentally retarded is disproportionate among African American children and leads to years of inferior education, and possibly incarceration in institutions.

Given the problems associated with standardized tests, practitioners must obtain corroborating and confirming evidence from nontest data, such as referral data and observations, language samples, and so forth. Once all evidence is evaluated and a child is viewed to have a problem, that child should be enrolled for clinical treatment. However, a recommendation for speech and language treatment is often considered to be tentative in that a problem is "suspected" but must await further testing for confirmation.

This approach constitutes an important aspect of what is referred to as diagnostic intervention (Seymour, 1986). Diagnostic intervention is the process by which information is gathered, and hypotheses are formulated and then tested. This is essentially a circular process in that tentative decisions are made regarding the existence of a problem and its nature, and therapy is begun while simultaneously conducting further testing. As more information is gained, therapy is revised and hypothesis formulation continues. Such an approach is advised for language treatment in general, but has particular merit with African American and other minority language groups.

What Is the Nature of the Problem?

The identification of a problem usually does not reveal the nature of the problem. The nature of the problem should be reflected in a thorough description of a child's strengths and weaknesses in using his or her native language. This determination usually requires a more in-depth and ongoing assessment. An important component in answering the second question is language sampling and probing. The SLP records the child in various speaking situations. This language sample is transcribed and analyzed, yielding descriptive information about the essential dimensions of language (i.e., syntax, phonology, semantics, and pragmatics). Once a descriptive profile is established for the child, language probes are used to elicit information not obtained in the language sample.

In many respects language sampling violates principles of whole language in that it focuses on the details, or components, of language (i.e., syntax, phonology, semantics, and pragmatics). However, this kind of information should lead to a clearer understanding of the child's language difficulty, which will inform and guide the treatment plan. It is in the treatment phase when whole language can be most effective. We take the position that a thorough and detailed assessment provides a necessary foundation for more directed and focused treatment using a whole language approach.

There is no specific time frame for determining the nature of the problem, although the objective is to arrive at a complete profile of the child's strengths and weaknesses as quickly as possible. The classroom can be an excellent setting for implementing diagnostic intervention. When teachers are partners in implementing a child's IEP, professionals can share insights about the child's strengths and weaknesses as they apply to curriculum demands. Hence, progress made in language can be linked to advancement in meeting the subject-content requirements.

What Should Be the Intervention Goals?

To determine the intervention goals, the professionals must focus on the child's weaknesses, which should be evident from a synthesis of all available diagnostic data. Weaknesses would constitute those behaviors that are clearly below what is expected for the child's age and language level. These behaviors would be inconsistent with expectations of AAE speakers. Of course, many

African American children do not speak AAE, in which case they would be expected to speak the dialect of their linguistic background, which for many African American children would be standard English.

Once weaknesses have been identified as intervention goals, they must be prioritized with respect to their importance because it is unlikely that all weaknesses will be worked on simultaneously. The classroom teacher can be helpful in making some of these decisions. How the child is performing academically and what the level of expectations is relative to curriculum needs can and should influence the focus of treatment.

Treatment

Whole language methods should dominate treatment and may be achieved best through integrating language intervention goals into classroom curriculum objectives. Whenever possible, African American experiential and cultural themes should be reflected in treatment and educational plans. With such an approach and in addition to meeting the specific language deficits of African American children with special needs, we aim to improve the child's attitude toward learning, self-esteem (relative to his or her language deficit), awareness of the importance of communication, perception of communicative capabilities, and positive awareness about the relationship among self, language, and culture.

A child's attitude toward language intervention activities in particular and education in general is critical to the success of any treatment plan. The infusion of culturally rich themes into treatment activities may be useful in improving the child's attitude. By introducing themes of relevance and interest, the SLP and classroom teacher enhance motivation while targeting deficit areas. For example, the goal of vocabulary concept development can be taught within a contextual theme that exposes African American children, beginning with early childhood programs, to their historical origins. Lessons on the African continent can have meaning when discussed in terms of ancestors and linkages between Africans and African Americans.

Indeed, the way in which history is told can be of great importance in bolstering a child's sense of worth and self-esteem. There is much about which African Americans can be proud. Despite the devastation brought about by slavery, one can point out with pride the bravery and dignity exhibited by slave resistors such as Nat Turner and Harriet Tubman in the early days of slavery, and the valiant civil rights fighters in more recent times. Also, important lessons can be conveyed about how slavery inflicted mental damage on African Americans and how, despite its eradication, new forms of mental slavery are now present in the form of drugs, as an example. Perhaps children can be taught to resist these new forms of slavery by learning more about their heritage, while simultaneously improving their communicative skills. The important point is that almost any language facilitation treatment plan can be carried out within a culturally relevant context.

The use of historical accounts and a child's cultural experiences provides a meaningful and contextually rich environment in which academic and linguistic concepts can be learned naturally and with ease. There is much evidence of this natural learning process when applying whole language philosophy to reading. According to Palincsar and David (1991), in discussing the views of Phelps (1988), written language can be processed as effortlessly and unconsciously as the learning of spoken language. Culture can be the support for a natural learning process in that it provides "the meaningful contexts and experiences of written language events that stimulate the learner's own construction of the symbol systems and strategies we call literacy" (p. 108).

These meaningful cultural contexts may be presented and highlighted by focusing on the experiences and accomplishments of role models who are real and tangible in children's lives. Athletes, singers, and movie stars are possible choices, but role models might also include local persons of significance to children, such as teachers, parents, doctors, dentists, nurses, and cab drivers. A good source for identifying key figures and building themes around them are African American publications, newspapers, and periodicals. These sources often provide photographs and stories about people of color that further enhance the child's perception that the successes obtained by these role models are a reality and, in fact, are attainable in their own lives. When children can identify with certain people, they can then project themselves into the roles those individuals fulfill, which can be a powerful force for learning. Moreover, when activities are presented in a holistic and child-centered manner, the treatment setting may be viewed as a place where fun and interesting activities take place.

Another advantage to utilizing culturally relevant themes in treatment is that they can be useful in increasing awareness of the importance of communicative functioning. Activities may be designed to allow the child to see how effective one can be in conversational discourse. The SLP can demonstrate how certain types of communication work positively for the child—how to be persuasive, to ask questions, to argue a point of view, and so forth. Also, the consequences of being inarticulate can be demonstrated. Activities might include modeling of alternate and different communication "styles" by the SLP, teacher, and children. The children then describe and figure out which communicative styles are most beneficial in specific contexts and situations. For example, children can conduct job interviews in which they alternate roles as interviewer and interviewee; judgments about effectiveness can then be evaluated and discussed. Again, examples should include important figures who are African American and for whom communicative acumen is evident.

The various activities and goals noted above should lead to an awareness and heightened appreciation of the relationship among self, language, and culture. This awareness may not be overt or even conscious, particularly among young children. Yet, this awareness and appreciation will exist when children think of themselves and their way of talking as an extension of the cultural hue of their own family and community. Once children have this awareness, evidence an understanding of the importance and power of communication, and have a firm grasp of their own capacity, they can be introduced to the idea of a standard English. This introduction to standard English need not and should not be too academic. There is a simple idea to convey: that there is a kind of "school talk" and a form of "home talk," either of which may be used when in certain speaking situations. In order to use both, one must know how to "code switch."

Code switching may be defined as alternation in use between two language or dialect systems. It is often governed by social constraints, such as speaking in very informal and relaxed settings versus more formal settings in which there are perceived expectations with respect to speaking style (Seymour, 1986). Speakers of AAE code switch by using AAE in certain contexts and standard English in others. The extent to which such switching is possible depends on one's capacity to speak standard English. Although not an immediate goal for children with language disorders, code switching may be thought of as a future and long-range goal. To this end, SLPs can be useful in assisting teachers in the more general educational goal of standard English instruction.

However, we caution against such endeavors until the child has a positive self concept about his or her own dialect and understands that this dialect need not be eradicated when acquiring standard English skills. Once assured about the child's self-esteem, the SLP can collaborate with the teacher in creating interesting and fun-filled activities that demonstrate different styles of speaking. This may draw on the role playing skits discussed above, or can be modeled by the SLP and teacher. In any event, these endeavors afford an excellent opportunity to be integrated with language arts and grammar lessons where standard English skills may be highlighted.

It is this meshing of clinical activities and curriculum that must ultimately occur. When treatment complements the curriculum demands of the student, both treatment objectives and academic performance can be enhanced. Well-orchestrated integration of treatment goals into curriculum will increase the frequency of exposure to targeted skills, resulting in greater opportunities to experience the behaviors to be learned and to receive reinforcement from achieving positive results. All of this is best handled with a modified whole language approach in which learning proceeds from whole to part and work is accomplished in small groups via meaningful real tasks that enhance learning.

An additional advantage may occur when treatment objectives complement curriculum demands. Generalization of skills addressed in treatment may be improved. When skills are programmed in more than one setting, the child is less likely to isolate and associate specific tasks to specific learning contexts. Instead, the child is more likely to recognize that skills are applicable in a variety of contexts. Children begin to understand that what they do in speech class can help them in their classroom, on the playground, or at home. They start to see that communication skills are useful beyond the classroom and treatment context. Hence, curriculum complementation allows the child to perceive language holistically. They are able to realize that speech–communication is not an isolated event to be mastered only in treatment sessions, but that it carries over to and influences all aspects of their life.

CONCLUSION

Several important issues associated with AAE should be clearly understood by any educator working with African American children. First and foremost, there must be no equivocation about the legitimacy of AAE. This variety of English is as capable of communicating ideas purposively and forcefully as any other dialect. Unfortunately, this awareness is not widely held, and ignorance about language diversity relegates AAE to a stigmatized and substandard status. As a result, there are adverse social and educational consequences for speaking AAE, which take the following forms: (a) children and their speech community are demeaned; (b) children become less confident about their communicative capacity; and (c) children participate less in class activities.

These consequences also apply to the African American child with special needs, but with additional clinical implications. Most notably, too many African American children with special needs either go undiagnosed or are diagnosed as having problems that do not exist. In addressing these issues, we have proposed collaborative interaction between SLPs and classroom teachers. An important component of this collaboration is the integration of whole language treatment with general educational–curriculum demands.

REFERENCES

Ainsworth, M. S. (1967). *Infancy in Uganda: Infant Care and the growth of love* (pp. 459–462). Baltimore: Johns Hopkins Press.

American Speech-Language-Hearing Association. (1983, September). *Position paper on social dialects*. Rockville, MD: Author.

Bereiter, C., & Englemann, S. (1966). *Teaching disadvantaged children in the preschool*. Englewood Cliffs, NJ: Prentice-Hall.

Bogatz, B. E., Hisama, T., Manni, J. L., & Wurtz, R. G. (1986). Cognitive assessment of nonWhite children. In O. L. Taylor (Ed.), *Treatment of communication disorders in culturally and linguistically diverse populations* (pp. 135–153). Austin, TX: PRO-ED.

Brazelton, T. B., Koslowski, B., & Tronic, E. (1967). Neonatat behavior among Urban Zambians and Americans. *Annual Progress in Child Psychiatry, 15,* 97–107.

Children's Defense Fund. (1991). *The state of America's children* (Annual Report). Washington, DC: Author.

Cohen, R. (1969). Conceptual styles, culture conflict, and nonverbal tests of intelligence. *American Anthropologist, 71,* 828–856.

Coon, C. (1962). *The origin of races.* New York: Knopf.

Dandy, E. B. (1991) *Black communications: Breaking down the barriers.* Chicago: African American Images.

de la Reyes, M. (1991). A process approach to literacy instruction for Spanish-speaking students: In search of a best fit. In E. H. Hiebert (Ed.), *Literacy for a diverse society* (pp. 157–171). New York: Teachers College Press.

Delpit, L. D. (1988). The silenced dialogue: Power and pedagogy in educating other people's children. *Harvard Educational Review, 58,* 280–298.

Diana v. State Board of Education. Civil Action No. C-7037RFP (N.D.) California (January 7, 1970, and June 18, 1973).

Education for All Handicapped Children Act. (1975). S.6, 94th Congress (Sec. 613(a)(4) 1st Session, June). Report N. 94-168.

Evard, B. L., & Sabers, D. L. (1979). Speech and language testing with distinct ethnic-racial groups: A survey of procedures for improving validity. *Journal of Speech and Hearing Disorders, 44,* 271–281.

Freeman, Y. S., & Freeman, D. E. (1992). *Whole language for second language learners.* Portsmouth, NH: Heinemann.

Goodman, K., Bird, L. B., & Goodman, Y. M. (1991). *The whole language catalog.* Santa Rosa, CA: American School Publishers.

Hale-Benson, J. (1982). *Black children: Their roots, culture and learning styles.* Baltimore: Johns Hopkins University Press.

Heath, S. B. (1983). *Ways with words.* Cambridge, England: Cambridge University Press.

Herskovits, M. J. (1958). *Myth of the Negro past.* Boston: Beacon Press.

Hilliard III, A. G. (1983). Psychological factors associated with language in the education of the African American child. *Journal of Negro Education, 52*(1), 24–34.

Hilliard III, A. G. (1980). Cultural diversity and special education. *Exceptional Children, 46*(8), 584–588.

Holloway, J. (1991). *Africanisms in American culture.* Bloomington: Indiana University Press.

Ingle, D. (1964). Racial differences and the future. *Science, 146,* 375–379.

Jaynes, G., & Williams, Jr., R. (1989). *A common destiny: Blacks and American society.* Washington, DC: National Academy Press.

Jensen, A.R. (1969). How much can we boost I.Q. and scholastic achievement? *Harvard Educational Review, 39,* 1–117.

Labov, W. (1969). *The study of nonstandard English.* Urbana, IL: National Council of Teachers of English.

Larry P. v. Riles. (1972). Civil No. C-71-2270, 343 F. Supp. 1306 (N.D.). (1972).

Marable, M. (1983). *How capitalism underdeveloped Black America.* Boston: South End Press.

Martin Luther King Junior Elementary School Children et al. v. Ann Arbor School District Board. United States District Court, Eastern District of Michigan, Southern Division, Civil Action Number 7-71861, (1979).

Merriam-Webster concise school and office dictionary. (1991). Springfield, IL: Merriam-Webster.

Norris, J. A., & Damico, J. S. (1990). Whole language in theory and practice: Implications for language intervention. *Language, Speech, and Hearing Services in Schools, 21,* 212–220.

Palincsar, A. S., & David, Y. M. (1991). Promoting literacy through classroom dialogue. In E. H. Hiebert (Ed.), *Literacy for a diverse society* (pp. 122–140). New York: Teachers College Press.

Phelps, L. W. (1988). *Composition as a human science.* London: Oxford Press.

Sanford, A. (Speaker). (1993). *The deliberate miseducation of the African child* (Cassette Recording). Willingboro, NJ: Word for Word Productions.

Seymour, H., & Bland, L. (1991). A minority perspective in the diagnosing of child language disorders. *Clinics in Communication Disordes, 1*(1), 39–50.

Seymour, H. N. (1986). Clinical intervention for language disorders among nonstandard speakers of English. In O. L. Taylor (Ed.), *Treatment of communication disorders in culturally and linguistically diverse populations* (pp. 135–153). Austin, TX: PRO-ED.

Smitherman, G. (1977). *Talkin and testifyin'.* Boston: Houghton Mifflin.

U.S. Department of Commerce, Bureau of the Census. (1990). *Census of population.* Washington, DC: Author.

Vaughn-Cooke, F. B. (1983, September). Improving language assessment in minority children. *American Speech-Language-Hearing Association, 25,* 29–34.

West, C. (1993). Interview on McNeil and Lehrer Evening News.

Westby, C. E. (1992). *Whole language and learners with mild handicaps.* Boulder, CO: Love.

Wolfram, W., & Fasold, R. W. (1974). *The study of social dialects.* Englewood Cliffs, NJ: Prentice-Hall.

Young, V. H. (1970). Family and childhood in a southern Negro community. *American Anthropology, 72,* 269–288.

CHAPTER FIVE

Curricular and Pedagogical Procedures for African American Learners with Academic and Cognitive Disabilities

Helen Bessent Byrd

Statistical analyses of existing conditions and predicted trends among African Americans indicate the inadequacy of society's response to the needs of this group of America's populace. These data also reveal the challenge that confronts the nation's educational systems.

Regarding the nation's children, poverty is at the base of all of the societal ills. The Children's Defense Fund's (1993) analysis of data led to the conclusion that nearly 20% of all children in the United States and about 50% of African American children live in poverty. The likelihood of living in poverty is much greater among those who live in one-parent families than in two-parent families, and this circumstance exists in the families of over half of all American children.

Other alarming statistics on African American children document the present-day crisis (Children's Defense Fund, 1993):

- Every 95 seconds a Black baby is born in poverty.

- Every 3 minutes a baby is born to a Black mother who did not graduate from high school.

- Every 4 hours a Black child is murdered.

- Every 7 seconds of the school day a Black student is suspended from public school.

- Every 49 seconds of the school day a Black student drops out of school.

The proportions of other ethnic minority groups in the population are increasing similarly.

These cited statistics serve as a mandate for attention to cultural parameters in society and education. It is incumbent upon non–European American groups as well as European Americans to understand their own and other cultures (Howard, 1993). Apparently, some different procedures need to be implemented to instill in individuals the knowledge, skills, and abilities required to function effectively in a culturally pluralistic society.

This chapter outlines a historical perspective of attitudes toward cultural groups in the United States reflecting the movement from a very narrow ethnocentric view by the voluntary European settlers to the wider posture of acceptance held today. Within this context, indigenous characteristics and contemporary cultural patterns of African Americans are enumerated and described. Curricular considerations for African American learners are described. Several pedagogical procedures for effective instruction are posited. Finally, a scheme and exemplary interventions are provided. This content is designed to serve as a guide to the reader for the development of materials that address culture, curriculum, and pedagogy appropriate for each child.

HISTORICAL PERSPECTIVES SPIRAL

The history of response to the presence of varied cultural groups in the education system is parallel to the response of the larger society to the presence of minority groups. The events leading from the settling of the United States by a few disparate European religious and ethnic groups to the plurality of the nation today is briefly chronicled by Seelye and Wasilewski (1979), Hunter (1974), and others.

The historical approaches taken to addressing cultures in the educational system may be perceived as a widening spiral (see Fig-

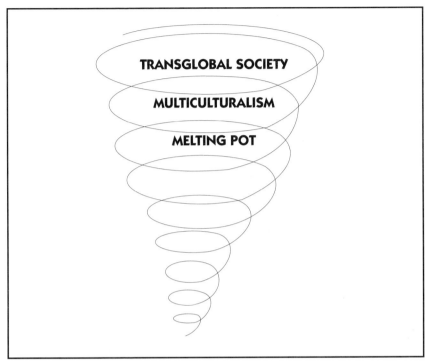

FIGURE 5.1. Historical perspectives spiral.

ure 5.1). The progression of thinking regarding minority children began with efforts to assimilate those with ethnic identities into the mainstream. This notion, termed the "melting pot" theory, is at the bottom of the spiral. It was built on the premise that all children would lose emphasis on their ethnic identity and become "American." The expectation was for enculturation of all groups and the termination of individuals' identity with any specific groups. Everyone would be American.

Widening of the spiral is evident in the shifts away from the melting pot theory. This progression began with recognition and assent to retention of ethnic groups. An ethnic group is a primarily involuntary group that "shares a common heritage and history, identity, belief system, and political and economic interests" (Banks, 1981, p. 53). Such a group usually has its roots in a specific geographical area of the world. Some persons may opt to identify with their ethnic group; others, whose ethnicity is obvious, may have little choice. Examples of ethnic groups include, among others, Greek Americans, Swedish

Americans, African Americans, and Mexican Americans. Ethnic *minority* groups are those non-White ethnic groups that are statistical minorities and are systematically discriminated against in American society. These groups are American Indians, Latin Americans, Asian Americans, and African Americans.

The second level of the spiral is multiculturalism. At this stage of history, culture was recognized as clearly differentiated from ethnic group. A group of persons who share a common culture may or may not represent a common ethnic background. *Culture* has been defined by educators, philosophers, anthropologists, and theorists from other disciplines. It is the common technical, social, aesthetic, ideological, and attitudinal preferences, including perceptions of disabilities, common to a group of people. It consists of shared beliefs, cognitive styles, languages, and religions, as well as preferences for sports, foods, and tools. Also included are other material and nonmaterial achievements of the group of people. Thus, the term culture is wide ranging, entailing all that enters into one's worldview. One's heritage and history as well as attitudes and actions shape the culture of that individual.

Hall (1976) enumerated three characteristics of culture: (a) it is not innate, but learned; (b) the various facets of culture are interrelated so that if a culture is touched in one place, everything else about that culture is affected; (c) it is shared by its members and, in effect, defines the boundaries of different ethnic groups. A culture is a common bond among a group of people. A university, a discipline, a business, and an ethnic group all represent cultural groups or subcultures.

The spiral widens to its apex, which represents the recognition of the interconnectedness and the interdependence of culture and political entities. The contemporary perception is that the peoples of the world are all transglobal citizens. Whatever happens to the peoples of the Western Hemisphere impacts those of the Eastern Hemisphere; any national disasters or special achievements among peoples to the North impinge on the lives of peoples in the South.

INDIGENOUS CHARACTERISTICS OF AFRICAN AMERICANS

To design a curriculum model and instructional strategies appropriate for each student, professionals must understand the student's individual and cultural characteristics. It follows that examination of the traits indigenous to African peoples and common among contemporary African Americans will aid educators in understanding the African American student in the classroom.

Significant exposition has been done on traditional characteristics of African Americans (Nichols, 1985; Patton, 1992). Traits that have been documented in the literature as indigenous among African peoples are, to a great measure, common among all indigenous peoples (the oppressed) when juxtaposed against those attributes evident among peoples who may be referred to as settlers (the oppressors). Table 5.1 charts the primary characteristics of the indigenous peoples and the settlers. Other peoples who share the characteristics of the indigenous peoples are the Dalits of India (Rajshakar, 1987), the Aborigines of Australia (Adler, Barkat, Bena-Silu, Duncan, & Webb, 1981; Pattel-Gray, 1991), the Africans of South Africa, and the American Indians in this nation.

African peoples, like other indigenous peoples, traditionally live in partnership with the land and property. They choose to protect and care for the environment as overseers for a higher power rather than abuse their holdings as sole owners. Also, African peoples have maintained that there is an interdependence in the relationships of humankind. This trait is seen in the caring reflected in the extended family structure, the authority over children (Bartz & Levine, 1978), the care for elders, and the reception of "new friends" (the feeling that no one is a stranger). Also, traditional African values hold that there is a unity among and between all things. Therefore, African peoples have an outer-directed rather than an egocentric focus. It follows, then, that indigenous African cultures also are more cooperative than competitive. Their orientation is to intragroup relations. Therefore, they use time and space

TABLE 5.1. Traditional Characteristics of Indigenous Peoples and Settlers

Indigenous People (Oppressed)	Settlers (Oppressors)
• Partners with nature	• Exploitative use of land
• Respectful of others	• Disrespectful of humankind
• Cooperative with others	• Competitive with others
• Holistic worldview; interrelatedness	• Cellular, fragmented perspective of world

to enhance the relations with others rather than being controlled by these factors (Nichols, 1985; Wilson, 1972).

CULTURAL PATTERNS COMMON AMONG CONTEMPORARY AFRICAN AMERICANS

Cultural patterns among contemporary African Americans are as diverse as the experiences of this large segment of the nation. Indeed, the cross-cultural fertilization that has occurred has resulted in as much intracultural variance among African Americans as there is intercultural variance between African Americans and other groups in this society. However, some generalizations retain validity regarding African American children. These children are more precocious in motor development than White Americans, and have different growth norms. Proclivity for certain diseases and genetic syndromes (e.g., sickle cell anemia, high blood pressure) is present in this group, whereas certain other diseases and syndromes (e.g., phenylketonuria, cystic fibrosis) are virtually absent.

African American children also possess unique patterns of the identifiable ethnic and cultural indices listed in Table 5.2 (Longstreet, 1978). A frequently referenced index of culture is intellectual mode or *cognitive style*. Although there is much individual variability, African Americans generally vary from White Americans in cognitive abilities and cognitive styles. Gardner (1983) theorized that there are multiple intelligences. Learning styles among children are, at a minimum, as varied as these intelligences. Individuals also tend to vary in their dependence upon the sensory modalities. Generally, however, the following pattern is evident among African Americans:

- More kinesthetic/tactile learning
- Preference for subdued rather than bright light
- Greater reliance on visual rather than auditory input
- Positive response to music and rhythm
- Greater response to cooperative learning

TABLE 5.2. Aspects of Ethnicity

Intellectual modes
- Ethnic influence on approach to learning
- Ethnic emphasis favoring development of intellectual abilities

Verbal communication
- Categories describing oral language
- Ethnic criteria for judging verbal communication with regard to socioeconomic status, intellectual capacity, sociability, etc.
- Discussion modes according to the kind of discussion

Nonverbal communication
- Diakinesic system (gestures and body language)
- Proxemics system (personal space)
- Haptics (touching)
- Symbols
- Signals

Orientation modes
- Body orientations
- Spatial architectural orientations
- Attention modes
- Time modes

Social value patterns
- Ways of participating in patterns
- Ways of evaluating patterns
- Nature of valuing

From *Aspects of Ethnicity* by W. Longstreet, 1978, New York: Teachers College Press.

In the United States, children's intellectual or cognitive abilities continue to be measured with instruments that place African Americans at a disadvantage. The traits that are valued and measured, as well as the choice of vocabulary and content in some of the test items, tend to exclude abilities and experiences of many African American children.

Communication systems also vary from culture to culture. Although Chapter 4 in this text focuses extensively on language and communication, several pertinent points are addressed here regarding verbal and nonverbal communication. Standard American English (SAE) is the language used for *verbal communication* in the education and business communities of the United States. Therefore, all children are expected to speak SAE. However, many Americans speak an English dialect or a native language other than English. Many African Americans, for example, speak Black dialect. These variances must be perceived as only a difference, not a deficit or deficiency. Children who speak other languages or dialects should be accepted with a positive attitude and aided in the mastery of SAE.

One notable characteristic of African Americans' discussion style is simultaneous talk instead of alternating talk, which is the European American style. An African American conversation often is analogous to jumping rope "double Dutch." As the rope is turning, the prospective jumper sways or rocks making motions that suggest entry into the ropes while awaiting the opportune moment for actual entry. Conversants jockey for an opportunity to enter the exchange. Most often a speaker starts talking before another one stops—as the rope jumper goes in before the other exits in double dutch. In the European American custom, most often a speaker waits for the talk to cessate before initiating comments.

Another trait of African American verbal communication is colorful language. Children learn early the art of verbal offense and defense that occurs in heated debates, "signifying" (i.e., making derogatory comments about a person to the person referenced), and "playing the dozens" (i.e., making denigrating statements about the person's genealogy). Educators should capitalize on this artful use of language in the classroom.

Nonverbal communication skills are also highly developed among African Americans. The creation of very intricate gestures and body language may have resulted from the need to keep the communication within the cultural group for security reasons. Other forms of nonverbal communication are proxemics (referring to one's personal space) and haptics (the proclivity and pattern of touching). Research reveals differences in use of these modes of communication across cultures. The expression "in your face" often used by African Americans suggests that one's personal space, physical and/or psychological, has been invaded.

Orientation refers to an individual's way of behaving in the absence of others. An example is the spatial orientation exemplified by the position and environment one chooses for study. While the European American culture emphasizes quiet for study, many African Americans prefer to study while music or conversation occurs in the room. Furniture arrangement can also affect learning for each child; the typical formal organization of the classroom and seating furniture may not be conducive to learning for all children. This matter should receive attention from educators at the preschool through secondary school levels.

Another orientation issue is that the attention span of children from some cultures may be out of synchrony with the class periods of the school day. Cultural groups also vary in their attitudes about time. Some may be strictly bound by time limits, perceiving that temporal constraints dictate behavior. Others see time as available solely for their own purposes; the interactions of the moment are more critical than any scheduled activity. Therefore, whatever is next on the schedule can wait. Indigenous African American preference has been for the latter behavior.

The final aspect of ethnicity cited by Longstreet (1978) is *social value patterns,* which includes many of the factors typically considered to characterize a culture. Examples are group preferences for food, sports, and religion, as well as the cultural definition of the role of the child. Additionally, the rites of passage (e.g., rituals associated with birth, courtship patterns, entry into adulthood, marriage, and death) define the ways one participates in a group's social value patterns. Ethical values also tend to be shared within a culture, as do maladaptive societal behaviors (types of delinquent acts, tendency toward suicide, etc.).

When the ethnic variables of the child and those of the mainstream society differ, as is the case for most African American children, disequilibrium is created within the child. The burden tends to rest upon the child to bring about balance. This should not be the case. Such a condition challenges the child to choose between the home and the school, the parents and the teacher.

Another challenge for the African American child with disabilities is the lack of judgment or skill to face the difficulties of the discrepant value systems. The child's limited abilities make it difficult to translate learning materials into the context of his or her culture, to grasp the meaning, and then to respond within the school's culture. The school personnel should assume the responsibility of preparing the way for the child to succeed in the learning environment. The teacher must teach the child in a fashion that is conducive to the child's fully developing potential and success in school.

CURRICULAR CONSIDERATIONS—WHAT TO TEACH

The purpose of understanding the varied aspects of ethnicity as they relate to each child's culture is to determine what to teach and how to teach it. A philosophical base must be established, from which a structure is formulated and the content is overlaid (Gay, 1977; Grant, 1983). The consideration of curricular issues is quite a challenge in this information age. In the following sections, the structural design, the breadth of content or cultural spiral, and the proposed child-centered curriculum are described.

Structural Paradigms

A major issue regarding what to teach is the selection of a structural paradigm for inclusion of curricular content. There are at least three alternatives for inclusion of multicultural content: (a) supplantation, (b) supplementation, and (c) permeation (see Figure 5.2).

Supplantation entails the replacement of existing course content with new content on cultures of specific ethnic groups. Many efforts to address this matter have been reported in the literature and some have been evaluated (Almanza & Moseley, 1980; Council for Exceptional Children, 1989). An example of supplantation would be to have all science content or social studies material center on a non-European culture. Thus, the curriculum would be monocultural as has been the usual case, except the culture would be a specific non-European culture.

A contemporary example of supplantation in the curriculum coupled with physical separation is the instruction of African American males in an Afrocentric curriculum apart from other children. This model has been implemented in several public school districts, including Detroit, Michigan, and Norfolk, Virginia. Additionally, some parents who are disaffected with the response of the public to the needs of their children have turned to the establishment of non-public schools that are more responsive to their children in content and delivery. Proponents of this paradigm in both public and non-public schools attest to its merit and success.

Supplementation is an alternative in curriculum design in which content of a non-European culture is added to the existing curriculum. Ethnic studies programs are an example of this strategy. The

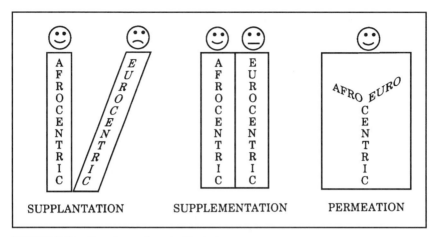

FIGURE 5.2. Paradigms of content inclusion.

primary curriculum remains intact, but courses in African American history, African art, or African American literature, for example, may be required or optional. Another example of supplementation is the flurry of varied activities during African American History Month.

The third alternative paradigm is *permeation.* This strategy involves the infusion or integration of the existing European American–centered curriculum with content about other ethnic groups. For example, in teaching the history of education, rather than stopping with an overview of Greek and Roman civilization, the teacher would also share information on the Mali empire of West Africa. In the study of biology, the contributions of George Washington Carver and Percy Julian would be interwoven into the course.

Too much emphasis is placed on supplantation and supplementation in most education systems. The strategy that has been found to be most appropriate is permeation (Fuchigami, 1980; Willis, 1992). It is important to consider how the contributions of different ethnic groups are interwoven to create a beautiful fabric. This approach also reflects the interrelatedness and interdependence of people upon each other.

Cultural Education Spiral

Several approaches have been used in addressing the matter of what content should be taught and in what paradigm the material should be delivered. Figure 5.3 depicts the sequence (spiral) of strategies used in responding to culture in the educational system. These approaches reflect the spirals of social philosophy, described earlier. During the melting pot era, there was intentional delivery of a monocultural curriculum in an effort to produce students with common values and belief systems. Harkness (1980) noted that this effort resulted from psychological theory relying on monocultural studies. Harkness called for a much more balanced view based on studies of child development among varied cultural groups which, to a large measure, has occurred.

The spiral of social thought widened in recognition and acceptance of specific ethnic groups. It follows that ethnic studies are investigations of the historical and contemporary aspects of specific ethnic groups. Ethnic studies, when effective, lead to enlightenment about and understanding of a people. The goal is to eradicate prejudice toward and discrimination against the ethnic group.

Multicultural education was the response of the education system to the trend toward recognition of a place in American society for cultural variance or pluralism. The best explanation of multicultural education was articulated by the American Association of Colleges for Teacher Education (1973), which stated that multicultural education values, not tolerates, cultural pluralism; rejects the melting pot notion; and "affirms that schools should be oriented toward the cultural enrichment of all children and youth" (p. 164). Additionally, the association noted that recognition of the right of these cultures to exist is even more important than mere acceptance. This emphasis on cultural plurality serves to restore the histories of African Americans and other ethnic groups to their rightful place in the human record (Hilliard, 1991–1992).

The widest level of the education spiral is global education, with its focus on issues relative to numerous cultures and subcultures. Global education refers to the study of ethnic, political, economic, religious, and linguistic groups around the world. The focus is on understanding the interrelatedness and interdependence of these groups, and includes such themes as hunger, international debt, world health, and the environment.

Care should be taken in the choice and promotion of these approaches. With global education, one must avoid dissipating the energies that need to be given to ensuring the rights and inclusion of ethnic groups that are systematically discriminated against

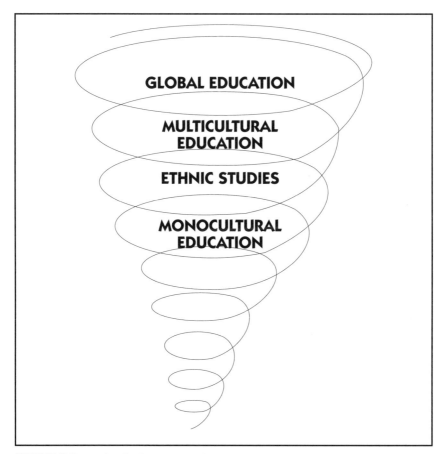

FIGURE 5.3. Cultural education spiral.

in U.S. society. Whereas ethnic studies appears to be a Band-Aid approach in that it gives concentrated attention to a selected ethnic group, multicultural education affords opportunity for integration of content about varied cultural groups. However, the outcome of multicultural education as it has been implemented over the last 20 years has not been satisfactory. It has been watered down in an effort to make it acceptable to both proponents and opponents. Therefore, education must modify this model. Banks (1993) discussed the concepts of multicultural education, debunking the myths and restating the basic tenets.

What must be emphasized in the education of all learners is a *culture-specific approach in the context of a multicultural education.*

A critical question becomes whether this proposal means that all teachers must know all cultures. This is certainly not expected. However, the teacher should know the various indices of ethnicity (Longstreet, 1978) and should become familiar with those traits as they are generally evident among European Americans, African Americans, Latin Americans, Asian Americans, and American Indians. Content on the history and variables specific to ethnic groups represented in the classroom should be included in the curriculum and instruction.

Child-Centered Curriculum

The issue of whether an Afrocentric curriculum is appropriate has been hotly debated (Asante, 1990, 1991–1992; Thomas, 1992). The focus, however, in the teaching–learning process should not be on the curriculum, but on the child. Indeed, when the child is the focus, the curriculum emphasizes and reinforces the worth of the individual culture of each child. Thereby, the child learns to value his or her own culture and to appreciate that of others.

If the teacher centers on the child while teaching, the child learns his or her individual culture and that of others. In this climate, the children learn to discern the universalities across cultures, and each child learns the individual and the common culture. The former must precede the latter, and both are requisites. The individual culture affirms the child's identity, builds self-esteem, and aids in understanding other individual cultures. This is especially important for the child with disabilities, who is very likely to have low self-esteem due to being presented with unfamiliar material and receiving negative feedback.

Indeed, children with disabilities should be taught in an environment that is receptive and accepting. Their need for a culturally compatible child-centered curriculum cannot be ignored on the assumption that they will not know the difference. Experienced teachers are aware that children with mild, moderate, or severe cognitive and academic disabilities often possess keen perceptions of the attitudes of others toward them. The old adage, "Children don't care how much you know; they want to know how much you care," is quite correct about *all* children.

Centering the curriculum on the child serves as the foundation for the child to grasp the common culture—that is, those principles and values that provide the cohesion in a citizenry that sustains a nation (Ravitch, 1991–1992). Indeed, if the teacher recognizes that the child should begin with self at the center, teaches the child to understand his or her own culture, and then moves to the common culture in approaching all curricular content, the teacher is affirming the value of an Afrocentric curriculum for the African American child, a Eurocentric curriculum for the European American child, an Asiaocentric curriculum for the Asian American child, and so on (see Figure 5.4). The outcome is a multicultural curriculum. When the curriculum centers on the child in a positive way,

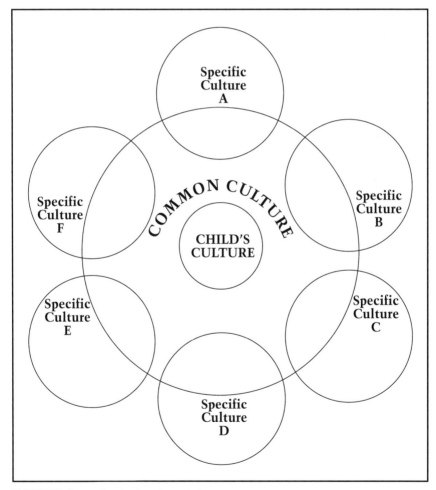

FIGURE 5.4. Cultural education spiral.

affirming the worth of the child, the child learns. It is mandatory that such learning environments be created and maintained in the schools for *all* children.

Pedagogical Procedures—How to Teach

In addition to knowing what structure to use and what to teach, the effective educator of the African American child must know how to teach the curricular content efficaciously. There are requisite teacher traits that will help African American students to do well. Efforts to enumerate these characteristics (Bessant, 1975; Bessant Byrd, 1980, 1989; Garcia & Malkin, 1993; Ladson-Billings, 1990) are compiled in Table 5.3.

Differentiated Instruction

The teacher who possesses the necessary traits is able to select and use strategies that are student centered. *Differentiated instruction* is a strategy that responds to the needs of the student. Appropriate differentiation requires *cognitive and cultural mapping and matching* (Bessant Byrd, 1989). Cognitive mapping involves ascertaining each child's intellectual level and cognitive style. Varied taxonomies exist for analysis of cognitive styles (Hoover & Collier, 1986). Determination of how children learn gives the teacher guidance regarding the mechanisms and strategies for instruction. The mark of a quality education system is the design and implementation of a program in which the curriculum and the pedagogy respond to the needs of the students, that is, a program in which both the content and the strategies are consonant with the traits of the individual children. The teacher and other members of the child study team for children with disabilities seek to ascertain the children's learning styles. This information is used to determine the appropriate teaching style for instructing the student.

Just as cognitive mapping and matching must take place, cultural mapping and matching must also occur. The teacher should examine the cultural background of the student, understand the teacher's own culture, study the cultural content of the school, and review these cultures for the presence of congruity. Should there be

TABLE 5.3.   Requisite Traits of Teachers of African American Children

Self-understanding
- Sees self as part of each child's community
- Models the behaviors expected of the child
- Evinces awareness of own values and belief systems
- Manifests awareness and control of own prejudices
- Exemplifies determination and commitment to teach African American children
- Maintains a sense of humor

Child focus
- Likes children
- Gives each child an identity base and enhances child's self-esteem
- Helps each child to develop prerequisite skills and abilities
- Promotes equitable teacher–student relationships
- Encourages children to learn collaboratively
- Makes expectations known to the child in a friendly, firm, calm, and confident manner
- Reacts appropriately to child's display of hostility
- Praises that which is praiseworthy
- Values multiple simultaneous exchanges; neither expects nor requires silence often

Content mastery
- Knows the sequence of developmental stages
- Understands cultural indices of the child and family
- Understands and recognizes the intellectual, emotional, social, and cultural strengths of the child
- Knows subject matter and relates it to the child's experience and life

Strategic proficiency
- Draws upon cultural experiences of the child and family to include authentic cultural perspectives in the curriculum
- Uses the child's culture to help the child to create meaning and understand the world
- Possesses a repertoire of varied teaching styles and adjusts them to accommodate varied learning styles among children
- Maintains participatory, dynamic, and spontaneous classrooms
- Displays flexibility in the context of a structured learning environment
- Maintains a high rate of academically engaged time
- Expands child's capacity to appreciate and deal with differences in others and helps child to perceive self in an international or global perspective

incongruity between the child's culture and that of the teacher and/or the school, the teacher should tailor the program to smoothly take the child from the familiar to the novel without indicating that the child's milieu for learning is inadequate. This accomplishes the cultural match.

After determining the appropriate cognitive and cultural maps and matches, the teacher may implement a curriculum model that gives consideration to these factors. The challenge is to orchestrate a student curriculum symphony in which there is consonance, not dissonance.

Alternative Curriculum Models

Teachers should begin cognitive and cultural mapping and matching as each child enters into the system. Early childhood educators must nurture every aspect of a child's identity and help children to be aware of both their unique and their common characteristics (Mitchell, 1990, p. 27). Throughout elementary, middle, and secondary levels, the curriculum should ensure positive and affirming experiences for all children.

This section contains brief descriptions of several curriculum models which have characteristics that commend them for instruction of African American students. This group is not comprehensive, and these paradigms are not mutually exclusive. The first, *integrative education,* emphasizes a coordinated use of brain functions. This model is based on Jung's organization of the human functions into thinking, feeling, physical sensing, and intuitive processes. The teacher who uses this model designs a responsive learning environment that includes individual assessment and instruction, self-directed activities, teacher–student planning, and implementation and evaluation (Clark, 1986).

Curriculum-based instruction is a model with some commendable traits for use with African American children with disabilities. This design focuses on a curriculum that is based on the child's performance, that empowers the child at varied levels of functioning to participate as fully as possible in school activities, and that allows children, through modification, to receive instruction fully (Choate et al., 1987).

Another strategy that complements traditional characteristics of the African American child is *cooperative learning.* This instructional approach is based on peer interaction. The children may engage in group projects, which entail sharing responsibilities to complete joint assignments. Another type of cooperative learning experience is parallel activity, in which children work in the same setting to complete individual and different tasks. Cooperative learning also may take the form of peer tutoring, in which a child aids another in review or practice of concepts that have been taught by the teacher. The merits of cooperative learning, including the increased acceptance of other racial and ethnic groups, have been cited in the literature (Slavin, 1992; Willis, 1992).

Another model that is especially valuable for a child with disabilities is *cooperative teaching.* In this case teachers rather than children become partners. The regular education and special education teachers share responsibility for instruction, classroom management, evaluation, and records management. The teachers may engage in team teaching, in which they jointly plan and teach the content to all students, or complementary teaching, in which the regular education teacher is responsible for the subject matter while the special education teacher ensures the personalizing of learning strategies by making the needed modifications (Bauwens, Hourcade, & Friend, 1989).

Contextual learning is another strategy that has significant merit in the instruction of African American children. This model responds to the tendency among African Americans to perceive the world holistically. Inasmuch as these children function from a perspective that emphasizes interrelationships and interdependence, the context becomes as important as the content. The psychological and pedagogical milieu of the lesson is critical because African American children place great value on interpersonal dynamics. The teacher should provide an affirming climate with purposive activities to help the child learn.

To help the African American child with disabilities to achieve potential, *familial encircling* is a useful strategy. The onus of responsibility rests with school personnel to work toward a positive relationship with the child's family. Although this may be a challenging task with some families, it is the key to the child's success. All parents and significant others in the home want to see the child succeed, although the desire may not be expressed in the manner preferred by school personnel. Indeed, there may be a discrepancy between the values and standards of the home and those of the school. The child should perceive that the teacher has a positive attitude toward both the child and the family. Forming a circle with the family that evinces care about and belief in the child often provides the child with motivation to succeed.

Education of the child, especially the young African American child with academic and cognitive disabilities, necessitates family-focused intervention. Major elements of this encircling of the family are enablement and empowerment (Dunst, Trivette, & Deal, 1988); that is, school personnel should provide opportunities for parents of young children to achieve competence and a sense of control. When these conditions occur for the family, in concert with the school personnel, the child and family sense that they are encircled in a caring, affirming, and positive environment that is conducive to learning by the child.

The final strategy discussed is *behavior self-regulation.* At the outset, the child must sense that the school personnel are authentic, caring professionals. The first step is to respect the child; such behavior commands respect in return. Then the child can be taught the skill of monitoring self. Joint planning and evaluation cause the child to become invested in change. Management systems can be devised to aid the child in developing proficiency in regulation of behaviors of self. When there are few interfering behaviors, the teacher is free to teach and the child is free to learn.

Numerous specific techniques have been proposed for instruction using the previously mentioned and other delivery systems (*Drawing on Diversity,* 1990; Hale-Benson, 1982; Kuykendall, 1989, 1992; McGregor, 1993; Ratleff, 1988; Shade, 1989; Wilson, 1991). The techniques suggested for instruction of African Americans tend to group into three categories: mnemonic activities, interactive activities, and movement-for-learning activities. Some of the specific techniques are listed in Table 5.4. Use of these techniques for instruction overall has been found by master teachers to be effective.

Exemplary Interventions

This section presents some specific learning activities that are exemplars of learning experiences that may be integrated into cur-

TABLE 5.4. Techniques for Teaching African American Learners

Mnemonic activities

- Audible recall: repeating information orally to facilitate recall
- Iconic learning activities: using pictures and figures of important data as memory aids
- Mediated learning: matching associated images to information to provoke recall
- Acronym or acrostic stimulated recall: first letter cueing to recall a series of terms

Interactive activities

- Keyboarding: using a typewriter, word processor, or computer
- Enactive learning: using manipulatives to aid learning
- Group learning: completing joint assignments working with others, peer tutoring

Movement-for-learning activities

- Theatrics: role playing, pantomime, theater rehearsal techniques
- Rhythmics: beating, clapping, or stepping to a pattern with recitation
- Locomotion: marching, dancing during instruction or recitation
- Creative content construction: writing content in poetry, creating and singing songs as a report, making up and performing rap as a lesson

riculum. The purpose of their inclusion is to motivate the reader to generate additional activities that may be infused in all subjects.

All of the activities discussed are designed specifically for the African American cultural group, although the schema may also be used for other groups. The learning activities are presented using a scheme that informs the teacher of the content to be taught and procedures to implement the activities. The categories of the schema are as follows: Curricular Content, Cognitive Ability, Objective, Procedure, and Assessment.

Activity 1

Curricular Content:	Language arts
Cognitive Ability:	Vocabulary development and structural analysis
Objective:	The student will identify compound words, pronounce them, and write them in complete sentences.
Procedure:	Select an excerpt from a biography of a famous African American which contains compound words. Write comple-

tion sentences omitting the compound words. Direct the student to read the story, circle the compound words in the story, then write the correct one in each sentence.

Assessment: Eighty percent accuracy.

Activity 2

Curricular Content: Arithmetic

Cognitive Ability: Introduction to money and its use for financial transactions

Objective: The student will know that cowrie shells were the legal tender for buying and selling in early civilizations.

Procedure: Read to the class of the use of cowrie shells as legal tender or money. They were counted and exchanged in business transactions in Ghana, West Africa, and other early civilizations. Also explain that in Ghana today the money is *cedi* bills (100 *pesawas* = 1 *cedi*, just as 100 *pennies* = 1 *dollar*).

Assessment: Eighty percent correct responses to oral questions.

Activity 3

Curricular Content: Language arts

Cognitive Ability: Vocabulary building

Objective: The student will recognize and be able to complete sentences using the following words: Martin, Coretta, dream, Nobel, marches, love, Atlanta.

Procedure: After reading a story about Martin Luther King, Jr., to the class and discussing it, each student is given a crossword puzzle to complete. Individual self-checking may be done using an answer key in the learning center.

Assessment: One hundred percent accuracy.

Activity 4

Curricular Content: Social studies

Cognitive Ability: Family membership

Objective: The student will demonstrate an understanding of the family by drawing the family of Sweetpea Whitaker and the student's own family.

Procedure: After the teacher reads newspaper stories, the teacher leads the class in discussing variance in size and membership of families. Have students name members of their own families and draw each of the two families in separate picture frames on a handout.

Assessment: One hundred percent accuracy of membership of Whitaker's family and self-report of own family.

Activity 5

Curricular Content: History

Cognitive Ability: Recall of historical facts about Africa

Objective: The student will recall specific facts about African culture.

Procedure: Use a teacher-designed game entitled "Africa," which is similar to "Bingo" except that words instead of numbers appear in lines and columns on the board. When the definitions of the words are stated by the teacher, the student covers the word with a marker. When all words in a vertical, horizontal, or diagonal line have been covered on a card, the student says "Africa" and wins the game.

Assessment:	Game performance.

Activity 6

Curricular Content:	Music
Cognitive Ability:	Ability to recognize and name percussion instruments
Objective:	The student will know three different percussion instruments from Ghana, West Africa—the talking drum, the hand piano, and the xylophone.
Procedure:	Each instrument is introduced, in series, with an explanation of its history, utilitarian purpose, and aesthetic value. The playing of each is demonstrated, and the students practice playing them.
Assessment:	Accurate responses to oral review questions.

Activity 7

Curricular Content:	Science
Cognitive Ability:	Increased understanding of space science
Objective:	The student will be able to describe the contributions of four African Americans to space science.
Procedure:	Organized in four cooperative learning groups, each assigned to study a different person, the students will research each scientist's life and contributions. Each group will make a presentation to their peers. The scientists for study are Christine Darden, Mae Jamison, Frederick Gregory, and Isaac Gilliam, IV.
Assessment:	Successful group presentation.

Activity 8

Curricular Content:	Social studies

Cognitive Ability:	States and capitals
Objective:	The student will be able to name the capital of each state in the United States.
Procedure:	After having the students sit in a circle, the teacher directs the students in establishing a 1, 2, 3, 4 rhythm by each person (1) patting the thighs simultaneously with both hands, (2) clapping the hands, (3) snapping the fingers on the right hand, then (4) snapping the fingers on the left hand. Once the rhythm is established, the teacher moves around inside the circle facing the students. The teacher stops in front of a student and says the name of a state on 1 and 2 of the rhythmic pattern; the student replies with the capital name on 3 and 4. *Note:* This activity can be used for numerous other review activities such as arithmetic facts.
Assessment:	Oral response during game.

CONCLUSION

This chapter has focused on curricular and pedagogical issues regarding the education of African American children. At the outset, an overview of the way in which this nation has responded to cultures was chronicled. After an enumeration of indigenous and contemporary characteristics of African American children, a parallel chronology of the response of the education system to this population was described. It was concluded that a child-centered multicultural education should be implemented in the schools. The "what" and the "how" of instruction were described. Finally, a schema for the preparation of interventions was outlined and some exemplary interventions were enumerated. The proposed instructional paradigm and the schema for interventions serve to guide the educator in providing an effective child-centered multicultural curriculum to African American children with cognitive and academic disabilities.

REFERENCES

Adler, E., Barkat, A., Bena-Silu, J., Duncan, Q., & Webb, P. (1981). *Justice for Aboriginal Australians.* Geneva: World Council of Churches.

Almanza, H. P., & Moseley, W. J. (1980). Curriculum adaptations and modifications for culturally diverse handicapped children. *Exceptional Children, 46*(8), 608–614.

American Association of Colleges for Teacher Education, Commission on Multicultural Education. (1973). No one model American. *Journal of Teacher Education, 24*(4), 264–265.

Asante, M. K. (1990). *Kemet, Afrocentricity and knowledge.* Trenton, NJ: Africa World Press.

Asante, M. K. (1991). Afrocentric curriculum. *Educational Leadership, 49*(4), 28–31.

Asante, M. K. (1991–1992). Afrocentric curriculum. *Educational Leadership, 49*(4), 28–31.

Banks, J. A. (1981). *Multiethnic education: Theory and practice.* Boston: Allyn & Bacon.

Banks, J. A. (1993). Multicultural education: Development, dimensions, and challenges. *Phi Delta Kappan, 75*(1), 22–28.

Bartz, K., & Levine, E. (1978). Childrearing by black parents: A description and comparison to Anglo and Chicano parents. *Journal of Marriage and Family, 40*(4), 709–719.

Bauwens, J., Hourcade, J., & Friend, M. (1989). Cooperative teaching: A model for general and special education integration. *Remedial and Special Education, 10*(2), 17–21.

Bessant, H. P. (1975). Interfacing special education multicultural education in a performance based teacher education model. In C. Grant (Ed.), *Sifting and winnowing: An exploration of the relationship between multicultural education and CBTE* (pp. 55–68). Madison, WI: Teacher Corps Associates.

Bessant Byrd, H. (1980). *Teacher competencies for educators of exceptional black children.* Paper presented at the Roundtable Exceptional Children sponsored by the Council for Exceptional Children Convention, Philadelphia.

Bessant Byrd, H. (1989). *Teaching urban educationally handicapped students.* Paper presented at Jackson State University, Jackson, MS.

Children's Defense Fund. (1993). *Moments in America for black children.* Washington, DC: Author.

Choate, J. S., Bennett, T. Z., Enright, B. E., Miller, L. J., Poteet, J. A., & Rakes, T. A. (1987). *Assessing and programming basic curriculum skills.* Boston: Allyn & Bacon.

Clark, B. (1986). *Optimizing learning: The Integrative Education Model in the classroom.* Columbus: Merrill.

Council for Exceptional Children. (1989). *Educating Exceptional Children Digest,* No. E 456. Reston, VA: Author.

Drawing on diversity: A handbook on teaching strategies for the multicultural classroom. (1990). Boston: North Zone Office, Boston Public Schools.

Dunst, C. J., Trivette, C., & Deal, A. (l988). *Enabling and empowering families: Principles and guidelines for practice.* Cambridge, MA: Brookline.

Fuchigami, R. Y. (1980). Teacher education for culturally diverse exceptional children. *Exceptional Children, 46*(8), 634–644.

Garcia, S. B., & Malkin, D. H. (1993). Toward defining programs and services for culturally and linguistically diverse learners in special education. *Exceptional Children, 26*(1), 52–58.

Gardner, H. (1983). *Frames of the mind: The theory of multiple intelligences.* New York: Basic Books.

Gay, G. (1977). Curriculum design for multicultural education. In C. Grant (Ed.), *Multicultural education: Commitment, issues and applications* (pp. 94–104). Washington, DC: Association for Supervision and Curriculum Development.

Grant, C. A. (1983). Multicultural teacher education—Renewing the discussion: A response to Martin Haberman. *Journal of Teacher Education, 34*(2), 29–32.

Hale-Benson, J. E. (1982). *Black children: Their roots, culture, and learning styles* (rev. ed.). Baltimore: Johns Hopkins Press.

Hall, E. T. (1976). *Beyond culture.* Garden City, NY: Anchor Press.

Harkness, S. (l980). The cultural content of child development. In C. M. Super & S. Harkness (Eds.), *New directions for child development: No. 8. Anthropological perspectives on child development* (pp. 7–13). San Francisco: Jossey-Bass.

Hilliard III, A. G. (1991–1992). Why we must pluralize the curriculum. *Educational Leadership, 49*(4), 12–15.

Hoover, J. J., & Collier, C. (1986). *Classroom management through curricular adaptations: Educating minority handicapped students.* Lindale, TX: Hamilton.

Howard, G. R. (1993). Whites in multicultural education: Rethinking our role, *Phi Delta Kappan, 75*(1), 36–41.

Hunter, W. A. (1974). Antecedents to development of and emphasis on multicultural education. In W. A. Hunter (Ed.), *Multicultural education through competency based teacher education.* Washington, DC: American Association of Colleges for Teacher Education.

Kuykendall, C. (1989). *Improving black student achievement by enhancing students' self-image.* Washington, DC: Mid-Atlantic Equity Center, The American University.

Kuykendall, C. (1992). *From rage to hope: Strategies for reclaiming Black and Hispanic students.* Bloomington, IN: National Educational Service.

Ladson-Billings, G. (1990). *Making a little magic: Teachers about successful teaching strategies for black children.* Paper presented at the Annual Meeting of the American Education Research Association, Boston.

Longstreet, W. (1978). *Aspects of ethnicity.* New York: Teachers College Press.

McGregor, J. (1993). Effectiveness of role playing and antiracist teaching in reducing student prejudice. *Journal of Educational Research, 86*(4), 215–225.

Mitchell, A. W. (1990). Schools that work for young children. *The American School Board Journal, 177*(11), 27.

Nichols, E. (1985). *Philosophical aspects of cultural difference.* Unpublished paper.

Pattel-Gray, A. (1991). *Through aboriginal eyes: The cry from the wilderness.* Geneva: WCC Publications.

Patton, J. (1992). Assessment and identification of African-American learners with gifts and talents. *Exceptional Children, 59*(2), 150–159.

Rajshakar, V. T. (1987). *Dalit: The black untouchables of India.* Atlanta: Clarity Press.

Ratleff, J. E. (1988). *Instructional strategies for crosscultural students with special needs.* Sacramento: Resources in Special Education.

Ravitch, D. (1991–1992). A culture in common. *Educational Leadership, 49*(4), 8–11.

Seelye, H. N., & Wasilewski, J. H. (1979). Historical development of multicultural education. In M. D. Pusch (Ed.), *Multicultural education: A cross cultural training approach.* LaGrange Park, IL: International Network.

Shade, B. J. (1989). *Culture, style and the educative process.* Springfield, IL: Charles C. Thomas.

Slavin, R. (1992). Getting results with cooperative learning. *Dialog, 2*(1).

Thomas, J. T. (1992). Is there a need for an Afrocentric curriculum? *InSyte, 1,* 7.

Willis, S. (1992). Cooperative learning shows staying power. *ASCD Update, 34*(3), 1–2.

Wilson, A. N. (1991). *Awakening the natural genius of Black children.* New York: Afrikan World Infosystems.

Wilson, T. (1972). Notes toward a process of African-American education. *Harvard Educational Review, 42*(3), 374–389.

CHAPTER SIX

Cultural Contexts, the Seriously Emotionally Disturbed Classification, and African American Learners

Mary Gresham Anderson and Gwendolyn Webb-Johnson

The way professionals and students interact in schools significantly determines educational contexts. The knowledge and values that professionals use to define educational contexts, however, are not culturally neutral. Professional groups and experts construct individual working definitions of children to "fit" their own cultural orientations and professional purposes (Anderson, 1994; Green, 1973; Hallahan & Kauffman, 1994). Although the concept of culture has many different definitions, in schools, the meaning of culture reflects the views of professionals, and their views are the standard against which students are judged (Rogoff & Morelli, 1989). In large measure, when the expressed cultural values, attitudes, beliefs, and aspirations of children differ from those of professionals, both the differences and the children are judged by professionals as "problematic" within regular classroom settings. Professional judgments about cultural differences, then, critically affect the educational treatment children receive.

Historically, African American children have been assessed, taught, and evaluated in public schools based on the social value system of middle class European Americans (Akbar, 1985; Delpit, 1988; Hilliard, 1988; Kneller, 1971). These values define differences as deficits and deficits as problematic (Anderson, 1992; Leone, 1990). Professionals perceive many African American learners as problematic or "difficult to teach" (U.S. Department of Education, 1992, p. 48). Children perceived by professionals as difficult are devalued, defined as deficit learners, and expected to fail. As Rosenberg, Wilson, Maheady, and Sindelar (1992) pointed out, "If a society is to maintain a social structure, violations of both implicit and explicit rules must be met with negative evaluation and punishment. Such practices ensure the continuation of a particular way of life and promote conformity to shared social expectations. It can be argued that all those who deviate from normative expectations, be they behaviorally disordered or criminal, share the fate of degradation and ostracism from society" (p. 23). Apparently, professional expectations influence which children will be treated differently, what the treatment will be, and how that treatment will define the context of their educational experiences.

The impact of professional expectations of failure for African American children was clearly evidenced in a 1990 cross-sectional estimate of children in "regular" grades 1–3, 4–6, 7–9, and 10–12. The estimate was that 48% of the African American public school population was not *expected* to "experience normal school progression without failure" (U.S. Bureau of Census, 1992, p. 4). An educational consequence of professional expectations of failure is a professional response to African American learners that too often includes diagnoses, classifications of disability, and special education placements (U.S. Department of Education, 1992). According to the U.S. Department of Education, "The reasons for [the] high disproportion of black children in special education has been an issue of national concern and debate. Congress, in its conference report on P.L. 101-476, suggested that the use of standardized assessment instruments which are racially biased are, at least in part, responsible. Some observers contend that school professionals are more likely to refer and place minority and poor children in special education because of lower expectations regarding the educability of these children" (p. 15).

To date, professional expectations of African American children often result in their overrepresentation within the seriously emotionally disturbed (SED) disability category. Disproportionate numbers of African American male learners are labeled and placed in SED classes before they complete third grade (U.S. Department of Education, 1992). Regular education professionals increasingly identify SED placements as "appropriate educational treatment" for this student population. Nationally, African American children comprise 16% of public school enrollments but account for 27% of all students in SED classes (National Mental Health Association, 1993). Unfortunately, despite the "special" treatment of SED settings, the school failure, dropout, incarceration, and stress rates of these students continue to increase.

We assert that failure to equate the cultural contexts of professional responses to the educational experiences of children is indefensible. The purpose of this chapter is to examine the impact of prevailing cultural views about African American learners on the educational treatment students identified as SED receive. An analysis of the relationship of these views to current and proposed federal SED definitions is subsequently addressed. Because neither definition is grounded in a cultural orientation compatible with African American cultural experiences, congruent relationships between aspects of Nichols's model of cultural differences, the artistic ideology, the theatre communication process, and compatible educational goals and instructional strategies are presented. These relationships structure an empowerment model of educational context, which is compatible with the study of child and adolescent development and the cultural context of African American learners. Finally, implications for future ethnographic and empirical research are proposed.

PREVAILING CULTURAL VIEWS

Dominant cultural views influencing professional perceptions about teaching African American children in our public schools are historically based (Asante, 1992; Boykin, 1993; Delpit, 1988; Hilliard, 1976, 1988, 1991). We identify four interrelated cultural views: the social view of cultural nonexistence, the legal view of teaching African Americans, the psychological view of learning, and the scientific view of testing. These views have influenced theoretical explanations of disordered behavior, namely sociological, ecological, psychodynamic, and behavioral. We address the critical educational implications these explanations have for African American children labeled SED.

The Social View of Cultural Nonexistence

The concept of culture includes both implicit knowledge and explicit expressions of purposeful thinking and feeling for a way of life. Banks (1988) described the components of culture as intangible aspects of human societies. Interrelated components of culture include institutions, language, games, symbols, meanings, beliefs, and values, as well as technological, ideological, and attitudinal products of human learning experiences shared by generations of people (S. D. Johnson, 1990; Pai & Morris, 1978; Washington, 1989). These cultural characteristics affect people at the levels of feeling, action, and prejudice.

Historically, the dominant European American response to the acknowledgment and acceptance of the existence of the African American cultural experience met and continues to meet with resistance. According to Holliday (1989), seminal studies on African Americans did not introduce the concept of African American culture. These early studies were "guided by a caste/class perspective" (p. 33) and emphasized the joint effects of race and social class. Furthermore, multidisciplinary approaches to the study of the "Negro" did not encourage development of a visible vehicle for interdisciplinary work on the African American cultural experience (Jones, 1991). In large measure, professional perceptions of the uniquely American culture did not include recognition of African American ways of life.

The current sociological explanation of disordered behavior defines problem behaviors as "deviations from arbitrarily determined social rules" (Rosenberg et al., 1992, p. 24). Children are expected to learn the value of the rules and follow them, within dominant social contexts, regardless of their cultural orientations. Adults are expected to transmit the dominant culture by modeling and rewarding appropriate behaviors. Children are expected to behave in ways that adults socially sanction. Simply, they are expected to comply with the diverse cultural expectations of professionals. Within this cultural context, the impact of the African American cultural experience on the educational context is largely nonexistent. In schools, a single culturally given body of knowledge, values, and behaviors still defines appropriate and inappropriate behaviors for children.

The Legal View of Teaching African Americans

Hilliard (1988) examined the legal implications of the African American educational experience. He presented his belief that no clear conceptual base or theoretical framework had been developed that could result in the significant improvement of education for millions of African American learners. He asserted that privilege and oppression dominated professional practice prior to the Supreme Court's decision in 1954 regarding *Brown v. Topeka, Kansas,* and included six major interrelated functions: (a) ideology of White supremacy, (b) political control, (c) systematic distortion and disrespect for history and culture, (d) uses of group identity, (e) uses of financial and human resources, and (f) physical segregation. The Supreme Court decision focused only on physical segregation. Hilliard contended that the problem of segregation was only a very small part of a generally pervasive system. He purported that the past 40 years of research were heavily focused on an aspect of the decision that may not have been the most important component of the problem.

Akbar (1985) further asserted that the 1954 Supreme Court decision promoted the following indefensible assumptions about teaching African American children:

1. It was psychologically unhealthy for "colored children to go to school only with one another";
2. Segregation promoted self-hatred and lowered motivation;
3. It was psychologically healthy for African American children to attend school with White children; and
4. Integration would improve African American children's self-concept, intellectual achievement and overall social and psychological adjustment. (p. 24)

Akbar continued by noting that the Supreme Court decision did not identify the reality that, in maintaining a system of segregation, not only were African American children hurt "by the thwarted opportunity and abuse, but Caucasian children were raised as delusional racists" (p. 25).

Nevertheless, a nation of African American children and their parents thought that desegregation would finally guarantee the quality education that had previously been denied. National educational organizations such as the National Association for the Advancement of Colored People (NAACP) and the Urban League supported this famous decision. A theoretical explanation that supports the court decision is the ecological view. From this perspective, children are defined "normal" when they achieve, generalize, and maintain a visible balance between their behaviors and the social expectations of their environments. Disordered behavior reflects an imbalance or mismatch between student behaviors and professional expectations for behaving. This explanation reflects the cultural notion that professional practice involves providing children labeled SED with opportunities to interact with the "right" people in the "right" environments. In this way, children could learn to match their behaviors to the appropriate behaviors of those in the acceptable environments and subsequently learn to behave appropriately across dominant social contexts.

The Psychological View of Learning

Researchers have attempted to respond to the ongoing implications of the legal view of teaching African American learners. Ogbu (1985) examined the universal model of educational intervention as it was currently used to study and determine the competencies of African American learners. Through the universal model, African Americans are studied in relation to problems they confront in the larger society (i.e., the expectations of others, lack of appreciation or utility of their culture in dominant educational contexts, personal life challenges). The environmental and the developmental components of this model continue to define the concept of difference as "deficit." Environmentalists believe that African American underachievement is due to a lack of cognitive, linguistic, motivational, and social competencies because African American parents do not use the same child rearing practices as Caucasian middle class parents (Bloom, Davis, & Hess, 1965). Developmentalists contend that African American underachievement might be due to a lack of cognitive competencies necessary for achievement (Jensen, 1969). Each model identifies the origin of the learning problem as something "lacking" within the African American child.

The psychodynamic explanation also focuses on the motivations or driving forces underlying behavior and emotions. Disordered behavior is believed to be an imbalance among the components of the intrapsychic events of the personality (Bootzin, 1980). Again, the notion of disorder is understood to be inherent within the child. The major source of the behavioral disturbance from this perspective is psychological instability.

The Scientific View of Testing

The passage of time and the experience of continued educational injustice have offered new perspectives on the ramifications of the 1954 decision. The use of the following more recent and more creative procedures to aid in education has become a persistent trend maintaining the deficit view and influencing professional perceptions about teaching African American learners:

1. Mental measurement emerged as a tool for continued segregation and special education placement.

2. Tracking, manifested by the overrepresentation of African Americans in lower level classes, increased.

3. Labeling (e.g., culturally different vs. culturally deprived, other advantaged vs. disadvantaged, educationally exposed vs. educationally deprived) evidenced the failure of school systems to understand cultural differences or appropriately address the unique needs of African American children (Bernstein, 1961; Hilliard, 1988; McIntyre & Pernell, 1985; Neil & Medina, 1989).

The behavioral explanation of disordered behavior defines disorder as a learned behavior maintained by external, environmental events. Behavior can be observed, measured, modified, predicted, and controlled external to the individual exhibiting the behavior. According to this explanation, the behaviors of children identified as SED can be identified (known), managed, and controlled for in social settings.

TRADITIONAL EDUCATIONAL TREATMENT

As a result of dominant cultural views and theoretical explanations, the educational treatment that students labeled SED receive consists of professionals trying to influence or control student behaviors. Professional strategies of control consist primarily of dominating classroom communication interactions with "a heavy use of commands and a high degree of direct instruction" (McDermott, 1977, p. 205). Secondary SED classrooms are particularly designed to restrict and control the social communication behaviors of students (Anderson, 1989; Bolton, 1984; Hymes, 1983). Popular and restrictive behavior modification or management interventions are implemented, monitored, and controlled by professionals so as to gain and maintain control of student social communication behaviors (Gresham, 1982; N. Johnson, 1990). These interventions or social skills training curricula "treat" surface communication behaviors by directly dictating predetermined, prosocial behaviors, and either reward students for using them or punish them for noncompliance (Newmann, 1981; Safran & Safran, 1985).

As a result, students labeled SED are given very little opportunity to control their social interactions during the school day. They can neither initiate social contacts nor escape undesirable ones. Such restriction of social role control can be disconcerting, particularly because it relates to "loss of privacy, loss of power and prestige, and restrictions of movement" for those being controlled (Lightfoot, 1973, p. 226). Additionally, the interpersonal relationships between teachers and students in SED classes are characterized by a number of calculated limitations. Neither children nor adolescents labeled SED are expected to evaluate, examine, or if necessary reject the dictates or responses of professionals without negative sanctions (Anderson, 1989; Robinson, 1980), and they are expected to interact virtually in a one-way communication pattern, with little room for negotiation (Strom, 1973). Unfortunately, professionally controlled communication interactions are clearly counter to both the developmental nature and the cultural needs of African American learners (Anderson, 1989; Kortering & Blackorby, 1992).

RELATIONSHIP OF CULTURAL VIEWS TO SED DEFINITION

In the following sections, we discuss the relationships among the identified cultural views, the theoretical explanations, and both current and proposed SED definitions. The relationships are further outlined in Table 6.1. The influence of these views on professional conduct and the educational treatment that African American students labeled SED receive are addressed in the discussion and outlined in Figure 6.1 (see page 170).

The Current SED Definition

The 1990 Individuals with Disabilities Education Act (IDEA) uses the term seriously emotionally disturbed (SED) to describe children and youth with behavioral disorders or emotional disturbances. The current federal definition is as follows:

> (i) The term means a condition exhibiting one or more of the following characteristics over a long period of time and to a marked extent which adversely affects educational performance:
>
> (A) An inability to learn that cannot be explained by intellectual, sensory, or health factors;
>
> (B) An inability to build or maintain satisfactory relationships with peers and teachers;
>
> (C) Inappropriate types of behavior or feelings under normal circumstances;
>
> (D) A general pervasive mood of unhappiness or depression; or
>
> (E) A tendency to develop physical symptoms or fears associated with personal school problems.
>
> (ii) The term includes children who are schizophrenic or autistic. The term does not include children who are socially maladjusted unless it is determined that they are seriously emotionally disturbed. (Hallahan & Kauffman, 1994, p. 208)

Culturally Based Problems

We have identified three clarifying explanations that illuminate culturally based concepts impeding the efficacy of the current definition, as discussed in the following text.

1. The terminology used in the definition has been invented to identify characteristics or behaviors of children as disturbing "conditions" inherent within the child. However, professional perceptions and expectations determine the existence of disturbance.

TABLE 6.1. Relationships Among Aspects of Current and Proposed SED Definitions, Cultural Views and Theoretical Explanations

Components	Current Definition	Proposed Definition	Cultural View/ Theoretical Explanations	Conceptual Limitations
Choice of terminology	Inability inappropriate "over a long period of time"; "to a marked extent"	Disability Co-exist with other disabilities	Social/Sociological— Differences are deficits; deficits are problematic	Open to varying negative interpretations Affective reactions to expressed behaviors
Origin of disability	A condition A tendency	Consistently exhibited More than a temporary expected response	Legal/Ecological Deficits are inherent within the child	Lack of widely acceptable measuring devices Many observable behaviors are the same for large numbers of children who have not been identified as having learning or behavior problems
Performance expectations	"Inability to learn"	"Unresponsive to direct intervention in general education"	Psychological/ Psychodynamic Behaviors pose problems for others	Ill-defined Open to interpretation Presumed differences Faulty evidence
Observational evidence of disorder	"Inappropriate types of behaviors and feelings"	"So different from appropriate age, culture, or ethnic norms"	Scientific/Behavioral Identify and target deficit behaviors for intervention	Lack of clear distinction between normal and deviant Lack of strategies related to diagnosis

When a diagnosis of an emotional or behavioral "inability" is determined, the concluding evidence does not take into account the transactions that occur between the professionals identifying the behavior as disordered and the student being identified. Washington (1989) acknowledged that within every culture there is a point at which deviancy is not tolerated. Professional expectations of "ability" are based on cultural beliefs and values about how much deviance is acceptable. Professionals use a social view that defines acceptability from a single definition. Thus, it is the beliefs and values inherent in both the training and the cultural views of professionals rather than significant differences between or among the behaviors of children that determine which children are defined (Anderson, 1992; Bullock, Wilson, & Campbell, 1990; Gajar, 1979; Hallahan & Kauffman, 1977; Russell & Tanguay, 1981; Safran & Safran, 1985) and which terms are used to define children (Smith & Luckasson, 1992). These views have cognitive, affective, and behavioral components.

When professionals cognitively and affectively react to the behavioral characteristics of children, they count and classify the behaviors they reacted to. Their reactions, then, are constitutive of and influential to how students are classified. In large measure, the behavior is not a problem or an "inability" without these professional reactions (Anderson, 1992; Ditton, 1979). The *same* student behaviors may be considered disturbing in one social situation but not in another because of preconditions such as differences in adult interpretations of and expectations for behavior, subjective teacher attitudes and perceptions, adult rules for conduct, adult ways of interacting with children, adult consequences for rule breaking, and even adult interpretations of the behavior of other children in the immediate environment (Gallagher, 1988; Kauffman & Hallahan, 1981).

2. Although neither the current federal definition nor the terminology used to construct it is "clear nor comprehensive enough to determine appropriate eligibility in this category" (Forness & Knitzer, 1990, p. 4), professionals continue to assess, place, and treat children in SED settings because of their reactive responses to the communicative behaviors of the children.

Professionals differentiate observable behaviors or social characteristics based on their individual expectations of normal or appropriate social communication behaviors (Fielder & Knight, 1986; Simpson, 1989). Their individual motives, perceptions, and intentions are inherent in their expectations and in the diagnostic data they report.

Professional expectations influence what professionals observe as well as the data they report. Because there are no standardized tests that determine behavioral or emotional disabilities (U.S. Department of Education, 1992), behavioral profiles are determined from information based on clinical/behavioral observation data (i.e., self-reports or behavioral rating scales). Professionals, then, maintain the scientific view of using procedures to search for the deficit behavior and preserve the dominant cultural view. This perspective also reflects the psychological view that directs professionals to study the deficit behavior and the child in relation to the problems that professionals confront.

Clinical/behavioral observations result in differences in data reporting practices, identification criteria, and policies and programs. These differences reflect professional expectations that are uncritically treated in diagnostic analysis. They also include professional disagreements about evaluational protocol, nomenclature, informational content, and interpretation (Sinclair & Kheifets, 1982). Despite the differences, disagreements, and violations, diagnostic data and special education research methods continue to be used to determine eligibility and educational treatment.

Chenault (1975) asserted that the trend to identify African American learners as "special" exemplifies a macroscopic psychological and educational construct that may have "provided the theoretical foundation for questionable educational diagnosis and inappropriate placements" (p. 93). The problems inherent in Chenault's assertion are congruent with the problems with the SED classification. Chenault pointed out that the two theoretical models applied to assessment and research in special education—the medical and the psychometric—have utilized "quantitative statistical techniques to generate qualitative conclusions" (p. 94). The ongoing effectiveness of practices that perpetuated and maintained inequity in education calls into question theoretical foundations grounding their continued use. Hilliard (1976) concluded that the educator must embrace and know history to inform theory. He further contended that "empirical observations by observers or ethnographers must address the real world and know our children" (p. 42). Woodson (1933) and Hilliard (1988) noted that theories about equity (like those maintaining inequity) must be based on both historical and "real world" student outcomes as the primary evidence for validating their effectiveness. As a result, theorists and practitioners of special education are to be challenged because the bases of their educational assessment findings have not consistently reflected this violation of methodology.

3. Because of the cultural context underlying theoretical explanations of disordered behavior and the SED label, other children do not experience the educational process in ways that parallel the experiences of African American learners.

In 1990–1991, a total of 392,559 children and youth, ages 6 to 21, were identified with serious emotional disturbance (U.S. Department of Education, 1992). According to the observational data, the largest group of children and adolescents labeled and receiving SED services are those whom "regular" teachers identify as having disruptive behaviors or conduct disorders (Forness & Knitzer, 1990). African American learners are labeled SED twice as often as their peers (U.S. Department of Education, 1992). Teachers and other professionals report that when students exhibit deficits in social skills performances (Leone, 1990; Schonert-Reichl, 1993), they experience difficulties in their interpersonal relationships and should be identified and targeted for intervention (Asamow, 1988; Parkhurst & Asher, 1992; Rubin, Hymel, LeMare, & Rowden, 1989). After identification and placement in SED settings, African American students are least likely to earn academic credit in regular education courses, are significantly more likely to receive failing grades and be retained (Wagner, Newman, & Shaver, 1989), and are more likely to exit school by dropping out than any other student population (U.S. Bureau of Census, 1992; U.S. Department of Education, 1992; Walker et al., 1988). Thus, the legal view of difference that defines African American children as lacking in competencies focuses on deficit areas of performance, and intentionally counts and reports frequencies of student failures but recognizes no service responsibility for the educational outcomes these students experience.

Proposed Definition

Because the federal definition has been widely criticized, in 1990 a second definition was proposed by the National Mental Health and Special Education Coalition. The proposed definition follows:

(i) The term emotional or behavioral disorder means a disability characterized by behavioral or emotional responses in school so different from appropriate age, cultural, or ethnic norms that they adversely affect educational performance. Educational performance includes academic, social, vocational, and personal skills. Such a disability

(A) is more than a temporary, expected response to stressful events in the environment;

(B) is consistently exhibited in two different settings, at least one of which is school related; and

(C) is unresponsive to direct intervention in general education, or the child's condition is such that general education interventions would be insufficient.

(ii) Emotional and behavioral disorders can co-exist with other disabilities.

(iii) This category may include children or youth with schizophrenic disorders, affective disorders, anxiety disorders, or other sustained disorders of conduct or adjustment when they adversely affect educational performance in accordance with section (i). (Forness & Knitzer, 1992, p. 13)

Although the coalition is currently working to have the proposed definition and terminology adopted as federal law and regulation, the problems inherent in this definition, like its predecessor, continue to reflect the concept of differences as deficits. These problems are as follows:

1. Neither definition embraces the reality that prevailing topologies of student characteristics (i.e., *differences* in cognitive, linguistic, motivational, and social competencies) reflect distinctive cultural frames of reference within which students behave (Ogbu, 1986). Even within cultural contexts, differences can and do occur.

2. Neither definition establishes a common understanding of "order" and/or acceptability consistent with the diverse experiences of the children they define. The following questions need to be considered: In the face of socioeconomic, intracultural, and adult psychological/emotional health differences, who is going to determine *what is* "so different from appropriate age, culture, or ethnic norms" for individual children? When are professionals going to recognize that

the realities of homelessness, abuse, physiological and/or intellectual differences, maleness, or African American heritage "adversely affect" the life priorities of children *separate* from educational performances?

3. Neither definition explains causes of behavior. Both describe student characteristics as if the differences inherent in school-related factors that influence professional behaviors were inconsequential.

4. Neither definition addresses the incongruencies between professional interpretations of observed behaviors and culturally sound student-generated motives and explanations for behaving.

5. Both definitions are grounded in the search-for-and-reduce-or-eliminate-the-deficit perspective of student behaviors.

Thus, professional perceptions and expectations continue to be focused on problematic or disordered *children.* Despite the content of student profiles and the concepts of differences as deficits, both the current and the proposed SED definitions continue to rest on the legally accepted evidence of professional perceptions and expectations about how children should behave.

Rethinking and Redesigning the SED Definition

For professional observations, analyses, and practices to be less professionally biased, a more proactive rather than reactive educational context is needed. We offer in this section seven components of a redesigned context.

First, professional reactions should be collected, collated, and treated as additional resources upon which the effects of the identified difference can be based. Such treatment would begin to yield a more representative understanding of the contributing factors influencing diagnostic data, professional decisions, and the nature of the educational treatment that African American learners receive.

Second, help is needed in separating behaviors and skills that facilitate school success and later socioeconomic success from behaviors and skills that imply assimilation and threaten cultural identity (Ogbu, 1985). Holliday (1985) examined a study investigating competence and ecology and found that parental expectations of competence related to African American children were quite different from the competence expectations of teachers. She found nonsignificant relationships between academic performance and competence at home. She wrote, "Mothers' perceptions of the children's skills bear no relationship to the children's academic achievement. But teachers' perceptions of children's skills are highly predictive of children's academic achievement. In the home and neighborhood, children's roles most frequently demand problem-solving skills. But at school, children's interpersonal skills, as well as academic excellence, are in great demand" (p. 123). Holliday's findings suggest that, while competent in roles at home and the community, these children were nevertheless experiencing persistent problems in school.

Third, the concept of difference could be defined as "context," not as it relates to the culture of one population as a standard (Boykin, 1986, 1993). This concept reflects a cultural ecological model of child rearing and development. It is an interrelated context that includes effective environment, subsistence tasks, and survival strategies that lead to child-rearing techniques in various settings. Proponents of the model have argued that "minority" groups have their own distinct cultural patterns of child-rearing practices and learning competencies (Boykin, 1983; Hale, 1980; Hale-Benson, 1986). They define the concept of difference as "other" and suggest that children fail in school because "schools do not recognize and utilize their unique competencies for teaching, learning, and testing" (Ogbu, 1986, p. 49). Ogbu (1986) suggested that the development of a cultural ecology that "enables us to discover distinctive [B]lack competencies, and the relationship of these instrumental competencies to [B]lack child-rearing competencies as well as to [B]lack school experiences" (p. 49) would be educationally appropriate.

Fourth, teachers must begin to acknowledge and accept that many of the behaviors they identify as disordered or problematic actually characterize normal physical, social, emotional, and intellectual stages of development (Despert, 1965; Kauffman & Hallahan, 1981; National Middle School Association, 1982; Strom, 1973). For example, a central developmental goal of adolescence is self-determination, which is most meaningfully evidenced by emancipation from authoritarian control and influence (Despert, 1965). A chief characteristic of this goal is autonomous behavior. When adolescents attempt to manage their communication behaviors, they often do not allow others to control aspects of their lives even indirectly, without trying to influence decisions (Knoblock, 1983). Consequently, autonomous adolescent behavior "often runs counter to the social expectations of adults" (National Middle School Association, 1982, p. 6). Thus, professional definitions and expectations for behavior should emerge from the particular age, experience, and cultural orientations of the child rather than from professional preferences for student behavior.

Fifth, school professionals could provide children with numerous and diverse opportunities to make sense of their life experiences. To date, millions of African American children have entered classrooms in which teacher expectations have been based on what these children *cannot* do academically and socially within the context of the school arena, rather than on the integrity and strengths they bring with them to school (Boykin, 1993). Professionals need to acknowledge that identifying the behavior is not more important than what they do as a result of their reactions to it. Clearly, professionals should search for the strengths of children and use the integrity of the children's life experiences to promote social development and academic achievement.

Sixth, although the SED definition and label are currently under reconsideration, the qualifying phrases "labeled" or "identified as" could precede the new label as a means of recognizing the transactional role of professionals in the diagnosis. In this way the language used would redirect the focus of the problem or disorder away from the thinking that "something is wrong with the child" (i.e., "SED child" or a child *with* SED") and toward the thinking that "something has been identified as problematic by someone other than the child" (specifically, "a child *labeled* SED" or "a child *identified as* SED"). These qualifying phrases, which we have used throughout this chapter to preface the SED label, could be equally qualifying if used in conjunction with other educational labels (i.e., "learning disabled" and "mentally retarded").

Finally, seventh, because exit criteria from SED placements rest heavily with professional interpretations of student social communication behaviors, a significant change in a student's social communication behavior is a precondition necessary for prompting a reassessment of his or her communicative competence. The reassessment would facilitate exits from SED classes

(Anderson, 1992). A significant result of improving the social communication skills of African American learners labeled SED would be the "replacement of many students into regular classrooms" (Anderson, 1992, p. 133).

COMPONENTS OF A COMPATIBLE EDUCATIONAL CONTEXT

In the previous section, we identified seven components necessary for rethinking and redesigning the SED definition. The following discussion identifies an educational context compatible with African American cultural orientations. The components of this context, specifically Nichols's (1976) model of cultural differences, the artistic ideology, and aspects of the theatre communication process, structure congruent relationships between cultural, developmental, and academic differences. The relationships reflect the concept of empowerment and help to redefine educational context as an empowering communication paradigm for all students across grade levels. Appropriate modifications for the developmental differences of children are necessary for successful utility of the educational context offered.

Empowerment

The idea of empowerment is concerned with the process by which families and individuals manage to function effectively under difficult or demanding circumstances (Edelman, 1985). The process also involves providing opportunities to acquire the competencies needed to *change* the nature of the experiences children and families manage. Hilliard (1991) and Woodson (1933) reminded professionals that if African Americans are to empower themselves "to do for themselves," their power must be drawn from the knowledge of their history and the real-world outcomes they experience within African American and "other" cultural communities. Educators could create instructional programs that embrace the strengths children bring to school and define the larger patterns of continuity effecting the generalization of cultural theory as empowering practices.

Nichols's Model

Currently, cultural differences present cross-cultural problems because children from one ethnic group are expected to employ problem-solving strategies considered of value or "supreme" by another group. Nichols (1976) postulated that damages in the experiences provided for students in the educational system occur because many educators fail to constructively use important cultural differences between African American and European American learners (see Figure 6.1). He developed a model for examining the philosophical aspects of the cultural differences between European Americans and African Americans that helps to clarify the impact of cultural contexts on the educational treatment that African American students labeled SED receive (see Figure 6.1).

The first area of Nichols's model highlights the *axiology* of a group, the differences in the values individuals possess. For example, European Americans' axiological referent has been identified as "Man to Object." The highest value lies in the object or the acquisition of the object, be it land, work, time, or money. African Americans' axiological referent is "Man to Man." The highest value lies in the interpersonal relationships between persons. One seeks to interact and understand the social environment.

The second area of Nichols's model highlights the *epistemology* of the two groups. Each group knows knowledge differently. The African American knows through symbolic imagery and rhythm. Knowledge is predominantly processed through an affective framework that is used intuitively. An individual sees the whole before he or she attends to the parts of the whole. However, European Americans know through counting and measuring. The individual processes knowledge predominantly through attendance to the parts en route to encountering the whole. Traditional curriculum and instruction in math offer a "counting and measuring" pedagogy. The significant failure of African American children in the area of math may be partly due to a lack of alternative methods of instruction that incorporates affective symbolic imagery and rhythm into teaching practices.

The third area of the model is *logic.* African American logic systems tend to be epistemology, characterized by the union of opposites. European American logic systems are characterized by dichotomy and are expressed as either/or.

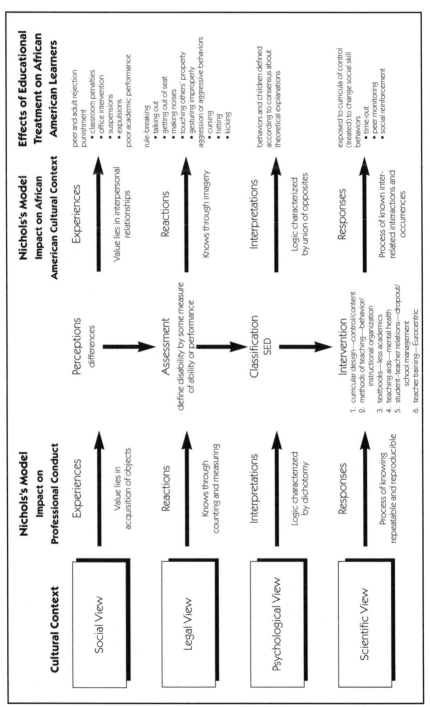

FIGURE 6.1. Impact of cultural context on educational treatment of students classified as seriously emotionally disturbed (SED).

The fourth area of Nichols's model is the *process of knowing.* African Americans tend to associate this process through ntuology. All sets of interactions and occurrences are interrelated through human and spiritual networks. European Americans, in contrast, tend to process knowledge through technology. All sets of occurrences and interactions are repeatable and reducible.

The cultural components of Nichols's model provide a framework within which the critical aspects of cultural differences between African Americans and European Americans can be examined. The identified principles and perspectives define a knowledge base for understanding and using educational theory and the existence of culture to promote educational success among these student populations.

Artistic Ideology

The way students communicate in schools influences the nature of their educational treatment. To date, the educational treatment that students labeled SED have received includes loss of privileges, corporal punishment, physical control, some action by fellow students, forced apologies, teachers lowering grades, isolation, or after-school detentions (Campbell, Dobson, & Bost, 1985). Behaviors such as cursing, fighting, truancy, willful disobedience, being out of seat, talking out, or other rule-breaking or "aggressive" acts are generally cited as measurable reasons for coercive methods of teaching self-control (Campbell et al., 1985). The same evidence is often used to maintain students in SED placements. However, if students learn how to change the way they think about interactions and change the way they actually interact, then they will, in turn, be empowered to influence the way they are perceived and judged by others. They will also be empowered to change the nature and consequences of their social interactions by changing the way they participate in and contribute to ongoing interactions.

Students labeled SED could learn to facilitate their memberships into more inclusive and less restrictive educational environments if they learned "how to portray *themselves* in the most successful and rewarding way" (Wood, 1976, p. 254). "Learning how" requires an artistic rather than a control ideology. The artistic ideology is based on the thinking that, although student actors cannot control many of the contextual influences imposed upon them, they can learn to calculate and organize the way they think about and participate in social communication interactions such that the nature of their participation benefits them. This ideology characterizes an empowering communication paradigm. The paradigm embodies the premise that each person is the source of his or her own meaning-making power (Benedetti, 1981; Goffman, 1959; Hagen, 1991; Kauffman & Hallahan, 1981; Way, 1976). The premise directs each social communicator to use the artistic ideology "to see familiar things [specifically, the way they communicate], in unfamiliar ways" (Anderson, 1992, p. 137).

The process of "seeing," calculating, and organizing the nature of one's participation in social interactions is clearly a matter of individual choice. Choosing the nature of one's participation is congruent with student developmental needs to communicate for reasons separate from the content and dynamics of adult controls (Luria, 1967). The observable behavioral choices of students as social actors can facilitate personally and academically rewarding communication consequences for them (Anderson, 1992; Goffman, 1959). Apparently, self-control is dependent upon an actual emphasis on the intellectual, affective, and active experiences of each learner.

Thus, the partnership between the needs of students to self-regulate and the artistic ideology could significantly benefit the development of desirable social self-controllers among African American learners labeled SED. The artistic ideology could therefore be used to shift educational context away from authoritarian power and influence, and toward contexts of individual organization and self-control (Goffman, 1967). It can be used by both professionals and students as an educative tool for explicitly presenting, understanding, and *changing* the implicit nature of their social interactions. The changed behavior influences both teaching and learning processes. This educational tool could be understood as a cognitive–affective–behavioral intervention process that results in real or authentic changes in individual behaviors. The changes would be both qualitative and quantitative.

Aspects of the Theatre Communication Process

Inherent in the artistic ideology are aspects of the theatre communication process. This process structures an interactive way of thinking about and learning how to communicate with increased competence. Because communication competence is critical to student social and academic success, empowering students to effectively self-regulate and influence the way they learn and change communication performances is fundamental to educational purpose. Three primary aspects of the theatre communication process—namely, intention, performance, and consequences—are compatible with Nichols's (1976) model of cultural differences (see Figure 6.2). Six interrelated questions (shown in Figure 6.2) provide a concrete and patterned way for students to use the aspects of the

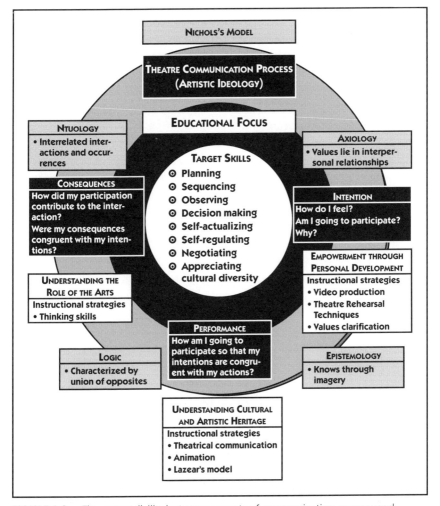

FIGURE 6.2. The compatibility between aspects of communication process and Nichols's cultural differences.

process. The questions direct students to think about, talk about, experience, create, and make decisions about how to change the nature of their interpersonal relationships. The visible presentational format of each aspect provides students with explicit ways of "seeing how to" self-regulate implicit concepts of interaction.

Both the questions and the presentational formats presented illuminate educational goals compatible with the cultural, developmental, and learning style differences of African American learners. These compatible goals facilitate self-regulated social communication competencies for students labeled SED as well as their nonlabeled peers. This is because the goals are defined to include students in rather than separate students from the empowering communication process. The goals direct professionals to search for, encourage, and appreciate student differences in learning. They also provide students with opportunities to learn to use the empowering paradigm themselves to investigate and understand the efficacy of their communication choices and influence social and academic consequences. The educational goals identified in this discussion have been defined by Heathcote and were outlined in Pfeuffer and Kingsley (1982). These goals help to clarify each aspect of the process. Compatible empowering competencies and instructional strategies are presented to further define the utility of the goals, thus guiding the process inherent in the paradigm.

Intention Aspect

The first aspect, intention, is structured to bring about a synthesis between feelings and thoughts. It is addressed by involving students in sequentially answering the following three questions:

1. How do I feel about the interaction?

2. Am I going to participate?

3. Why? (What are my reasons for participating?)

The educational goals for addressing these questions are as follows: "to give children an opportunity to examine their own living problems with a new perspective" (Pfeuffer & Kingsley, 1982, p. 66), and "to accept, support, and then challenge decisions the class makes" (p. 66). These educational goals focus on empowering students through *personal fulfillment and development* by providing opportunities for them to:

- Learn through their individual talents
- Challenge perceptions about feelings, interests, and the things they know
- Understand their cultural/artistic heritage
- Focus on intentions of context
- Explore feelings that promote a sense of power and control through personal accomplishments
- Create a disciplined environment
- Develop a knowledge of structure

These opportunities offer explicit educative ways for students to experience how to alter reactive relationships between feelings, thoughts, and behavior performances. Students labeled SED, like stage actors, could learn to select and express emotion in social situations, in a deliberate manner for a particular purpose. Intention, then, serves mainly to define the details or characteristics of the action rather than the performer (Goffman, 1959). By keeping their attention on the details of their actions (their intentions), actors and students can learn to use or control emotion objectively, and to express a selected purpose within a given social situation. From a theatrical perspective, action comes by way of intention or purpose (Benedetti, 1981).

Instructional Strategies

Three instructional strategies are suggested that help students answer the three questions and gain the competencies that define the intention aspect. First, the video-making experience provides students with opportunities to keep their attention on their intention and control the details of changing behavior. Black's (1989) book *Kid Vid* describes nine video production lessons, complete with student and teacher objectives. The teacher-oriented, conversational format of the text makes this resource ready to use across grade levels and content areas. The possibilities for students to select, construct, express, control, and change their cognitive and affective perceptions are endless.

Another instructional strategy is to use improvisational theatre rehearsal technique (TRT) activities. Elliott (1986) pointed out that if people were to change and control the way they act or behave, they must begin by breaking the domination of their ordinary habits of conceiving and perceiving their own behavior. Thorngate (1976) further clarified that although people do not always think before they act, if they are to intentionally change the action, they must think first, in order to "de-automatize" the behavior expressed and influence the perceptions of others. He noted that learned perception gives rise to a particular set of images or thoughts, which must be taken into consideration if changes or shifts in ordinary habits of conceptualizing are to take place.

Anderson's (1985) article describes a TRT activity called "Car Wash," which translates Elliot's (1986) and Thorngate's (1976) theories into practical classroom application. This particular TRT is very difficult for students to experience, however, because many students "feel" uncomfortable intentionally accepting a compliment or saying something nice to someone else. This activity requires that students think first and change their ordinary habits of feeling, thinking, and behaving *during* the interaction. A description of "Car Wash" follows:

> I begin this activity by saying, "Please divide yourselves into two groups so that you form two straight lines facing each other, leaving an aisle between you. A person from either side may begin but whoever starts must come down the aisle, turning to each side alternately. Each person you turn to must tell you something that they like about you. You can only answer "Thank You." Afterwards, you quietly turn and face the person in the other line and wait for their compliment. When you get to the end of the aisle, take a place at the end of your line and the person from the other side will begin coming down. Remember, whatever is said to someone must be a true compliment. No one is allowed to pass. [No one is allowed to repeat a compliment to a person coming down the aisle.] You can always find at least one nice thing to say about someone else. The other person can not leave until you give a compliment."
>
> Compliments range from "I like your shoes," "I like your shirt," to "I like your smile," or "I like the way you care about

how I feel. You are a fair and honest person and I am glad to be your friend." It is not unusual for people to hug each other, shake hands, or even cry. By the time we have all come down the aisle [Yes, even the professional], everyone is aware of feeling better. (p. 23)

The third instructional strategy is to use the activities described in Simon, Howe, and Kirschenbaum's (1972) book, *Values Clarification*. These activities involve students in the ongoing process of transforming their perceptions about the way they think, feel, and act in order to redefine and use new meanings to understand common interactions.

Performance Aspect

The second aspect of the process, performance, is based on an understanding of behavior as communication action. Students are provided with opportunities to explicitly address the question, How am I going to participate so that my intentions are congruent with my actions? The educational goals for the performance component are "to help students discover that they know more than they thought they knew" (Pfeuffer & Kingsley, 1982, p. 66), and "to lead students to see the real world more clearly in light of what is revealed by the imagined one" (p. 66). These goals focus on understanding their artistic/cultural heritage by providing opportunities for students labeled SED to:

- Recognize the value of multiple ways to learn

- Create opportunities for choice

- Explore roles and aspects of personality

- Promote social relations

- Promote self-expression

- Appreciate symbolic performances (i.e., gesture as language)

- Draw on multiple intelligences as multiple ways of communicating

- Learn to set standards for self

The competencies focus on student abilities to "see" and use ideas, knowledge, and perceptions common to experiences inherent in their everyday lives in ways that promote their successes.

Three instructional strategies are offered to provide professionals with visible approaches for providing students with opportunities to share experiences and learn to negotiate self-satisfying consequences for themselves. First, Johnson and O'Neil's (1985) text entitled *Dorothy Heathcote* provides professionals with a resource for gaining enhanced understandings about negotiating meaning through a theatrical communication process in the classroom. The interactional nature of the activities provides students with opportunities to visualize and negotiate meaning based on public and personal expectations. The expectations are clarified as they relate to integrated relationship between art and science. Heathcote's understanding "goes beyond little divisions of knowledge competing with each other for space in the curriculum" (p. 7). She supports an anthropological rather than a psychological emphasis when she points out that professionals must "join in" the learning process as a critical component of her risk-taking methodology. Heathcote works out of respect for the learner and respect for the learning process.

A second strategy is the use of animation methodology. The experimental method of learning to animate objects demands a personalization of techniques. The creative authority of each individual becomes the base upon which new interactional responses are constructed and presented in a showing way (Laybourne, 1979). Students learn to select and assess the effects of behavioral performance. Computer-assisted animation techniques further define the possibilities of behavioral choices and visual consequences (Thalmann & Thalmann, 1990).

The third strategy is to use Lazear's (1992) model, which describes seven ways of knowing. It reflects the artistic ideology and promotes a respect for diverse capacities for knowing. Lazear examined intelligence as performance related to the child. The utility of using this model is the practical implications for teaching and learning. The intelligences are defined as logical, verbal, intrapersonal, interpersonal, musical, body, and visual, and professionals can explicitly address the skills of each intelligence capability as deliberately as one would teach "the keyboard" (p. 14).

Consequence Aspect

The third and final aspect of the theatre communication process, consequences, explicitly addresses the following questions: How did my participation in the interaction contribute to the consequences of the interaction? and Were my consequences congruent with my intentions? The educational goal for the consequence aspect of the process is "to help students capture more and more of what is implicit in any experience" (Pfeuffer & Kingsley, 1982, p. 66). The goal focuses on understanding the role of the arts in society by providing opportunities for students to:

- Receive data from the environment

- Establish values and beliefs

- Gain more specialized skills in problem solving, ways of knowing, and using sensory data

Competencies in skill areas include, but are not limited to, sequencing, observing, listening, following directions, executing choices, making decisions, reflecting, selecting, cooperating, appreciating cultural diversity, expressing oneself, and recognizing problems. All of these skill areas are applicable across content areas and grade levels.

The consequences aspect focuses on congruent relationships among knowledge, comprehension, analysis, and self-assessment as necessary elements for changing thinking, knowing, and behaving. The degree to which the intentions and performances of students as social actors result in congruent consequences for them, is dependent upon the degree to which the people with whom they communicate respond reciprocally to their meaning or definition of the social situation. Achieving congruency between intention, performance and consequences, then, demonstrates some degree of reciprocity in the social communication interaction. However, in many instances, the consequences have already been determined, and student behaviors will not change the outcomes of the interaction. A student's understanding of the imbalance of power in the existing social reality is critical for maintaining authentic, self-regulated perceptions of self within social interactions. Blos (1970) pointed out that "Mastery of the world concretely, symbolically, and conceptually, begins to serve as a self-regulatory source of self-esteem" (p. 961).

The instructional strategy of focusing on higher order thinking skills would provide students with diverse opportunities to self-regulate in ways that are congruent with the developmental and cultural strengths of African American learners. Rath, Wassermann, Jonas, and Rothstein's (1986) book, *Teaching for Thinking*, is a fundamental resource for professionals working to understand and respond to classroom interactions in ways that enhance the strengths and capacities of their students. Students could be empowered to intentionally change the outcomes of their interactions by intentionally changing the way they think and feel. The authors of this text offer exemplary teaching and learning strategies for promoting intentional changes in the way learners think, feel, act, learn, and achieve in both elementary and secondary classrooms.

Discussion

Communication behaviors, like cultural perspectives, are learned. Individuals interact differently, and the social attitudes and feelings that motivate behavior vary. The major components of our proposed educational paradigm—specifically, Nichols's (1976) model; the artistic ideology; and the intention, performance, and consequence aspects of the theatre communication process—structure an educational context based on the use of individual differences to enhance rather than impede the teaching–learning process. The components of the paradigm are common to all forms of social endeavors. The structure of the paradigm provides students with opportunities to invent, replicate, express, and change communication choices in and out of school settings and throughout their life experiences.

The utility of the paradigm in schools is that it creates opportunities to talk about talk and examine communication competence as an empowering and clarifying educational experience. The paradigm provides opportunities for both teachers and students to investigate the feelings and motives underlying their cultural perceptions and social conduct, as well as the social behaviors and cultural differences of others. The content and context of empowering goals, competencies, and instructional strategies suggested are based on the everyday social interaction experiences of students and are appropriate to their diverse interests and developmental differences. By using the paradigm, from the empowerment perspective, students labeled SED can learn to use their perceptions and experiences to create an explicit context for discovering, testing, constructing, changing, and using their personal knowledge of the communication process to facilitate successful social and academic interactions. From this perspective, students can learn to plan and execute their degree of participation in the interaction. Ongoing flexible thinking and action are necessary such that the plan, or the intent of the interaction, matches the student's desired consequences.

Every content area could be enhanced by utilizing the paradigm to explicitly connect the perceptions, motives, and actions of real people to the thoughts and feelings underlying communication interactions. Professionals could use the paradigm to identify elements inherent in their own personal concepts and conduct and their communicative effect on others. Examining the degree of congruency between intent and consequences would provide information necessary for altering their professional perceptions and practice. Clearly, if the generalizability of classroom learning experiences continues to be perceived as a critical measure of effective educational practice, then professionals must begin to acknowledge and accept the interactive nature of professional and student attitudes and habits of thinking and behaving as culturally, personally, and educationally valid in the teaching–learning process.

Finally, African American students identified as SED could learn to see themselves objectively as they critically analyze academic content and gain competencies in understanding how and why people interact the way they do in social situations. The paradigm would provide students with a scientific way of distancing themselves from the interaction in order to determine the nature and degree of participation they and others may choose to contribute. By knowing how to "take oneself out" of communication interactions and analyze interactions objectively, students would control their abilities to plan and make changes in the way they feel, think, act, and react *during* their own social communication interactions and *about* the social interactions of others. Empowering both students and teachers to communicate among themselves with increased competencies, which include appreciation for cultural differences, would facilitate social and academic outcomes that declassify African American learners identified as SED, as well as benefit those at risk for the SED label.

CONCLUSION

Although diverse learning and motivational styles are found within all ethnic groups and social classes, researchers have to be careful about reaching "a delicate and different balance between using generalizations about groups to better understand and interpret the behavior of groups, and using that knowledge to interpret the behavior of a particular student" (Banks, 1988, p. 466). The cultural views and relationships identified in this chapter are not an effort to stereotype further the interactions, skills, and competencies of African American learners. These views and relationships were presented to structure an educational context within which professionals can initiate effective interactions, in a collaborative process of educating African American learners with respect, quality, and equity. Future research has the potential to "traditionalize" this context. Current research can now be examined in terms of its degree of congruency with the proposed context. As professional change agents, educators have the responsibility for making the differences that benefit the real lives of all the children served. Awareness of the problem is not enough, and "knowing how" is not enough. Changing what educators do, why it is done, and how it is done, redefines what is meant by American education. Children are *still* waiting for the change to benefit them.

REFERENCES

Akbar, N. (1985). Our destiny: Authors of a scientific revolution. In H. P. McAddo & J. L. McAdoo (Eds.), *Black children: Social, educational, and parental environments* (pp. 17–31). Newbury Park, CA: Sage.

Anderson, M. G. (1985). "Hey Miss Gresham . . . That's not right!" No room for blind faith in language education. *English Language Arts Bulletin, 26*(2), 21–23.

Anderson, M. G. (1989). Perceptions about the use of selected theatre rehearsal technique activities: Resources for socially emotionally disturbed adolescents (doctoral dissertation, Kent State University, 1989). *Dissertation Abstracts International, 50,* 1622A.

Anderson, M. G. (1992). The use of selected theatre rehearsal technique activities with African American adolescents labeled "behavior disordered." *Exceptional Children, 59*(2), 132–140.

Anderson, M. G. (1994). Behavior disorders in the context of the African American community. In R. C. Peterson & S. Ishii-Jordan, *Multicultural issues in the education of students with behavior disorders.* Cambridge, MA: Brookline.

Asamow, J. R. (1988). Peer status and social competence in child psychiatric inpatients: A comparison of children with depressive, externalizing, and concurrent depressive and externalizing disorders. *Journal of Abnormal Child Psychology, 16,* 151–162.

Asante, M. K. (1992). Afrocentric curriculum. *Educational Leadership, 49*(4), 28–31.

Banks, J. A. (1988). Ethnicity, class, cognitive, and motivational style: Research and teaching implications. *Journal of Negro Education, 57,* 452–466.

Benedetti, R. L. (1981). *The actor at work.* Englewood Cliffs, NJ: Prentice-Hall.

Bernstein, B. (1961). Social class and linguistic development: A theory of social learning. In A. H. Halsey, J. Floud, & C. A. Anderson, *Education, economy, and society* (pp. 288–314). New York: Free Press.

Black, K. (1989). *Kid Vid.* Tucson, AZ: Zephyr Press.

Bloom, B. S., Davis, A., & Hess, R. (1965). *Compensatory education for cultural deprivation.* New York: Holt, Rinehart & Winston.

Blos, P. (1970). *The young adolescent: Clinical studies.* New York: Free Press.

Bolton, G. M. (1984). *Drama as education.* Durham, England: Longman House.

Bootzin, R. R. (1980). *Abnormal psychology: Current perspectives.* New York: Random House.

Boykin, A. W. (1983). The academic performance of Afro-American children. In J. Spence (Ed.), *Achievement and achievement motives* (pp. 324–371). San Francisco: W. H. Freeman.

Boykin, A. W. (1986). The triple quandary and the schooling of Afro-American children. In U. Neisser (Ed.), *The school achievement of minority children* (pp. 57–92). Hillsdale, NJ: Erlbaum.

Boykin, A. W. (1993). The sociocultural context of schooling for African American children: A proactive deep structure analysis. In E. Hollin (Ed.), *Formulating a knowledge base for teaching culturally diverse learners.* Philadelphia: Association for Supervision and Curriculum Development.

Bullock, L. M., Wilson, M. J., & Campbell, R. E. (1990). Inquiry into the commonality of items from seven behavior rating scales: A preliminary examination. *Behavioral Disorders, 15,* 87–99.

Campbell, N. J., Dobson, J. E., & Bost, J. M. (1985). Educator perceptions of behavior problems of mainstreamed students. *Exceptional Children, 48,* 298–303.

Chenault, J. (1975). Special education and the black community. In L. A. Gary & A. Favor (Eds.), *Restructuring the educational process: A black perspective* (pp. 93–98). Washington, DC: Institute for Urban Affairs and Research.

Delpit, L. (1988). The silenced dialogue: Power and pedagogy in educating other people's children. *Harvard Educational Review, 58,* 280–298.

Despert, J. L. (1965). *The emotionally disturbed child—Then and now.* New York: Vantage Press.

Ditton, J. (1979). *Contrology.* London: Macmillan.

Edelman, M. W. (1985). The sea is so wide and my boat is so small: Problems facing Black children today. In H. P. McAdoo & J. L. McAdoo (Eds.), *Black children: Social, educational, and parental environments* (pp. 72–82). Newbury Park, CA: Sage.

Elliott, R. (1986). Making children moral. *Educational Theory, 36,* 289–299.

Fielder, J. F., & Knight, R. R. (1986). Congruence between assessed needs and IEP goals of identified behaviorally disabled students. *Behavioral Disorders, 12,* 22–27.

Forness, S. R., & Knitzer, J. (1990). *A new proposed definition and terminology to replace "Serious Emotional Disturbance" in Education of the Handicapped Act.* Workshop on Definition, The National Mental Health and Special Education Coalition, Alexandria, VA.

Forness, S. R., & Knitzer, J. (1992). A new proposed definition and terminology to replace "serious emotional disturbance" in Individuals with Disabilities Act. *School Psychology Review, 21,* 12–20.

Gajar, A. H. (1979). EMR, LD, ED: Similarities and differences. *Exceptional Children, 45,* 470–472.

Gallagher, P. A. (1988). *Teaching students with behavior disorders* (2nd ed.). Denver, CO: Love.

Goffman, E. (1959). *The presentation of self in everyday life.* New York: Doubleday.

Goffman, E. (1967). *Interaction rituals: Essays on face-to-face behavior.* New York: Doubleday.

Green, M. (1973). *Teacher as stranger.* Belmont, CA: Wadsworth.

Gresham, F. M. (1982). Misguided mainstreaming: The case of social skills training with handicapped children. *Exceptional Children, 48,* 420–433.

Hagen, U. (1991). *A challenge for the actor.* New York: Macmillan.

Hale, J. (1980). De-mythicizing the education of Black children. In R. Jones (Ed.), *Toward a black psychology* (pp. 221–230). New York: Harper & Row.

Hale-Benson, J. E. (1986). *Black children: Their roots, culture and learning styles.* Baltimore: Johns Hopkins University Press.

Hallahan, D. P., & Kauffman, J. M. (1977). Labels, categories, behaviors: ED, LD, EMR reconsidered. *Journal of Special Education, 11,* 139–149.

Hallahan, D. P., & Kauffman, J. M. (1994). *Exceptional children.* Needham Heights, MA: Allyn & Bacon.

Hilliard III, A. G. (1976). *Free your mind: Return to the source, African origins.* Atlanta: Georgia State University.

Hilliard III, A. G. (1988). Conceptual confusion and the persistence of group oppression through education. *Equity and Excellence, 24*(1), 36–43.

Hilliard III, A. G. (1991). Do we have the will to educate all children? *Educational Leadership, 24*(3), 18–25.

Holliday, B. G. (1985). Toward a model of teacher–child transactional processes affecting Black children's academic achievement. In M. B. Spencer, G. K. Brookins, & W. R. Allen (Eds.), *Beginnings: The social affective development of black children* (pp. 117–130). Hillsdale, NJ: Erlbaum.

Holliday, B. G. (1989). Trailbrazers in Black adolescent research: The American council on education's studies on Negro youth personality development. In R. L. Jones (Ed.), *Black adolescents* (pp. 29–48). Berkeley, CA: Cobb and Henry.

Hymes, D. (1983). Report from an underdeveloped country: Toward linguistic competence in the United States. In B. Bain (Ed.), *The sociogenesis of language and human conduct* (pp. 189–224). New York: Plenum Press.

Jensen, A. R. (1969). How much can we boost IQ and scholastic achievement? *Harvard Educational Review, 39*(1), 1–117.

Johnson, L., & O'Neil, C. (1985). *Dorothy Heathcote.* London: Hutchinson.

Johnson, N. (1990). School consultation: The training need of teachers and school psychologists. *Psychology in the Schools, 27,* 51–56.

Johnson, S. D. (1990). Toward clarifying culture, race, and ethnicity in the context of multicultural counseling. *Journal of Multicultural Counseling and Development, 18,* 41–50.

Jones, A. C. (1991). Psychological functioning in African Americans: A conceptual guide for use in psychotherapy. In R. L. Jones (Ed.), *Black psychology* (3rd ed., pp. 577–589). Berkeley, CA: Cobb and Henry.

Kauffman, J. M., & Hallahan, D. P. (1981). *Handbook of special education.* Englewood Cliffs, NJ: Prentice-Hall.

Kneller, G. F. (1971). *Foundations of education* (3rd ed.). New York: Wiley.

Knoblock, P. (1983). *Teaching emotionally disturbed children.* Boston: Houghton Mifflin.

Kortering, L., & Blackorby, J. (1992). High school dropout and students identified with behavioral disorders. *Behavior Disorders, 18*(1), 24–32.

Laybourne, K. (1979). *The animation book.* New York: Crown.

Lazear, D. G. (1992). *Teaching for multiple intelligences.* Bloomington, IN: Phi Delta Kappa Educational Foundation.

Leone, P. E. (1990). *Understanding troubled and troubling youth.* Newbury Park, CA: Sage.

Lightfoot, S. L. (1973). Politics and reasoning: Through the eyes of teachers and children. *Harvard Educational Review, 2*(43), 197–243.

Luria, A. R. (1967). The regulation function of speech in its development and dissolution. In K. Salzinger & S. Salzinger (Eds.), *Research in verbal behavioral and some neurophysiological implications* (pp. 405–422). New York: Academic Press.

McDermott, R. P. (1977). Social relations as context for learning in school. *Harvard Educational Review, 2*(47), 198–213.

McIntyre, L. D., & Pernell, E. (1985). The impact of race on teacher recommendations for special education placement. *Journal of Multicultural Counseling and Development, 13*(3), 112–120.

National Mental Health Association. (1993). *All system failure.* Washington, DC: Author.

National Middle School Association. (1982). *This we believe.* Macon, GA: Omni Press.

Neil, D. M., & Medina, N. J. (1989). Standardized testing: Harmful to educational health. *Phi Delta Kappan, 70*(9), 688–697.

Newmann, F. M. (1981). Reducing student alienation in the high schools: Implications of theory. *Harvard Educational Review, 51,* 546–564.

Nichols, E. J. (1976). *Cultural foundations for teaching Black children.* Paper presented at the World Psychiatric Association and Association of Psychiatrists in Nigeria Conference.

Ogbu, J. U. (1985). A cultural ecology of competence among inner-city blacks. In M. B. Spencer, G. K. Brookins, & W. R. Allen (Ed.), *Beginnings: The social and affective development of black children* (pp. 45–66). Hillsdale, NJ: Erlbaum.

Ogbu, J. U. (1986). The consequences of the African American caste system. In U. Neisser (Ed.), *The school achievement of minority children* (pp. 19–56). Hillsdale, NJ: Erlbaum.

Pai, Y., & Morris, V. C. (1978). The concept of culture: Is transcultural education possible? In *Cultural issues in education* (pp. 21–27). CA: National Dissemination and Assessment Center.

Parkhurst, J. T., & Asher, S. R. (1992). Peer rejection in middle school: Subgroup differences in behavior, loneliness, and interpersonal concerns. *Developmental Psychology, 28,* 231–341.

Pfeuffer, D. B., & Kingsley, R. F. (1982). *Enhancing learning for the handicapped through the arts.* Columbus, OH: Department of Education.

Rath, L. E., Wassermann, S., Jonas, A., & Rothstein, A. (1986). *Teaching for thinking.* New York: Teacher's College Press.

Robinson, K. (1980). *Exploring theatre and education.* London: Heinemann Educational Books.

Rogoff, B., & Morelli, G. (1989). Perspectives on children's development from cultural psychology. *American Psychologist, 44,* 343–348.

Rosenberg, M. S., Wilson, R., Maheady, L., & Sindelar, P. (1992). *Educating students with behavior disorders.* Needham Heights, MA: Allyn & Bacon.

Rubin, K. R., Hymel, S., LeMare, L., & Rowden, L. (1989). Children experiencing social difficulties: Sociometric neglect reconsidered. *Canadian Journal of Behavioral Science, 21,* 336–350.

Russell, A. T., & Tanguay, P. E. (1981). Mental illness and mental retardation: Cause or coincidence? *American Journal of Mental Deficiency, 85,* 570–574.

Safran, S. P., & Safran, J. S. (1985). Classroom context and teacher's perceptions of problem behaviors. *Journal of Educational Psychology, 77*(1), 20–28.

Schonert-Reichl, K. A. (1993). Empathy and social relationships in adolescents with behavioral disorders. *Behavioral Disorders, 18*(3), 189–204.

Simon, S. B., Howe, L. W., & Kirschenbaum, H. (1972). *Values clarification.* New York: Hart.

Simpson, R. G. (1989). Agreement among teachers in using the Revised Behavior Problem Checklist to identify deviant behavior in children. *Behavioral Disorders, 14,* 151–156.

Sinclair, E., & Kheifets, L. (1982). Use of clustering techniques in deriving psychoeducational profiles. *Contemporary Educational Psychology, 7,* 81–89.

Smith, D. D., & Luckasson, R. (1992). *Introduction to special education.* Needham Heights, MA: Allyn & Bacon.

Strom, R. D. (1973). *Education for affective achievement.* London: Rand McNally.

Thalmann, N. M., & Thalmann, D. (Eds.). (1990). *Computer animation '90.* Tokyo: Springer-Verlag Tokyo.

Thorngate, W. (1976). Must we always think before we act? *Personality and Social Philosophy Bulletin, 2,* 31–35.

U.S. Bureau of Census. (1992). *School enrollment—Social and economic characteristics of students.* Washington, DC: Author.

U.S. Department of Education. (1992). *To assure the free and appropriate public education of all handicapped children* (14th Annual Report to Congress on the Implementation of the Handicapped Act). Washington, DC: Author.

Wagner, M., Newman, L., & Shaver, D. (1989). *The national longitudinal study of special education students: Report on procedures for the first wave of data collection (1987).* Menlo Park, CA: SRI International.

Walker, D. K., Singer, J. D., Palfrey, J. S., Orza, M., Wenger, M., & Butler, J. A. (1988). Who leaves and who stays in special education: A 2-year follow-up study. *Exceptional Children, 54,* 393–402.

Washington, E. D. (1989). A componential theory of culture and its implications for African American identity. *Equity and Excellence, 24*(2), 24–29.

Way, B. S. (1976). *Development through drama.* Atlantic Highlands, NY: Humanities Press.

Wood, B. S. (1976). *Children and communication: Verbal and non-verbal language development.* Englewood Cliffs, NJ: Prentice-Hall.

Woodson, C. G. (1933). *The miseducation of the Negro.* New York: Amsterdam Press.

CHAPTER SEVEN

Restructured Teacher Education for Inclusiveness: A Dream Deferred for African American Children

Norma J. Ewing

African American children in U.S. schools do not yet enjoy equal educational opportunities. Race, ethnicity, and socioeconomic status still matter today (West, 1993). Despite some recognized gains made by U.S. schools in recent years, there is general agreement that educational programs still need considerable improvement for African American children to succeed in school (Obiakor, Patton, & Ford, 1992). Repeated pallid education reform efforts have surfaced for decades, but they appear to have failed to improve both academic achievement and social climates of classrooms, schools, and communities. For schools to enhance educational outcomes for all students, teacher education programs must make bold, visionary changes that elevate the quality of general and special educators needed for the 21st century (American Association of Colleges for Teacher Education [AACTE], 1988). Changes are needed in the Eurocentric curriculum and faculty, in the nature of field-based experiences, and away from endorsement and perpetuation of nonacademic programs that create enormous inequities in educational opportunities for many African Americans. Recent educational reform efforts appear to have conspicuously denied the value of culture as an important educational phenomenon for facilitating academic achievements for African American children. How can teacher education programs respond to increasing demand for serious, sensible, deliberate changes that value and incorporate the culture of African Americans and other dominant minority groups in every aspect of U.S. schools? This chapter responds to this question in an in-depth fashion.

PERSISTENCE OF SCHOOL FAILURE FOR AFRICAN AMERICANS

Over the years the failure to educate African American students in the schools has been persistent, pervasive, and disproportionate (Lomotey, 1990). The unfortunate education dilemma of these children has not gone unobserved, as the nation has received repeated notice that certain children in the schools experience disparities in opportunities to learn. Two decades ago, in *Deschooling Society*, Ivan Illich (1971) poignantly focused the nation's attention on the issue of the failure of U.S. schools to educate minorities and children of the poor. A decade later the National Commission on Excellence in Education (1983) released the report, *A Nation at Risk*. This influential report delivered an excruciating message, a portion of which corroborated Illich's salient message. The report indicated that 13% of all 17-year-olds and 40% of minority youths were functionally illiterate (Haynes, Comer, & Hamilton-Lee, 1989). The commission cautioned that there was a "rising tide of mediocrity" in U.S. schools (Nelson, Carlson, & Palonsky, 1993). This critical account of schooling was an alarming second "wake-up" call for the entire nation. It is credited with catapulting the current school reform movement, including efforts to create change in teacher training programs.

A few years later the Carnegie Foundation for the Advancement of Teaching (1988) issued *An Imperiled Generation: Saving Urban Schools*. This account of the status of urban schools concluded that the education reform movement, launched to improve the status of education, was useless for many children, largely African Americans and Hispanics (Shujaa, 1990). Again, a prevailing message seems to have gone unheard.

The latest account of the failure of schools to educate poor and minority students is described in *Savage Inequalities* (Kozol, 1991). In this book Kozol indicated that the United States is moving backward in the field of education. He makes a strong plea for fairness and decency in the way minorities and children of the poor are educated. His strong appeal is for equity in education of children from poor families—children who are being starved intellectually in schools. He postulated that schools of today are more segregated and less equal than in 1954, the year of the *Brown v. Board of Education* decision, which mandated an end to separate and unequal educational institutions. Kozol concluded that the rich still get a richer quality of education while the children of the poor get less. The message becomes even more distressing when one pauses to acknowledge that popular education program options such as special education, Chapter I, and tracking, have facilitated the maintenance of separate and unequal education opportunities for African Americans and other children of the poor. There is blatant disregard for the academic plight created by the educational system for some children.

Clearly, the status of education for African Americans and others of similar social status has not improved over the years. Mounting criticism of the failure of public schools to educate African Americans and other children of similar status has not prompted sufficient change in teacher education programs to enhance school outcomes for these students. Teacher education programs have failed to produce the quality of educators required to improve school outcomes for African American students. Traditional teacher education programs continue to prepare ethnocentric teachers and administrators who serve as major barriers to improving school outcomes for African American children. It is a major responsibility of schools, colleges, and departments of education to ensure that knowledge and information applicable to culturally based learning and behavioral styles, teaching styles, culturally sensitive proactive educational practices, and family and community values be incorporated in teacher education programs. The failure of many students will persist unless teacher educators are prepared to act as conduits of educational change that will improve school climate and academic achievement for African Americans.

EDUCATIONAL REFORMS AND AFRICAN AMERICANS

Since 1983 school reform has been at the top of the national agenda (Carnegie Foundation for the Advancement of Teaching, 1988). However, past education reform efforts have indubitably favored enhanced school outcomes for children of the privileged in U.S. society. Changes that bolster academic achievement for African Americans and others shouldering low social class status have not emerged, partially because teacher education programs have adhered tenaciously to theories and practices that support the idea that poor education achievement is caused primarily by cultural, family, or biological circumstances. The results of poor education achievement cannot, however, be explained solely by cultural or family circumstances (Nieto, 1992), although biological aspects not unique to any racial or ethnic group can have an impact on capacity to acquire knowledge and skills. It is heartless and inhumane to perpetuate the notion that certain groups of students are inherently deficient and hence an appropriate explanation for academic failure.

Teacher education programs have played a major role in creating the current school debacle for many African American children. Endorsement of perfunctory, repressive educational changes, such as special education, compensatory programs, and remedial tracks, has fostered low teacher expectations for some students and paved the way for permitting limited access to high-quality academic opportunities. Through the years teacher education programs have portrayed African American children and others holding similar social class status as "hard to teach" and lagging in cognitive development. This prejudicial viewpoint has been an albatross in teacher education and has aided in producing teachers ill prepared to teach all children. Teacher education programs have basically exonerated teacher educators and teachers as strong forces that contribute to the underachievement of some students. Traditional programs have engendered reluctance and resistance to academically challenging African American children with powerful learning experiences.

Reform in teacher education programs and schools has faltered in dealing with the root causes of school failure and disaffection with education among African American youth (Comer, Haynes, & Hamilton-Lee, 1989). Changes have not provided evidence of intent to confront some basic problems facing education (Corrigan, 1985). Separating and sorting students for differential programming, stricter high school graduation requirements, or more stringent teacher education program entry criteria are not the answers to the more evasive, complex myriad of problems that must be challenged to improve academic achievement and school outcomes for African American children.

Accelerating indicators of insipid failure of African American students are undeniable evidence that the current education system is ineffective and of declining worth for many students. Evidence of school failure is sobering and reaching frightening proportions. For African American children data indicate inadequate academic achievement, staggering school dropout rates, unbalanced suspensions and expulsion rates (Brown, 1992), and an increase in the disproportionate representation of minority children labeled for inclusion in special education (Chinn & Hughes, 1987; "New Faces at School," 1991). African American children are three times more likely than European American children to be placed in classes for the educable mentally retarded and one half as likely to be in classes for the gifted (Nieto, 1992). These data are heartwrenching and provoke intense feelings of dissatisfaction, despair, and outrage in the African American community. It is well known that school outcomes for African Americans do not correspond to the power-engendering outcomes for children of the privileged in U.S. society. Teacher educators have not come to grips with the intrepid nature of systemic barriers that are contributing factors to the failure occurring in the schools.

The cumulative effect of the failure of teacher education programs to equip educators with adequate skills and knowledge to educate African Americans has emerged as a menacing malady best described as accelerating educational misery. This misery factor, created in part by inequities in schooling, has generated a festering undercurrent in schools and society. The undercurrent has promoted an obvious threat to personal safety; eroded middle class status; eroded the freedom and leisure life-style of the privileged; deteriorated race relations; and created burgeoning caseloads in social services agencies, juvenile court systems, and prisons. If allowed to persist, these conditions will devastate the political, social, and economic infrastructure of our nation and negate any efforts to successfully compete in international markets.

PITFALLS OF OUR SCHOOLS

African American students, parents, families, and communities are cognizant of, though they often feel powerless to effect change in, the pitfalls of U.S. schools. The perils that exist divest African

American students of educational opportunities that are inalienable rights of passage to a productive adult life. African Americans have traditionally depended on the formal educational process to serve as a vehicle for social mobility (Hilliard, 1989). However, as many proceed with schooling, the academic success needed to accomplish social mobility becomes an elusive reality (Lomotey, 1990). As a result of the dire effects of schooling for a significant number of students, schools and teachers have suffered a significant loss in integrity and respect. Voices and echoes from the powerless in society vehemently express diminishing faith, trust, respect, and appreciation for teachers and schools. The calamity of the situation is overwhelming and has created the need for the presence of a "police" force in many of our schools.

As a precursor to gradual disillusionment with school, African American children harbor dreams of successful endeavors "when they grow up." Their dreams include employment as an adult, economic security, and a sense of respect and value. After entering school, dreams of these ideals slowly erode and inevitably vanish. Inadequacies in teacher education programs contribute to the process of demoralizing students and halting academic achievement. Teachers in the schools are too often responsible for destroying the passion for learning that African Americans bring to school (Grant, 1988).

The entire nation is painfully aware that a growing number of students experiencing school failure are African American. A considerable measure of academic peril for these students is created by teachers' diverse cultural ineptness, improper attitudes, and differential behaviors toward children of color (Nieto, 1992). These teacher-related factors can adversely affect students' internal motivation to achieve, self-esteem, respect for the privileged, and desire to remain in school. For African American students, school experiences under current conditions are too often an incessant, degrading, exasperating, endless nightmare that leaves many frightened, disenchanted, alienated, detached, disenfranchised, and unwilling to engage in constructive school activities. The aggregate effect of overwhelming negative school experiences inevitably is loss of zeal for schooling. Over time, the school misery index increases, academic performance diminishes, and an exorbitant price is paid by society in perpetuity.

Our nation is unprepared for the consequences of a growing mass of students who have endured prolonged periods of anguish and disappointment in schooling and who recognize the diminutive value in inferior educational experience. Creating schools that genuinely demonstrate equity in education experiences for all children is a challenge teacher educators and politicians cannot chance surrendering to the next generation. The destiny of these children is bound up in the nation's future. To continue to neglect them is to soil our nation needlessly (Kozol, 1991).

TEACHER EDUCATION REFORM: KEY TO IMPROVED EDUCATION OUTCOMES

There is an undeniable relationship between the preparation of education personnel and what transpires in the schools. More specifically, the professional preparation of educators is inextricably linked to academic improvement in the schools (Brown, 1992; Corrigan, 1985; Smith, 1987). Although educators cannot be held entirely responsible for student achievement, they are an absolute major circumscribing force in creating quality education for all children. The linkage between teacher preparation and educators in schools determines to a large extent educational outcomes of African Americans. Certainly, African American parents, families, and "community" should assume some responsibility for motivating and encouraging students to pursue academic achievement. However, many educators (administrators and teachers) seem to vehemently resist empowering parents, families, and others to become active partners in the education of their children. The notion appears intimidating and creates a sense of loss of power. For the most part, educators and schools are perceived by many African American parents as extremely unfriendly and intimidating.

A vast chasm exists between our schools and the parents, families, and community of African American children. The distance is a formidable barrier to achieving improved school outcomes for many children. This predicament leaves educators with the awesome task of assuming primary responsibility for academic achievement of students often misunderstood in many ways.

Reform in teacher education is needed that will embrace the kind of democracy that values and endorses full and free discussion with African American parents, families, and community leaders. This notion of democracy seems to unfold ideally in school-based management reform efforts (Maxcy, 1994). A school-based management philosophy espouses the notion of egalitarian participation to empower African Americans as stakeholders in our schools.

Preservice and inservice education programs must devote more attention to the important role that home, parents, and community play in the education of *all* children, including African Americans (Garibaldi & Bartley, 1989). Parents should be involved in schools, consulting with educators and monitoring the progress of their children (Carnegie Foundation, 1988). Teacher educators must prepare educators to actively pursue a working relationship and collaborate with parents and significant others in the African American community. It seems that teacher education programs have not yet clearly embraced the idea that a school–home–community partnership is needed to ease the strife in schools and concomitantly improve the educational opportunities for many students.

Preservice and inservice students must be adequately prepared to execute appropriate strategies required to build effective coalitions and partnerships with relevant forces in the African American community. Prominent organizations such as the National Association for the Advancement of Colored People (NAACP), the Urban League, the Black Coaches Association, African American fraternities and sororities, the Association of Black School Psychologists, health care agencies, and churches are examples of influential bodies that should be approached for collaborative efforts aimed at improving schooling for African American children. These viable constituencies can make significant contributions to teacher education programs and schools focused on improving school outcomes for African American students.

Improved teacher education is the primary vehicle for improving schools for children at risk of academic failure (Boe & Gilford, 1992). Until there is wholehearted acceptance of the idea that major changes must occur in teacher education to improve schools for African American children, there is little promise for ameliorating the intensifying education debacle currently facing the nation. The growth in gang affiliation and the accelerating rate of serious violence and crimes committed by school-age youth will continue to spiral out of control, unless education opportunities become a positive force in the quest for dignity, respect, and success. Change in teacher education programs does not guarantee improvement, but unless there is relevant change, the current status of schooling for African American and other children holding similar status will remain dismal. Those who feel a false sense of insulation from crime and violence will eventually discover they too are unprotected from the depravity of poor schooling, poverty, and unemployment.

No one exemplary teacher training paradigm currently exists (Brown, 1992). However, it is reasonable to expect vital changes to emerge incrementally and in the aggregate within a few years produce teacher education models containing necessary components for improving the quality of teachers needed for the 21st century. It is criminal to delay action on a national problem that can be revamped with determination, objective insight, unfeigned commitment, and elimination of society-based problems that are embedded in traditional training programs. There is absolutely not justification for delay.

Producing New Cadre of Educators

The teacher education profession is bound by moral principles to initiate immediate steps to prepare a cadre of teachers and administrators who can make schools a better place by providing a setting where all students have equal opportunity to excel in academics and develop exposure and knowledge needed to respect and tolerate individuals from diverse cultures. The new breed of educators must be prepared to improve the school climate; promote the empowerment of African American students, their families, and community (e.g., churches, civic organizations, community-based businesses); and recognize and counteract social forces that impede equal education opportunities for all students. These improvements are absolutely required to improve school outcomes for African American children.

Critics charge teacher education programs with the lack of necessary standards, competence, substance, and academic rigor to do a quality job of training teachers (Evertson, Hawley, & Zoltnik, 1985). There is little doubt these criticisms are warranted but rather constricted in scope. It is nonsense to solely target mundane, easily manipulated factors in isolation from other powerful, dynamic, complex forces known to exert tremendous influence on school outcomes for African American students. Improving school outcomes for African American children requires taking brave, bold, unusual steps that conclusively target political, social, and economic factors that relegate a definitive group of students to a vulnerable position in school and society.

Schools have changed drastically the past few decades. Cultural diversity has increased significantly, classrooms accommodate larger numbers of students, peers in classrooms demonstrate a vast range of achievement levels, and classrooms include an increasing number of students with varying exceptionalities (e.g., gifted and talented to severely or profoundly mentally challenged). These prominent and influential changes in schools have been accompanied by tangential federal and state mandates and policies that require multidisciplinary collaboration in the classroom. It is imperative that teacher educators acknowledge and value changes that continue to occur in schools and prepare educators for the emerging new frontier (AACTE, 1988).

The challenge to prepare quality teachers to teach all students and prepare administrators to provide leadership that advocates change that enhances educational opportunities for African American children should invigorate the profession. Encouragement can be drawn from the reality that enormous strides have been made on other frontiers in U.S. society. If sufficient intellect exists in the nation to place persons in orbit in space for weeks, develop star-wars defense system, contrive complex schemes to win wars on foreign soil, and develop super advanced computer technology, it is reasonable to expect teacher training paradigms to emerge that will produce the cadre of educators needed to improve school outcomes for students described by Kozol (1991) as defenseless emblems of hope and promise for the nation's future.

Effecting Changes for African American Children

To improve the schooling of African American children, teacher education programs must excel in preparing teachers and administrators who have an elevated level of authentic knowledge of African American culture; a deeper understanding of the impact African American culture has on behavior, learning styles, and preferred teaching styles; and a genuine appreciation for the valuable repertoire of experiences African American children bring to school. These pivotal professional qualities are needed to diminish the enormous cultural dissonance that exists between children, curriculum, teachers, and administrators. To accomplish the critical level of multiculturalism in our schools, teacher educators are compelled to provide preservice students and inservice personnel sufficient opportunities to acquire adequate information regarding African American children, families, and community agencies, organizations, and businesses.

To accumulate the knowledge and information needed to improve school outcomes for African American students, preservice students must be immersed in extended, direct, real-life experiences in the African American milieu (Ford, 1994). Useful resources for gaining experiences, knowledge, and appreciation for African American cultural treasures systematically neglected in our schools include summer community-based programs; after-school community-based student and parent learning centers; student teaching experiences; Big Brother–Big Sister programs; Urban League and NAACP community programs; and church-affiliated elder care, preschool day care, and after-school child care programs. An ongoing blend of experiences in cultural, socioeconomic, racial, and geographic settings should be provided throughout the teacher education program (Trumble, 1993).

Over the past decade, traditional teacher education programs have engaged preservice students and inservice teachers in isolated, prepackaged activities that depict African American children, families, and other significant forces in the community. This conventional practice typically includes perusal of vignettes, case studies, and video accounts of settings and activities associated with African American culture. These capsuled activities are of limited value for several reasons. Ensuing discussions and reactions to abridged information are prone to perpetuating myths, stereotypes, and misconceptions about African Americans. The sterile approach to multicultural education also permits preservice education students to maintain a critical measure of insulation and detachment from conspicuously unfamiliar cultural experience. In addition, directed learning experiences from written or media materials are usually explained or interpreted through the eyes of European American faculty encapsulated in ethnocentricity.

Teacher education program faculties are 91% White (Zimpher & Ashburn, 1992) and few have firsthand experience and knowledge related to the African American culture. A more effective method of preparing teacher educators and public school personnel to work effectively with African American children is through direct immersion in unadulterated African American culture. Without absolute absorbing experiences, teachers will continue to lack sufficient knowledge and understanding of African American students to improve academic outcomes for those not faring well in schools.

In addition to gaining quality experiences in the African American culture, teacher educators, teachers, and administrators must understand the importance of creating a positive school climate. For African American students in particular, school climate plays a significant role in their adjustment to school and the ability to perform well (Haynes et al., 1989). Research has provided evidence of significant correlations between achievement and perceptions of classroom climate among African American students in particular (Haynes et al., 1989). To develop the capacity of educators to create a positive school climate, schools, colleges, and departments of education are obliged to place strong emphasis on modifying teacher attitudes, understanding and embracing diverse cultural values, and improving ways of interacting between educators and African American students in schools. Teachers must be prepared to create a climate that is receptive, hospitable, challenging, and conducive to high academic achievement for African Americans. Shouldering the responsibility for providing effective leadership in schools, administrators must also be prepared to create and maintain an overall positive school environment for African American children.

Teacher educators need to prepare preservice and inservice teachers to employ a variety of instructional and assessment practices, not merely those created by mainstream educators and effective for mainstream students (Dilworth, 1992). Quality teachers must be prepared to use information gleaned from research and practice regarding effective teaching strategies for some African American children. For example, effective use of peer tutoring, inductive presentation of subject matter, and cooperative learning activities tend to be effective when implemented with minority and low-income students (Johnson & Johnson, 1990; McIntyre, 1993). Teacher candidates must be informed through lectures and provided real-life opportunities to practice matching teaching style with culturally based learning styles of African American students. Results from culturally relevant research demonstration projects should be recorded and reported to parents, teachers, and preservice students. Although laboratory schools affiliated with teacher education programs have diminished in number, existing schools with a representative sample of African American children would be ideal for conducting research and demonstration projects related to effective instructional and assessment strategies. Preservice students must also be taught to critically examine the culturally based behavior of African American children and engage in culturally sensitive proactive behavior management strategies that are fair, equitable, and designed to promote a positive school climate. Teacher educators must emphasize the potential for engendering increased cooperation and motivation to learn when teachers use instructional strategies that recognize and value strong cultural influences for African American children.

Revisiting Special Education Teacher Education Programming

Special education teacher education is a distinct common subsystem in general teacher education programs. As a component subsumed within general teacher education programs, special education teacher education embodies the same frailties that afflict general preservice teacher education. The major difference associated with the pervasive frailties is the heightened degree to which they exist in the special education profession. Teacher expectations of students' academic achievement are decidedly lower; teachers are unduly underprepared to promote overall equitable academic achievement of children with mild disability labels; school climate associated with special education breeds contempt, fear, and more powerful rejection of a disproportionate number of the students; and curriculum deficiencies extend beyond the disabling effect of the dominating Eurocentric focus to include markedly reduced academic content—generally referred to as a "watered-down" curriculum. The frailties of teacher education programs examined in the context of special education suggest even more profound inequities in educational opportunities for a growing number of African American children channeled into special education programs.

Other major obstacles associated directly with special education teacher education programs impede academic achievement of many African American children. As a part of the current education reform efforts, some glaring problems warrant prompt serious examination and remedy. The spiraling increase in the number of African American students with disability labels and the parallel increase in special education preservice teacher education programs are morally indefensible. The overall thrust of special education in terms of purpose, mission, and outcomes requires reexamining and changes made to improve the plight of a growing number of African American students trapped in virtually deadened nonacademic programs.

There is growing evidence of the ineffectiveness of special education. That alone accentuates the need to rethink the nature and value of special education teacher education and special education school programs. Research findings (Edgar, Levine, & Maddox, 1986; Hasazi, Gordon, & Roe, 1985; Mithaug, Horiuchi, & Fanning, 1985) indicate that school outcomes for students who have received special education services throughout their schooling strongly suggest that the programs are not effective. Such findings provide justifiable reason for questioning the wisdom of preparing an increasing number of special education teachers rather than preparing a cadre of superior quality teachers to teach all students.

According to the National Information Center for Children and Youth with Disabilities (1993), research findings in the mid-1980s indicated high dropout rates, low employment rates, and social isolation of students who received special education. More recent data from the National Longitudinal Transition Study support the findings of previous studies (Wagner, 1991). Results from the study indicate that students with a disability drop out of school at a higher rate than their nondisabled peers. Few of these students, including those labeled as having mild disabilities, are employed or participate in postsecondary training or education. The disappointing outcomes of schooling for students who have received special education services dictate the need to critically examine the underlying premise that supports the production of an increasing number of special education teachers.

Bold teacher education reform that diminishes the ethnocentricity of the teaching force will probably improve school achievement for African Americans. As the quality of all teachers improves, theoretically fewer African American children will be sorted and placed into special education tracks. As changes occur that improve schooling for many African American students, the accelerating demand for special education teachers should decrease. Stronger emphasis must be placed on aiding preservice students to overcome parochialism, modifying the prominent Eurocentric curriculum, and clarifying and strengthening the regular teachers' role and responsibilities for educating all children. Under existing circumstances, the philosophy, mission, and special education teacher education practices justify educational practices that segregate, stigmatize, and limit the academic growth and school outcomes of too many African American students. Special education teachers are prepared in increasing numbers today and licensed as school agents to produce individuals who will have limited intellectual or economic power in adulthood.

The entire teacher education profession needs to enter serious deliberations with African Americans (e.g., parents, school psychologists, sociologists) and other groups most affected by special education teacher education and school programs. The efforts should focus on developing reasonable, powerful steps aimed at alleviating the continuing pernicious practice of undereducating too many African American students held captive in special education programs. Too many of the students are victimized by educational practices that are to a large extent questionable and appear worthless when judged on the basis of school outcomes. Yet many of the practices are taunted as "best practices" and perpetuated through current special education teacher education programs.

Special education teacher educators and teachers must carefully appraise existing self-serving personal and professional concerns (e.g., job security) and consider the overall effects on society of continuing ineffective special education programs for a growing number of African American students. Under current conditions special education programs are inflicting irreparable harm on many African American students. The pernicious effect on a disproportionate number of African American students is sufficient reason to advocate immediate reform in special education, including special education teacher education. Reform efforts must focus not only on philosophy and mission of special education but also on governance, student outcomes, accountability, instructional practices, curriculum, teachers' ethnocentricity, and the role of other personnel responsible for delivery of services to children who are failing in school.

The sparsity of African American special education teacher educators and teachers is another critical problem. A pronounced inverse relationship exists between the proportion of African American students assigned to special education and the percentage of African Americans in the teaching workforce or in preservice education programs. According to a report by AACTE (1988) of the total number of undergraduate special education majors in schools, colleges, and departments of education, 78.8% were White and only 11.2% were African American. An increase in African American special education and regular education teachers is essential for transforming schools into better places for children, many of whom are misclassified as mentally retarded or emotionally disturbed. The positive impacts of training a more diverse cadre of all teachers, including special education personnel, are as follows: (a) teachers of color will be less likely to mislabel culturally diverse students as disabled ("New Faces at School," 1991); (b) teachers of color can foster improved cross-cultural understanding and diverse cultural tolerance; (c) teachers of color can provide culturally relevant diverse on-site collaboration for European American teachers; (d) the presence of teachers of color can encourage the development of a positive school climate that meets the academic, cultural, social, and emotional needs of African Americans and other students of color; and (e) a culturally diverse cadre of teachers can provide an on-site avenue for divergent views to be recognized and considered when important curriculum matters (e.g., textbook committee decisions, field trips to support learning, program and policy issues) are deliberated (Education Commission of the States, 1990). A culturally diverse teacher force is needed to help bridge the cultural gap in U.S. schools. It is through educators and schools that the nation should choose to pursue enlightened ends for all its people and it is here that the battle for the future of the United States will be won or lost (Carnegie Foundation, 1988).

Traditional special education preservice education prepares personnel to provide students with the greatest academic needs the least academics (Brady, Swank, Taylor, & Frieberg, 1992; Oakes, 1985). It is imperative that teacher educators consider the overall devastating impact of systematically undereducating many African American children. The results of such practices are having a menacing impact on the nation as a whole. The problems created are no longer problems for the African American communities. Escalating crime, unemployment, poverty, and ineffectiveness of the schools create a portrait of inequality for African American children. The portrait has been created in part by the impact of special education programs sustained by current special education teacher education programs.

CONCLUSION

Teacher education programs must recognize the role that traditional training practices have played in creating the grim educational outcomes of many African American children. Sensible, deliberate, visionary changes are needed in teacher education programs to restore the dreams deferred for a growing mass of children marking time in U.S. schools. Without a conscious, powerful shift in thinking regarding preservice teacher education curriculum, field experiences, diversity and quality of faculty and students, and nature of policies that drive programs, there is little hope for improved school outcomes for a growing mass of children who are certain to have major impact on the future of our nation.

REFERENCES

American Association of Colleges for Teacher Education. (1988). *Teacher education pipeline II: Schools, colleges, and departments of education enrollments by race and ethnicity.* Washington, DC: Author.

Boe, E., & Gilford, D. (Eds.). (1992). *Summary of conference proceedings in teacher supply, demand, and quality: Policy issues, models, and data bases.* Washington, DC: National Academy Press.

Brady, M. P., Swank, P. R., Taylor, R. D., & Frieberg, J. (1992). Teacher interactions in mainstream social studies and science classes. *Exceptional Children, 58,* 530–540.

Brown, C. (1992). Restructuring for a new America. In M. Dilworth (Ed.), *Diversity in teacher education* (pp. 1–22). San Francisco: Jossey-Bass.

Carnegie Foundation for the Advancement of Teaching. (1988). *An imperiled generation: Saving urban schools.* Princeton, NJ: Author.

Chinn, P., & Hughes, S. (1987). Representation of minority students in special education classes. *Remedial and Special Education, 84,* 41–46.

Comer, J. P., Haynes, N., & Hamilton-Lee, M. (1989). School power: A model for improving Black student achievement. In W. Smith & E. Chunn (Eds.), *Black education: A guest for equity and excellence* (pp. 187–200). New Brunswick, NJ: Transaction Publishers.

Corrigan, D. (1985). Politics and teacher education reform. *Journal of Teacher Education, 36,* 8–11.

Dilworth, M. (1992). *Diversity in teacher education: New expectations.* San Francisco: Jossey-Bass.

Edgar, E., Levine, P., & Maddox, M. (1986). *Statewide follow-up studies of secondary special education students in transition.* Seattle: CDMRC, University of Washington.

Education Commission of the States. (1990). *New strategies for producing minority teachers.* Denver, CO: Author.

Evertson, C., Hawley, W., & Zoltnik, M. (1985, May–June). Making a difference in educational quality through teacher education. *Journal of Teacher Education, 36,* 2–12.

Ford, B. A. (1994). *Educating African American exceptional learners: Collaboration and consultation with African-American parents and communities.* Paper presented at the National Association of the Council for Exceptional Children Convention, Denver, CO.

Garibaldi, A., & Bartley, W. (1989). Black school pushouts and dropouts: Strategies for reduction. In W. Smith & E. Chunn (Eds.), *Black education: A quest for equity and excellence.* New Brunswick, NJ: Transaction.

Goodlad, J. (1990). Connecting the present to the past. In J. Goodlad, E. Soder, & K. Sirotnik (Eds.), *Places where teachers are taught* (pp. 3–39). San Francisco: Jossey-Bass.

Grant, C. (1988). The persistent significance of race in schooling. *The Elementary School Journal, 88*(5), 561–569.

Hasazi, S., Gordon, L., & Roe, D. (1985). Factors associated with the employment status of handicapped youth exiting high school from 1979–1983. *Exceptional Children, 51*(6), 455–469.

Haynes, N., Comer, J., & Hamilton-Lee, M. (1989). School climate enhancement through parental involvement. *Journal of School Psychology, 27,* 87–90.

Hilliard III, A. G. (1989). Reintegration for education: Black community involvement with Black students in schools. In W. Smith & E. Chunn (Eds.), *Black education: A quest for equity and excellence* (pp. 201–208). New Brunswick, NJ: Transaction Publishers.

Illich, I. (1971). *Deschooling society.* New York: Harper and Row.

Johnson, D., & Johnson, R. (1990). Cooperative small-group learning. *NASSP Curriculum Report, 14*(1), 1–4.

Kozol, J. (1991). *Savage inequalities: Children in America's schools.* New York: Crown.

Lomotey, K. (1990). Introduction. In K. Lomotey (Ed.), *Going to school: The African-American experience* (pp. 1–9). New York: State University of New York Press.

Maxcy, S. (1994). Democracy, design, and the new reflective practice. *NASSP Bulletin, 78,* 46–50.

McIntyre, T. (1993). Reflections on the new definition for emotional or behavior disorders: Who still falls through the cracks and why? *Behavioral Disorders, 18,* 148–160.

Mithaug, D., Horiuchi, C., & Fanning, P. (1985). A report on the Colorado statewide follow-up survey of special education students. *Exceptional Children, 51*(5), 397–404.

National Commission on Excellence in Education. (1983). *A nation at risk: The imperative for educational reform.* Washington, DC: U.S. Department of Education.

National Information Center for Children and Youth with Disabilities. (1993). *Including special education in the school community.* Washington, DC: Author.

Nelson, J., Carlson, K., & Palonsky, S. (1993). *Critical issues in education.* New York: McGraw-Hill.

New faces at school: How changing demographics reshape American education. (1991, August 28). *Education of the Handicapped, 17*(18, Suppl.), 4.

Nieto, S. (1992). *Affirming diversity: The socio-political context of multicultural education.* Longman, NY: Longman.

Oakes, J. (1985). *Keeping track: How schools structure inequality.* New Haven, CT: Yale University Press.

Obiakor, R., Patton, J., & Ford, B. A. (Eds.). (1992). Educating African-American learners [Special issue]. *Exceptional Children, 59*(2), 97–176.

Shujaa, M. (1990). Policy failure in urban schools: How teachers respond to increased accountability for students. In K. Lomotey (Ed.), *Going to school: The African-American experience.* New York: State University of New York Press.

Smith, G. P. (1987). The impact of competency tests on teacher education: Ethical and legal issues in selecting and certifying teachers. In M. Haberman & J. Bakus (Eds.), *Advances in teacher education* (Vol. 3, pp. 218–247). Norwood, NJ: Ablex.

Trumble, J. (1993). *Preparing and supporting teachers for the 21st century.* Dekalb: Illinois Association of Colleges for Teacher Education Forum.

Wagner, M. (1991). *The transition experience of youths with disabilities: A report from the National Longitudinal Transition Study.* Menlo Park, CA: SRI International.

West, C. (1993). *Race matters.* New York: Vintage Books.

Zimpher, N., & Ashburn, E. (1992). Countering parochialism in teacher candidates. In M. Dilworth (Ed.), *Diversity in teacher education* (pp. 40–62). San Francisco: Jossey-Bass.

PART III

The Home–Community–School Pyramid Connection

CHAPTER EIGHT

African American Families

Beth Harry

T his chapter addresses the issue of African American families' interaction with the special education system. An understanding of the dynamics involved is crucial for two reasons. First, it is the children of African American families who are predominant in special education programs across the country (U.S. Department of Education, Office for Civil Rights, 1993). The most recent figures on the placement of students in special education programs show that African American students continue to be overrepresented nationwide in the educable mental retardation (EMR) category, and in many states in the learning disability (LD) and severely emotionally disturbed (SED) categories. Furthermore, these students continue to be underrepresented in gifted programs in all states.

Second, African American families have long been cast in a deficit light by mainstream professionals. At the base of this perspective was the belief, proposed by Frazier (1948), that the Black family had been so decimated by slavery that there was nothing left but a domineering matriarchy with no functional family structure. Glazer and Moynihan (1963) retained this view while arguing that Black families, having no cultural basis, were simply dysfunctional American families: "The Negro is only an American and nothing else. He has no values and culture to guard and protect" (p. 51). This belief supported the development of the concept of "cultural deprivation" commonly used to interpret the academic and social difficulties of Black children (Reissman, 1962). In 1965, the Moynihan study, commissioned by the U.S. Department of Labor to investigate the status of Black families, resulted in a report that pulled together a collection of these stereotypes and described Black families as representing a "tangle of pathology."

The response of Black scholars to the latter report was immediate and strident. In particular, Billingsley (1968) and Hill (1971) argued that, despite the undermining effects of slavery, Black families in the United States had developed distinct strengths, many of which represented adaptations to the experience of oppression. These characteristics included strong kinship bonds, informal adoptions of children and other relatives, adaptable adult family roles based on an egalitarian pattern, a tradition of working mothers, strong achievement orientation, and a strong religious orientation. More recently, scholars have emphasized that Black family patterns should be viewed as unique cultural products rather than successful or unsuccessful versions of White families (Adams, 1978; Aschenbrenner, 1978). Other scholars have focused on the role of surviving traditional African features, such as the extended family (Shimkin, Louie, & Frate, 1978) and an emphasis on biological rather than conjugal ties (Sudarkasa, 1981).

Despite these responses, stereotypical negative views are still common among mainstream professionals in education. In special education, professionals' interactions with African American families have been detrimentally affected by the combination of the traditional deficit view of Black families with the deficit model of learning difficulties on which special education policy is built (for a fuller discussion, see Harry, 1992b). It is common to hear professionals exclaim, "These families just don't care about their children!" or "You just can't get them to come to the school!" Professionals who stop to ask why families appear this way may find that their interpretation of the families' behavior is based on deep-seated stereotypes developed by people who had no understanding of the cultural patterns, family structures, or value systems of African Americans (see also Harry, Torguson, Katkivich, & Guerrero, 1993). Furthermore, because of the imbalance of power between professionals and parents generally (see an excellent analysis of this by Gliedman & Roth, 1980), it is clear that families who hold low status in the society are at a particular disadvantage. Thus, the perpetuation of negative stereotypical beliefs is seriously detrimental to communication between professionals and African American families.

If the legal mandate for parental participation is to be fulfilled, it is crucial to combat these attitudes. Indeed, legislation in early intervention calls for services to be built on the family's resources, priorities, and concerns, and professionals are being expected to provide "family-focused" services (see, e.g., Wolery, 1992). This cannot be accomplished without understanding of and respect for families' cultural beliefs and traditions.

AFRICAN AMERICAN FAMILIES
IN A CHANGING SOCIETY

An important first step in seeking knowledge about African American families is to be sure that one set of stereotypes is not simply replaced with another. Like all other groups in this increasingly multicultural society, African Americans are by no means a homogeneous group. Because in the United States the designation African American is applied to any individual with any amount of African heritage, regardless of the extent of racial mixture in that heritage, it is evident that the term is not purely a statement about race; for example, to be biracial is still to be Black in America. Rather, the term represents a complex construct that includes racial mixture, cultural affiliation, and one's sense of personal identity. Certainly, African Americans come in many shades of color, are from all socioeconomic classes, and represent a wide variety of family structures and ways of functioning (Billingsley, 1968; Frasier, 1980; Landry, 1987).

These variables, as well as gender, educational status, religious affiliation, and the overall level of acculturation to the dominant ethos of White, middle class America, have a tremendous impact on the values, goals, expectations, and life-styles of African Americans. Inevitably, such variables will also impact the way these families view and interact with the special education system. This caveat should be kept in mind throughout this chapter, and the term "traditional" will frequently be used to indicate a feature that has been observed among many African American families, with the understanding that all such features will be modified by the variables mentioned previously.

In this chapter, I attempt to answer the following questions:

1. What is known about the way African Americans define disabilities, and does this conflict with institutional/educational definitions of what constitutes a disability?

2. What is known about African American families' attitudes to children's disabilities? Furthermore, do family attitudes vary according to the type or severity of the disability?

3. What is known about African American families' participation in special education decision making and their overall levels of knowledge about special education systems and procedures, and parental rights within these systems? How do the attitudes and interactions of professionals influence parental participation?

4. In what ways do these definitions, attitudes, and levels of participation and knowledge differ from those of other groups of parents in U.S. society? How are these factors modified by variables such as social class; acculturation to White, middle class values and life-styles; and geographic location?

I address questions 1 through 3 in turn, and include a discussion of question 4 in each section. Each section also includes a discussion of implications for professionals; these implications are offered in a general vein and are intended to apply to professionals providing services under all aspects of the law—early intervention, school age, and transition to adulthood. I conclude the chapter with an overall evaluation of educators' knowledge, and some recommendations for restructuring interactions with African American families so as to alter the balance of power.

AFRICAN AMERICAN PARENTS' DEFINITIONS OF DISABILITIES

I begin this discussion with the question: Why ask about definitions of disability? Are disabilities not actually factual phenomena that can be identified by objectively administered evaluation procedures? This is not a new question, but without addressing it, educators run the risk of assuming that a parent who says "My child is not disabled/retarded" is engaging in what professionals like to call "denial." Although there are some parents who deny features in a child that are evident to everyone else, I believe that most often two dynamics are operating. First, parents may be seeing strengths in the child that are not perceived by the professional and, second, parents are often disagreeing with the value placed by professionals on the child's condition; that is, parents see the same features that the professional sees, but value them differently. Nevertheless, the so-called denial phenomenon is a frequent source of conflict between parents and professionals.

This discrepancy is understandable when one recalls Mercer's (1973) distinction between developmental anomalies that can be scientifically verified and those that cannot. Mercer emphasized that the latter are based on social judgments regarding what is normative and, perhaps more important, what is valued by the society. Indeed, even in the case of a verifiable biological etiology, whether the condition is perceived as constituting a "disability" depends on a number of factors, such as the extent to which the individual is able to perform tasks valued by the society, the extent of stigma attached to the condition, and the presumed causes of the condition.

My question here is: To what extent might African American parents' definitions of disabilities differ from school definitions because of particular cultural assumptions, experiences, expectations, or life goals? The disability classifications used in special education are based on mainstream developmental and learning norms; students thought to fall outside the parameters of those norms are considered disabled. However, these parameters may be narrower than those found in communities whose behavior patterns and career expectations differ significantly from those of the school.

Some evidence exists to suggest that this is so. In three studies with families of color, I found that parents' definitions of normalcy were much broader than those used by the school system. For example, case studies (Harry, 1988) of the views of four mothers on welfare revealed rejection of the SED label on the grounds that their children's behavior was socially unacceptable, but not abnormal. A White mother, whose daughter was mixed Caucasian and African American, strongly rejected this label, exclaiming, "Oh, she's a bad 'un alright. That's all she is; she's normal as anybody. Just bad, not disturbed. I mean she *is* wild, but not crazy!" Similarly, an African American mother said, "Well, he just has a bad temper, always did. He likes to fight a lot and that's why they had to put him in a special class." These views support Anderson's (1992) argument that the seriously emotionally disturbed/behavior disordered label is determined by "teachers' cultural notions about how people should behave" (p. 132).

A similar discrepancy was found regarding the terms mental retardation and learning disability among a group of 12 predominantly Black, Puerto Rican parents (Harry, 1992a). Most of these parents rejected the notion that mild learning or behavior problems constituted "disabilities." Rather, they defined such difficulties as falling within the range of acceptable individual differences, and were often viewed as part of a family's identity. The same pattern was evident among a group of 24 African American parents of low to low-middle income, (Harry, Allen, & McLaughlin, 1995). For example, a 26-year-old African American father, who makes a stable living as a truck driver, strongly disagreed with the application of this label to his 5-year-old son. He offered the following definition of the term: "To me mental retardation means like that they're slow. I mean very slow, to the point where they seriously need some heavy personal attention. . . . But I guess in the school the least little bit of difference, or whatever, they use that term" (Harry et al., in press).

Similar findings have emerged from a recent study by Smith-Lewis (1993), whose interviews with 127 randomly selected African Americans in New York City revealed a strong trend to define mental retardation as a readily visible condition based on a biological etiology often related to parental behavior, such as abuse of drugs or alcohol. Asked by the researchers to define mental retardation, the majority of respondents did not express a concept of mild mental retardation. Furthermore, and in support of my point, the few respondents who did express a concept of a "milder" form were engaged in professional or quasi-professional occupations. Thus, I believe that African American parents who have imbued values, expectations, and goals based on school success are more likely to share the school's narrower definition of normalcy. Those who hold wider criteria for success—for example, the ability to earn a living from unskilled labor—are more likely to reject school definitions.

Another source of discrepancies between parental and professional perspectives is the adequacy of the assessment process. The issue of inappropriate use of standardized assessment instruments has been at the center of three decades of debate surrounding the overrepresentation of minority students in special education programs (e.g., Dent, 1976; Hilliard, 1991; Mercer, 1973), and landmark litigation (*Larry P. v. Riles,* 1979) has ruled that IQ tests are culturally biased. The problem of adequate assessment is equally relevant in early intervention, where parental knowledge of a child's skills should be at the center of the process. In the study of African American parents cited above (Harry et al., 1995), there were numerous examples of what I refer to as the "he can do that" discrepancy, in which parents would actually come to the school to demonstrate to the teacher that their preschool child could, in fact, perform tasks that the teacher's assessment had said he or she could not do.

In sum, parents who define disabilities differently from professionals, as well as those who disagree with the outcome of assessments, run the risk of gaining yet another professionally generated label, that of being "in denial"!

Comparisons to Other Groups

The literature on parental definitions of disabilities does not directly address comparisons among ethnic or social class groups. However, studies on this topic have focused on White, middle class families, and have shown that parents would accept disability labels provided they indicated specific rather than global impairments; hence, labels such as brain injured or learning disabled were acceptable to parents whereas the label mental retardation was not (Barsch, 1961; Pollack, 1985; Smith, Osborne, Crim, & Rhu, 1986; Wolfensberger & Kurtz, 1974).

Furthermore, it is well known that middle class, White parents were very involved in the establishment and recognition of classifications such as learning disability (Sleeter, 1986) and attention deficit/hyperactivity disorder. The rapid growth in the acceptance of these classifications suggests that such parents have tended to engage in refining disability classifications rather than rejecting them. A study by Gottleib, Gottleib, and Trongone (1991) compared the occurrence of teacher and parent referrals to special education among 439 students in an urban school system. The study found that White parents referred their children at a similar rate to teachers, and were significantly more likely to refer than were African American or Hispanic parents. Furthermore, teachers were almost five times more likely to refer Black students for exclusively behavioral reasons than were their parents. Although the study gave no information on social class factors, the data certainly suggest that White parents are more likely to share the cultural value system of the school than are parents from minority backgrounds.

Overall, current definitions of disabilities reflect the underlying values of a technological society—for example, literacy, without which one is considered disabled, or an emphasis on a medical framing of human behavior, by which features such as poor attention, hyperactivity, or alcoholism, which used to be seen as behavioral issues, are now interpreted as disease (Conrad & Schneider, 1980). African American and other families from non-mainstream cultures are likely to inculcate such belief systems as their level of acculturation increases. For those who hold more traditional beliefs, home–school conflicts will continue to be common unless professionals become more sensitive to cultural differences.

Implications for Professionals

What are the implications for professionals of differing parental definitions? First, professionals must begin by relinquishing the well-known automatic response that the parent is in denial. A good way to start is to find out to what extent the parent and professional are observing the same features in the child. Do they agree that the child is currently performing particular actions or tasks? If so, the professional can begin to find out how the parent views the importance of these tasks at this point in the child's life, and how the parent values such development in terms of family goals and expectations. Parent–professional differences can then be discussed openly as differences in point of view, rather than being treated as weaknesses on the part of the parent. It is also the responsibility of professionals to see that parents are given all appropriate information regarding child development, so that they can have the advantage of shared knowledge. Thus, the parent can begin to understand the educational definition of the disability. If, on the other hand, a parent and professional do disagree on a child's current capabilities, every effort must be made to ascertain the truth of the parent's assessment, rather than relegating the parent's judgment to the realm of "subjectivity" or "wishful thinking." To do this, professionals must be willing to include parents in the assessment process, in order to produce more realistic profiles of children's learning and behavior.

PARENTAL ATTITUDES TO DISABILITIES

The issue of defining disabilities overlaps to some extent with the question of what attitudes parents hold toward disabilities. On the one hand, the question is whether a parent agrees that the child's performance constitutes a disability; on the other, the question is how the parent feels about, or values, an identified disability. This distinction is illustrated by the following quotation from a single mother of a 6-year-old girl with mild cerebral palsy (Harry et al., 1995):

> He (the psychologist) said that she's in the retarded range or something. . . . I know that she's slow, but people who are retarded are people who really can't do a lot. But Arlethia—I mean, she remembers things. If she say someone did something to her, and I ask her what happened, she can tell me what happened, the whole story, and I don't think someone retarded can do that. . . . Of course, I wouldn't care if she's retarded or not. She's mine, you know. It wouldn't matter to me. But I just don't see that she's retarded.

The statement, "I wouldn't care if she's retarded or not," represents a much more positive approach than is typically expressed in the literature on parental reactions. Many of the reactions have come from accounts written by parents themselves, the vast majority of whom have been White parents, sufficiently educated to get their accounts published (e.g., Featherstone, 1980; Greenfeld, 1978; Park, 1967; Pieper, 1981). Although varied, these accounts have generally reflected an initial sense of profound grief experienced by such parents, as well as an ongoing struggle to gain acceptable classifications and services for their children.

Meanwhile, professional analyses of parental reactions have succeeded in establishing a general view of parents as going through relatively predictable and recurrent phases of reaction (Solnit & Stark, 1962; Wolfensberger & Kurtz, 1974). A somewhat different view, originally propounded by Olshansky (1962), suggested the notion of "chronic sorrow," rather than succeeding phases that result in some amount of resolution.

As Marion and McCaslin (1979) pointed out, the vast majority of the literature that led to theories of shock and grief reactions was based on studies of non-minority parents. Although it seems reasonable to assume that these patterns would have some amount of universal applicability, since it is axiomatic that parents hope for the best for their children, it is by no means self-evident that identical patterns hold across cultures. Indeed, parental reactions are influenced by the way disabilities are interpreted. For example, it is known that some Asian groups attribute the existence of congenital abnormalities to supernatural retribution for past wrongs (Chan, 1986), and may experience a deep sense of shame because of this interpretation. By contrast, some groups interpret certain abnormalities as a blessing rather than a punishment, such as the case of the Hmong interpreting the occurrence of club feet as a blessing (*Omaha World-Herald*, 1991).

Comparisons to Other Groups

Against this background, it is important to ask in what ways African American parents may tend to differ from others in their reactions to children's disabilities. The existing literature has focused mainly on African American, "Hispanic" (nationality not always specified), and White samples. This body of literature does suggest some differences.

Marion and McCaslin (1979) found that parents of culturally diverse children with handicaps were not as negatively affected by the occurrence of a handicapping condition as is typically reported in the literature. These authors attributed feelings of protection and acceptance of the child to the support of extended family structures and religious beliefs. Three studies comparing attitudes among White, African American, and Hispanic families, reported variations on this theme. Vasquez (1973), using a parental acceptance–rejection scale with 60 low income families, found that Mexican American and African American mothers were significantly more accepting than White mothers. Mary (1990) also compared attitudes among 60 mothers from these three ethnic groups and found that structured questionnaire items revealed a common trend to early feelings of shock and sorrow, with no significant differences across groups; however, in response to open-ended questions, the African American mothers showed the least amount of emotional distress, and African American fathers the least denial of the disability. Hanline and Daley (1992) investigated coping strategies among these three groups, and found that the presence of a child with a disability did not negatively affect either family pride or family accord among African American and Hispanic families, whereas it did have a negative effect on family pride and accord within the White families in the sample. Wallace-Benjamin (1980), comparing attitudes among 20 White and 20 African American mothers (Wallace-Benjamin, 1980), found no significant differences in the mothers' acceptance of their children with retardation, but did find that the African American sample showed significantly more positive attitudes to maintaining their children at home. Furthermore, Wallace-Benjamin found greater consistency among the African American mothers, regardless of social class, and greater variability among the White mothers according to social class.

Looking at the views of African American adults more generally, a study by Grand and Strohmer (1983) reported greater acceptance of disabilities by Black male students than by their White counterparts. Smith-Lewis (1993), in interviews with 127 randomly selected African Americans in New York City, found that, although most respondents emphasized that they would be shocked and hurt by the occurrence of mental retardation in their child, they stated that they would have no problem dealing with and accepting the condition. This study did not compare groups.

Overall, it seems reasonable to speculate that a tendency to greater acceptance would be in keeping with what is known about traditional African American family life. Hill (1971), for example, included in a list of strengths a pattern of strong kinship bonds and the frequent absorption of children by informal adoption. These attributes, along with a strong religious orientation, would seem to provide fertile ground for ready acceptance of disabilities. This notion was supported by Turner (1987) and Willis (1992), who suggested that certain cultural traditions among African American families may contribute to effective coping strategies; Turner specified extended family support, open expression of emotion, religious support, and a greater value on personal interaction than on academic achievement. Furthermore, the fact that African American families have traditionally been accustomed to adapting to societal hardship and to holding a wide range of expectations for their children's success, makes such acceptance even more likely.

Thus, the nature of parental attitudes to disability varies with cultural, educational, and social class background. Although one cannot, at this time, come to any definitive statements about how African American parents compare with others on this dimension, the literature points to some salient differences in the direction of these families' greater resilience in the face of disability.

Implications for Professionals

The fact that cultural, religious, and social class background may make a significant difference in parents' attitudes to their children's disabilities means that professionals need to approach each family in an individual way. Assumptions about how a family reacts to and interprets a disability should be held in abeyance while the professional takes a genuinely open-ended approach to understanding family attitudes and values. The earlier discussion on implications of differing parental definitions is also applicable to this concern.

AFRICAN AMERICAN PARENTS' PARTICIPATION IN SPECIAL EDUCATION

The legal mandate for informed parental consent makes parent participation of central importance to practitioners. However, several studies have documented low levels of knowledge of special education rights and procedures, as well as low participation, among African American parents. Explanations of these patterns have focused most often on logistical and life difficulties, such as lack of transportation, child care, and competing priorities, as well as on negative feelings, such as low self-confidence and lack of information (Lynch & Stein, 1987; Marion, 1979; Patton & Braithwaite, 1984). The study by Patton and Braithwaite, in particular, indicated that parents presented an impression of apathy which masked their real feelings of being overwhelmed.

Harry et al. (1995) suggested that matters have not improved much over the last decade. Using ethnographic interviews and participant observations of Individualized Education Program conferences, this 3-year study of 24 inner-city African American families found low levels of knowledge of parental rights, although written versions of these rights were routinely given to parents. Parent conferences were conducted in such a pro forma and superficial manner that parental participation and confidence in dealing with the system diminished over the course of children's passage from preschool to first-grade special education classes. Overall, the study found that late notices, inflexible scheduling of conferences, the brevity of conferences, an emphasis on documents rather than participation, the use of jargon, and the asymmetrical power relationships between parents and professionals combined to form a powerful body of deterrents to parental initiative, participation, and advocacy.

Comparisons to Other Groups

Studies directly comparing the participation of African American families with other groups are few. Lynch and Stein (1987), in a study of families in the Southwest, reported that African American parents' participation fell lower than that of Whites but higher than that of Hispanics. The researchers noted that professionals tended to describe the minority families as being "apathetic" and "uninterested," whereas those parents spoke of difficulties in communicating with the professionals. In terms of direct discouragement of parental participation, Tomlinson, Acker, Canter, and Lindborg (1977) documented a pattern of differential treatment of parents: They found that professionals initiated significantly more contact with White parents than with African American and

Native American parents, and offered the latter groups a narrower range of service options.

Whether or not professionals actively discriminate against parents from particular backgrounds, more subtle forms of disregard seem inevitable in light of the widespread derogatory view held by many professionals of poor and, in particular, poor African American families. Indeed, I believe that professional and system-based deterrents to effective parental participation are widespread, and are by no means limited to African American parents. Rather, they appear to be common in professional interactions with other low income or low status populations, such as Mexican American (Lynch & Stein, 1987), Caribbean Latino (Bennett, 1988), Puerto Rican American (Harry, 1992a), Native American (Connery, 1987; Sharp, 1983), and Chinese American families (Smith & Ryan, 1987). Of course, it is true that middle class families may also feel excluded from the process, but it is also true that they have more ready access to resources that can enable them to exercise their rights. Generally, such parents have had more successful experiences in schools, and are therefore more comfortable and skillful in dealing with professionals (Lareau, 1989).

Certain features common to low status groups are particularly influential in maintaining the distance between parents and professionals; these include different home languages, unfamiliarity with the technical language and processes of special education, inflexible work schedules, and limited child care and transportation. More subtle are psychological features, such as lack of confidence, often based on the parents' own experiences in school or on societal status differentiations. Still more invisible is trust—a crucial factor that can be problematic in quite different, even opposite, ways.

Certain cultural groups, notably those from traditional Latino backgrounds, have been described as being very trusting of school authorities (Correa, 1989; Figler, 1981; Lynch & Stein, 1987). Recent studies (Bennett, 1988; Harry, 1992a), however, have observed that such traditional trust was easily undermined by uncaring behavior by professionals. When trust was lost by these families, however, traditional respect for authorities prompted parents to continue to behave in a deferential manner to school authorities. Similar patterns have been described among traditional Asian families (Chan, 1986; Leung, 1988).

Studies of Native American (Connery, 1987; Sharp, 1983) and African American families, on the other hand, suggest a clear pattern of mistrust, based on the historical experience of discriminatory treatment. However, Siddle-Walker (1991) and Marion (1979) observed that trust in school authorities was traditional among African American parents prior to the integration of schools in 1954, but was severely undermined by the prejudicial and rejecting ethos of many school systems into which African American students were placed. Furthermore, parents' awareness of the overrepresentation of African American students in special education may have further contributed to the undermining of their trust in school authorities (Marion, 1979).

Overall, African American families' participation has much in common with other cultural minority groups, but may be exacerbated by particularly ingrained negative stereotypes common among professionals.

Implications for Professionals

The common view of African American families has been based on a deficit model that envisaged the need for educating and training parents in middle class styles of parenting, in order to better prepare children for school. Although compensatory education programs were based on this model, they also gave parents considerable influence by mandating that they must be represented on advisory boards and be given preference in hiring of program personnel (Keesling & Melaragno, 1983). More recently, these programs have also made considerable attempts to make parent training more culturally appropriate to traditional African American parenting styles (Linn, 1990).

None of this applies in special education, however, where the mandate for parental participation requires only that parents' informed consent be gained and that parents be invited to attend annual conferences. Thus, when a deficit model of African American parents is combined with special education's deficit model of children, the prejudices engendered in many professionals is very deep. If practice is based on the notion that both the parents and the children are deficient, how many professionals are truly able to approach parents as potential partners in decision making? How many educators are even aware of holding these assumptions? An article by Harry et al. (1993) revealed the feelings of a group of graduate students who confronted, for the first time, their own deeply held prejudices against such families.

How can prejudicial practices be counteracted? Certainly, the development of respectful behavior and the observance of parental rights are essential. However, courtesy, even kindness, can be used as a manipulative tool to silence parents' disagreement (Gliedman & Roth, 1980), whereas "rights" can be observed in such a pro forma manner as to be meaningless (Harry et al., 1995). The remedies urgently needed go far beyond the surface behavior of professionals.

Essentially, the way parental participation is structured will influence the balance of power between professionals and parents. As mentioned earlier, legislation in the field of early childhood education now requires a focus on families. Recent developments in the Individualized Family Service Plan (IFSP) process (Wolery, 1992) should provide the field with models of new participation structures that can be utilized at all levels. In a more thorough discussion of restructuring for participation (Harry, 1992b), I have proposed the development of the following four parental roles appropriate to both the IEP and the IFSP processes.

The first role is parents as *assessors,* in which parental participation in, or at least observation of, the actual assessment procedure should be required. The inclusion of parents in the assessment has precedent in the requirements of many exemplary projects funded by the Handicapped Children's Early Education Program (Karnes, Linnemeyer, & Myles, 1983), and is very appropriate to the IFSP process. In the current formulation of parental participation at the school level, however, parents give consent to the evaluation, then wait to receive professional judgment on their child's condition and educational needs. Most often, parents receive this information via a school psychologist in a formal conference, and in language largely unknown and often incomprehensible to the average parent.

Second, parents should be included as *presenters of reports* and accorded an official place on the agenda, so that parental views can be given equal status with those of professionals. This report should not be expected to be formal or written, but it should be made clear to parents that their views of their child's needs and progress will be explicitly sought during the conference, will be entered into the official record, and will be included in decision making.

Third, parents should be included as *policymakers,* through school-based, parent advisory committees (PACs) developed for special education programs. Such parental roles are well established in compensatory education programs such as Head Start and Follow Through, as well as in bilingual education programs (Keesling & Melaragno, 1983). In special education, PACs have typically been advisory to the local education authority, and are thereby far removed from the immediate concerns of individual schools or families.

PAC members could also contribute to the fourth role suggested—that of parents as *advocates and peer supports*—by providing liaison with other parents and supporting parent-to-parent advocacy activities. Chapter I programs already include parent liaison activities; these could be extended to encourage collaboration among parents of children in special education programs.

The implementation of the foregoing features is absolutely within the intent of the law, and could be done successfully by all schools. Although all of these roles could be perceived as threatening by professionals who are afraid to share decision-making power with parents, those who truly value parental input and who are open to collaborative practice will welcome the genuine inclusion of parental perspectives.

CONCLUSION

My concern in this chapter has been with a particular group of parents and their relationship to special education. The discussion is driven by the belief that African American parents constitute a group with particular concerns or features that affect both the way they experience their childrens' special education placement and the way they are perceived by special education professionals. I have also emphasized, however, that cultural differences are mediated by variables such as social class and level of acculturation to the mainstream of society.

Furthermore, the concept of culture may be conceptualized at many levels. Banks (1991), for example, argued that individuals belong to many different cultures simultaneously. The fact that being a professional initiates one into a culture that assures middle class status adds another layer to the discussion of relations between African American parents and special education professionals. In other words, difficulties between parents and professionals do not occur only when there are racial and/or cultural differences between these two groups. Although it might be expected that professionals who share cultural features with parents will more quickly understand certain of the issues facing parents, their affiliation with both school culture and middle class culture may negatively affect their views of parents—in particular, those from low income backgrounds. Indeed, the well-known "we–they" way of talking about parents is quite readily heard from African American professionals, and Harry et al.'s (1995) study shows that some African American professionals engage in practices that exclude African American parents from genuine participation.

The problem is that issues of power and authority are at the center of parent–professional relationships. For most professionals, no matter how well meaning, two self-protective mechanisms are operating in their dealings with parents. First, many professionals fear that, if given an inch, parents will take a mile, and that to share power with parents will really be to lose it to them. This fear leads professionals to protect their right to decision making. Second, many professionals do not believe that parents' contributions are either necessary or beneficial, because they believe in the primacy of expert technical knowledge over what Vygotsky (1962) called "everyday knowledge." This leads professionals to protect their right to knowledge. In special education, the specific requirement for informed parental consent implies the sharing of both decision making and knowledge, providing professionals with a greater than usual challenge. It seems that most professionals will generally not relinquish this territory willingly. Rather than negotiate their territory with families, they become entrenched in a professional role identity that promotes exclusive rather than inclusive practice.

When negative stereotypes about parents are added to professionals' wishes to protect their own power, the gap between parents and professionals is even greater and more dangerous. This is why it is crucial for mainstream professionals to rid themselves of a deficit view of African American families, because this can only exacerbate the already tenuous negotiation that must take place between schools and communities. It is, however, no less crucial for African American and other professionals of color to guard against inculcating the mythologies of the mainstream as they acculturate to the culture of the school and take on the characteristics of their professional roles.

Finally, the culture of special education places professionals at even greater risk of interpreting cultural difference as a deficit, because educators are trained to look for and expect deficits. This field is based on a firm belief that children's difficulties reflect intrinsic deficits. Professionals with a more ecological perspective may argue that the deficiency is within the child's environment, which readily translates to mean the family. Families are quick to recognize such beliefs; for example, an African American, single mother in a study by Kalyanpur and Rao (1991) stated, "She is judging *me*. I met this lady once, *one time*, and she judged me. . . . She kept saying his environment is making him act like that. [But] I am his environment. So what is she trying to say? That I am not a good mother or something?" (p. 527).

This kind of conflict will be mitigated only by direct attention to teacher beliefs, values, and experiences. Professional development programs, whether preservice or inservice, must require students to directly address their own prejudices and stereotypes by engaging in face-to-face interactions with African American and other minority or low income parents. More than a decade ago, Marion (1980) described a teacher training approach that focused on sensitizing majority teachers to the needs of parents of African American children with educable mental retardation. Since then, very few such programs have been documented (see a recent effort by Harry et al., 1993). In view of the widespread negative images of African American family life, the need for such training is more urgent than ever.

Billingsley (1994) recently reiterated his belief in the "enduring strength" exhibited by African American families. Just as educators must recognize students' strengths in order to teach them, so must educators recognize families' strengths, if the two are to mutually benefit from each other's input.

REFERENCES

Adams, B. N. (1978). Black families in the United States: An overview of current ideologies and research. In D. B. Shimkin, E. M. Shimkin, & D. A. Frate (Eds.), *The extended family in Black societies* (pp. 173–180). Paris: Mouton.

Anderson, M. (1992). The use of selected theatre rehearsal technique activities with African-American adolescents labeled "behavior disordered." *Exceptional Children, 59*(2), 132–140.

Aschenbrenner, J. (1978). Continuities and variations in Black family structure. In D. B. Shimkin, E. M. Shimkin, & D. A. Frate (Eds.), *The extended family in Black societies* (pp. 181–200). Paris: Mouton.

Banks, J. A. (1991). *Teaching strategies for ethnic studies* (5th ed.). Boston: Allyn & Bacon.

Barsch, R. H. (1961). Social networks and Asian Indian families. In C. Jacobs & D. D. Bowles (Eds.), *Ethnicity and race* (pp. 18–33). Silver Spring, MD: National Association of Social Workers.

Bennett, A. T. (1988). Gateways to powerlessness: Incorporating Hispanic deaf children and families into formal schooling. *Disability, Handicap & Society, 3*(2), 119–151.

Billingsley, A. (1968). *Black families in White America.* Englewood Cliffs, NJ: Prentice-Hall.

Billingsley, A. (1994). *Climbing Jacob's ladder: The enduring legacy of African-American families.* New York: Simon & Schuster.

Chan, S. (1986). Parents of exceptional Asian children. In M. K. Kitano & P. C. Chinn (Eds.), *Exceptional Asian children and youth* (pp. 36–53). Reston, VA: Council for Exceptional Children and Youth.

Connery, A. R. (1987). *A description and comparison of Native American and Anglo parents' knowledge of their handicapped children's rights.* Unpublished doctoral dissertation, Northern Arizona University, Flagstaff.

Conrad, P., & Schneider, J. W. (1980). *Deviance and medicalization: From badness to sickness.* St. Louis: Mosby.

Correa, V. I. (1989). Involving culturally diverse families in the educational process. In S. H. Fradd & M. J. Weismantel (Eds.), *Meeting the needs of culturally and linguistically different students: A handbook for educators* (pp. 130–144). Austin, TX: PRO-ED.

Dent, H. (1976). Assessing Black children for mainstream placement. In R. L. Jones, *Mainstreaming and the minority child* (pp. 77–92). Minneapolis: Leadership Training Institute.

Featherstone, H. (1980). *A difference in the family.* New York: Penguin.

Figler, C. S. (1981, February). *Puerto Rican families with and without handicapped children.* Paper presented at the Council for Exceptional Children Conference on the Exceptional bilingual child, New Orleans. (ERIC Document Reproduction Service No. ED 204 876)

Frasier, M. (1980). A perspective on identifying black students for gifted programs. In C. J. Maker & S. W. Schiever (Eds.), *Critical issues in gifted education: Defensible programs for cultural and ethnic minorities* (Vol. 2, pp. 213–255). Austin, TX: PRO-ED.

Frazier, E. F. (1948). *The Negro family in the United States.* New York: Citadel.

Glazer, N., & Moynihan, D. P. (1963). *Beyond the melting pot.* Cambridge, MA: MIT Press/Harvard University Press.

Gliedman, J., & Roth, W. (1980). *The unexpected minority: Handicapped children in America.* New York: Harcourt Brace Jovanovich.

Gottleib, J., Gottleib, B. W., & Trongone, S. (1991). Parent and teacher referrals for a psychoeducational evaluation. *The Journal of Special Education, 25*(2), 155–167.

Grand, S. A., & Strohmer, D. C. (1983). Minority perceptions of the disabled. *Rehabilitation Counseling Bulletin, 27*(2), 117–119.

Greenfeld, J. (1978). *A boy called Noah.* New York: Holt, Rinehart & Winston.

Hanline, M. F., & Daley, S. E. (1992). Family coping strategies and strengths in Hispanic, African-American, and Caucasian families of young children. *Topics in Early Childhood, 12*(3), 351–366.

Harry, B. (1988). *Wild, but not crazy: A study of low-income parents' views of special education.* Unpublished manuscript, Syracuse University, Department of Special Education, Syracuse, NY.

Harry, B. (1992a). *Cultural diversity, families, and the special education system: Communication and empowerment.* New York: Teachers College Press.

Harry, B. (1992b). Restructuring the participation of African American parents in special education. *Exceptional Children, 59*(2), 123–131.

Harry, B., Allen, N., & McLaughlin, M. (1995). Communication versus compliance: A three-year study of the evolution of African-American parents' participation in special education. *Exceptional children, 61*(4), 364–377.

Harry, B., Torguson, C., Katkivich, J., & Guerrero, M. (1993). Crossing social-class and cultural barriers in working with families: Implications for teacher training. *Teaching Exceptional Children 26*(1), 48–52.

Hill, R. B. (1971). *The strengths of Black families.* New York: Emerson Hall.

Hilliard III, A. G. (Ed). (1991). *Testing African-American students: Special reissue of The Negro Educational Review.* Morristown, NJ: Aaron Press.

Kalyanpur, M., & Rao, S. (1991). Empowering low-income, Black families of handicapped children. *American Journal of Orthopsychiatry, 61*(4), 523–532.

Karnes, M. B., Linnemeyer, S. A., & Myles, G. (1983). Programs for parents of handicapped children. In R. Haskins & D. Adams (Eds.), *Parent education and public policy* (pp. 181–210). Norwood, NJ: Ablex.

Keesling, J. W., & Melaragno, R. J. (1983). Parent participation in federal education programs: Findings from the federal programs survey phase of the study of parental involvement. In R. Haskins & D. Adams (Eds.), *Parent education and public policy* (pp. 230–256). Norwood, NJ: Ablex.

Landry, B. (1987). *The new Black middle class.* Berkeley: University of California Press.

Lareau, A. (1989). *Home advantage: Social class and parental intervention in elementary education.* New York: Falmer.

Larry, P. et al. v. Wilson Riles et al. (1979). C-71-2270 FRP, 9th Federal District Court of California.

Leung, E. K. (1988, October). *Cultural and acculturational commonalities and diversities among Asian Americans: Identification and programming considerations.* Paper presented at the Ethnic and Multicultural Symposia, Dallas, TX. (ERIC Document Reproduction Service No. ED 298 708)

Linn, E. (1990, Spring). Parent involvement programs: A review of selected models. *Equity Coalition, 1*(2), 10–15.

Lynch, E. W., & Stein, R. (1987). Parent participation by ethnicity: A comparison of Hispanic, Black and Anglo families. *Exceptional Children, 54,* 105–111.

Marion, R. (1979). Minority parent involvement in the IEP process: A systematic model approach. *Focus on Exceptional Children, 10*(8), 1–16.

Marion, R. L. (1980). A cooperative university/public school approach to sensitizing majority teachers to the needs of parents of Black EMR children. *Journal of Negro Education, 49*(2), 144–153.

Marion, R. L., & McCaslin, T. (1979). *Parent counseling of minority parents in a genetic setting.* Unpublished manuscript, University of Texas, Austin.

Mary, N. L. (1990). Reactions of Black, Hispanic, and White mothers to having a child with handicaps. *Mental Retardation, 28*(1), 1–5.

Mercer, J. R. (1973). *Labeling the mentally retarded.* Berkeley: University of California Press.

Olshansky, S. (1962). Chronic sorrow: A response to having a mentally defective child. *Social Casework, 43,* 190–192.

Omaha World-Herald. (1991, January 1). Hmong family prevents forced surgery on son, p. 16.

Park, C. (1967). *The siege: The first eight years of an autistic child.* Boston: Little, Brown.

Patton, J. M., & Braithwaite, R. L. (1984, August). Obstacles to the participation of Black parents in the educational programs of their handicapped children. *Centering Teacher Education,* pp. 34–37.

Pieper, E. (1981). *Sticks and stones: The story of a loving child.* Syracuse, NY: Human Policy Press.

Pollack, J. M. (1985). Pitfalls in the psychoeducational assessment of adolescents with learning and school adjustment problems. *Adolescence, 20*(78), 479–493.

Reissman, F. (1962). *The culturally deprived child.* New York: Harper & Row.

Sharp, E. Y. (1983). *Analysis of determinants impacting on educational services of handicapped Papago students.* Tucson: University of Arizona, College of Education. (ERIC Document Reproduction Service No. ED 239 468)

Shimkin, D. B., Louie, G. J., & Frate, D. A. (1978). The Black extended family: A basic rural institution and a mechanism of urban adaptation. In D. B. Shimkin, E. M. Shimkin, & D. A. Frate (Eds.), *The extended family in Black societies* (pp. 25–148). Paris: Mouton.

Siddle-Walker, E. (1991, February). *Separate but equal: A case study of "good" pre-integration schooling for African-American children.*

Paper presented at the meeting of the Center for Urban Ethnography, Philadelphia.

Sleeter, C. E. (1986). Learning disabilities: The social construction of a special education category. *Exceptional Children, 53*(1), 46–54.

Smith, M. J., & Ryan, A. S. (1987). Chinese-American families of children with developmental disabilities: An exploratory study of reactions to service providers. *Mental Retardation, 25*(6), 345–350.

Smith, R. W., Osborne, L. T., Crim, D., & Rhu, A. H. (1986). Labeling theory as applied to learning disabilities: Findings and policy suggestion. *Journal of Learning Disabilities, 19*(4), 195–202.

Smith-Lewis, M. (1993). *What is mental retardation? Perceptions from the African-American community.* Unpublished manuscript, Hunter College, New York City.

Solnit, A., & Stark, M. (1962). Mourning and the birth of a defective child. *Psychoanalytic Study of the Child, 16,* 523–537.

Sudarkasa, N. (1981). Interpreting the African heritage in Afro-American family organization. In H. P. McAdoo (Ed.), *Black families* (pp. 23–36). Beverly Hills, CA: Sage.

Tomlinson, J. R., Acker, N., Canter, A., & Lindborg, S. (1977). Minority status, sex and school psychological services. *Psychology in the Schools, 14*(4), 456–460.

Turner, A. (1987, February). *Working with families of developmentally disabled high-risk children: The Black perspective.* Paper presented at the Infant Development Association Conference, Los Angeles.

U.S. Department of Education, Office for Civil Rights. (1993). *1990 elementary and secondary schools civil rights survey: National summaries.* Washington, DC: DBS Corporation.

U.S. Department of Labor. (1965). *The Negro family: The case for national action.* Washington, DC: U.S. Government Printing Office.

Vasquez, A. M. (1973). *Race and culture variables in the acceptance–rejection attitudes of parents of mentally retarded children in the lower-socioeconomic class.* Unpublished doctoral dissertation, California School of Professional Psychology, Los Angeles.

Vygotsky, L. S. (1962). *Thought and language.* Cambridge, MA: MIT Press.

Wallace-Benjamin, J. R. (1980). *Black mothers' attitudes toward their retarded children.* Unpublished doctoral dissertation, Brandeis University, Waltham, MA.

Willis, W. (1992). Families with African-American roots. In E. W. Lynch & M. J. Hansen (Eds.), *Developing cross-cultural competence* (pp. 121–150). Baltimore: Brooks.

Wolery, M. (Ed.). (1992). Family diversity. *Topics in Early Childhood Special Education, 12*(3).

Wolfensberger, W., & Kurtz, R. A. (1974). Use of retardation-related diagnostic and prescriptive labels by parents of retarded children. *Journal of Special Education, 8*(2), 131–142.

CHAPTER NINE

African American Community Involvement Processes and Special Education: Essential Networks for Effective Education

Bridgie Alexis Ford

Excellence in educational programming for African American learners, including the gifted and those with disabilities, cannot occur without meaningful collaboration between the public school system and the African American community.[1] Black youngsters, in particular those residing in communities described as troubled, who manifest positive self-concepts, maintain educational motivation, and are successful academically, do so in part as a consequence of support from and direct participation in critical community resources, which include various components of parental involvement (Barnes, 1991; Billinsley & Caldwell, 1991; Comer, 1985; Croninger, 1990; Jones, 1989; Lomotey, 1990; Mickelson & Smith, 1989; Nettles, 1991; Olion, 1980; Slaughter & Epps, 1987). This potential influence of community support on the academic outcomes of African American youth strongly illuminates the necessity of productive school and African American community networks.

---

[1]The terms *African American* and *Black* are used interchangeably in this chapter. *African American* or *Black community* will be used generically to encompass the local and the at-large community of African American individuals, institutions, and organizations, unless otherwise specified.

The educational system historically has assigned an inferior label to resources operating within African American communities. With few exceptions, this perception of deficiency is still mirrored and carried out in practices within teacher training programs. For example, in general a lack of attention in these programs is given to a critical component: educators' roles in the establishment of school–community collaborative endeavors (Mahan, Fortney, & Garcia, 1983). Even when this component is included, the resources present in African American communities have traditionally not been considered as a necessary element in school–community partnerships. Today, this deliberate disregard is targeted especially at economically poor Black communities. Several crucial factors, however, support the inception of decisive African American community–school linkages. They include but are not limited to the following:

- The projected increased enrollment of African American students in the public schools

- The severe shortage of African American teachers and administrators

- The potential escalation of African American learners into special education programs (and/or other remedial or low-level academic curriculum tracks) of questionable value

- The trend toward site-based managed schools and alternate organizational arrangements that encourage community involvement regarding decisions about curriculum and other managerial aspects

- The reduction of federal funding to public schools, as well as policy changes in states' allocation of funds to promote equity among local school districts

- The current charge for educational institutions to provide a liaison to social services for parents and children requiring help

- The advocating of policy for inclusive communities for individuals with disabilities

- The demand by the African American community for better performance, more broad-based education, and accountability from the school system

Community–school involvement is not a new phenomenon. Educators, in particular African Americans and other ethnic minority professionals, advocated its importance during the 1960s through the ideals and programmatic components embedded in the alternative social programs and community empowerment educational approaches. The aforementioned crises, however, have generated a renewed proclamation of community–school interactive processes. My own professional activities support the conclusions of other scholars, professionals, practitioners, and community activists pertaining to African American community resources— that is, regardless of the economic status of the local Black community, there usually exists a conglomerate of immediate or at-large Black community resources that can afford various systems of support to individual families. These human and financial assets consist of Black religious institutions, African American professionals, volunteer grassroots organizations, social and service clubs, Black-owned businesses, and community-based social agencies (Ascher, 1991; Billinsley & Caldwell, 1991; Epperson, 1991; Haynes & Comer, 1990; Nettles, 1991; Powell, 1989; Walton, Ackiss, & Smith, 1991).

The advancement of Black youth is fundamental to the community resources cited above; therefore, they can and should serve as valued elements in productive school–community networks. This chapter explores the formulation of these vital linkages. I divide the examination into four sections. First, I provide a brief overview of the historical involvement processes manifested by the African American community to obtain services for Black youth. Next, I present a condensed discussion of African American communities, in particular economically poor communities. The negative perceptions of the school system regarding these communities and the resulting implications are highlighted. Then I outline the significance of African American community involvement processes, focusing attention on African American *community-based educational programming* as an essential component in the delivery of quality educational services to African American youth and their families. The thematic content of these programs and advantages to Black students with exceptionalities are delineated. The special education classroom teacher can assume key roles in successful community–school enterprises. Examples of these specific roles are included. In the final section, I detail a knowledge base-to-practical experience community involvement model that I constructed to help facilitate adequate preparation of school personnel to form collaborative relationships with relevant organizations within local African American communities. Other chapters in this text focus extensively on Black parental involvement (e.g., Chapter 8) and restructuring of teacher training programs (e.g., Chapter 7). In this chapter, I discuss these two areas as they relate to African American community-sponsored programming and the establishment of appropriate school–community networks.

HISTORICAL OVERVIEW

Community Involvement as a Means to Foster Excellence for Black Youth

Historically, the African American community has placed great value on education as a dominant component to freedom and full inclusion in U.S. society (Anderson, 1988; Billinsley & Caldwell, 1991; Ford Foundation and John D. & C. T. MacArthur Foundation, 1989; Slaughter & Epps, 1987; Walton et al., 1991). Historian James Anderson (1988) provided an in-depth analysis of the intense struggle by ex-slaves to gain universal public schooling for themselves and their children. According to Anderson, the self-determination of ex-slaves escaped the attention of all but a few historians. In *Visions of a Better Way: A Black Appraisal of Public Schooling* (Ford Foundation et al., 1989), readers are provided with a historical perspective of the Black community's relationship to schooling. This essay assesses and chronicles the varied racist, economic, social, and political factors that direct the restrictive nature of educational services for African Americans.

Coleman-Burns (1989) proclaimed that, due to several social and economic reasons, the Black community's priority on education for Black women has been unprecedented from any similarly oppressed class. This high regard of education by the Black community-at-large is still prevalent today, in spite of the myriad of unresolved educational issues faced by most African American children, their families, and communities. The Black community has been a leading and persistent force in attempting to obtain equity in educational opportunities. Its pioneering actions continue to serve as a foundation for the educational rights of other underserved or excluded groups, such as children with disabilities.

The various collective mechanisms employed by the African American community to initiate and sustain involvement processes to produce educational gains for Black youth can be grouped into the following four nonexhaustive proactive and reactive categories:

1. Establishment of Black schools and institutions of higher education

2. Legal actions instituting the constitutional rights of Black youth to equal education

3. Litigation objecting to discriminatory policies and practices resulting in placement within inappropriate low-ability curriculum tracks and misclassification of Black youth into special education programs, especially self-contained classes for students with educable mental retardation, severe behavior disorders, and specific learning disabilities

4. Pervasive protests against the overall cognitive and psychologically damaging framework guiding the delivery of educational services to Black students and their families

Although some African American learners are achieving at average or high levels, the current state of affairs educationally for the majority of Black students enrolled in either general or special education programs is alarmingly discouraging and unacceptable. This phenomenon is especially grave considering that most African American youth enter the schooling process with adequate levels of motivation and cognitive abilities (Hale-Benson, 1989; Parham & Parham, 1989; Sanders-Phillips, 1989; Slaughter & Epps, 1987). Nevertheless, a significant number endure chronic academic failure and are continuously confronted with limiting program options, which include being involuntarily placed into remedial classes or special education programs and/or externally guided into self-enrollment in lower level general educational curriculum. These special classes and programs usually do not emphasize higher order thinking skills, methods of inquiry, control over one's environment, or maintenance of a positive sense of self.

As they are currently structured and operated, public schools are not meeting the needs of the masses of African American learners (Ascher, 1991; Hale-Benson, 1989; Boateng, 1990; Gill, 1991; Haynes & Comer, 1990; Obiakor, Algozzine, & Ford, 1993; Ogbu, 1978; Ratternay, 1990; Slaughter & Epps, 1987; Wikelund, 1990). A reframing and expansion of the present educational delivery framework is imperative. This is especially significant for those Black youth who are at greater risk for academic and social-emotional difficulties within the school environment.

Intensified community participation and active parental involvement at the local school district level are highly recommended by educators and mandated by federal legislation (Individuals with Disabilities Education Act of 1990 [IDEA]) as safeguards to promote adequate schooling. Both are considered to be particularly important variables to enhance the academic performance and overall development of African American youth with and without disabilities (Ascher, 1987; Barnes, 1991; Comer, 1985; Croninger, 1990; Epperson, 1991; Jenkins, 1989; Nettles, 1991; Parham & Parham, 1989; Ratternay, 1990; Sanders-Phillips, 1989; Slaughter & Epps, 1987; Walton et al., 1991; Wikelund, 1990). Outreach to and direct involvement of the community are deemed vital structural elements in the school's organization, in order to empower African American and other ethnic minority students.

In Cummins's (1986) examination of the variables associated with the empowerment of minority students, he stated that "a major reason previous attempts at educational reform have been unsuccessful is that the relationships between teachers and students and between schools and communities have remained essentially unchanged" (p. 18). He emphasized that the required changes involve *personal redefinitions* of the way classroom teachers interact with the children and the communities they serve. In addition, usage of community-based cultural programs to increase skill development for individuals with developmental disabilities is a research area that is increasingly being stressed by special education researchers (Braddock, 1988). In a compilation of strategies for interacting with Black parents of children with disabilities, Olion (1980) recommended that school personnel enlist the assistance of Black fraternities, sororities, and other community groups and persons as mediating agents between parents and the school.

A prevention and intervention model with a genuine interactive network between schools and targeted African American community resources is required. This conscientiously constructed school–parent–community partnership would incorporate the skills and resources of individual African American families, the African American community, and the school. Fundamental within the school would be competent, equity-oriented administrators, teachers, and other school personnel.

African American Community Involvement Processes

When attempting to provide proper services for Black youth and their families, special educators and other school personnel must be cognizant of and adequately respond to the fact that families exist within communities. Mahan et al. (1983) defined the term *community* as a multifaceted concept that includes all groups, individuals, and institutions that are touched by the school.

Nettles (1991) cited involvement processes as a main measurable feature of a community. Relative to schooling, community involvement "consists of the actions that organizations and individuals take to promote student development" (p. 133). She elaborated by stating that involvement may center around four basic processes:

1. Conversion—turning the [misguided] student around via a powerful message

2. Mobilization—complex activities, such as legal action, citizen participation, and neighborhood organizing that target change in institutions

3. Allocation—actions to increase students' access to resources, alter the incentive structure, and provide social support for students' efforts

4. Instruction—actions that support social learning and intellectual development

The African American community has steadily used all of these processes to promote the advancement of Black youth with and without disabilities. Before and after the Civil War, with and without the aid of the Freedman's Bureau, the African American community provided basic and higher levels of formal instruction for its people. This was accomplished while simultaneously seeking equal opportunity to a free public education. With a strong push by Black delegates to the Constitutional Conventions, the Reconstruction governments of the former rebel states established free segregated school systems in the South. However, during the period of 1880 to 1930, Black schooling in the South was brought almost to a halt through underfunding and neglect. The adoption of rigid segregation laws by Southern and border states resulted in disfranchisement of Black votes and the diversion of funding for Black education to separate schools for Whites (Ford Foundation et al., 1989). As discussed by Comer (1985), during the 1930s four to eight times as much money was being spent on the education of a White child as that of a Black in the eight states that held 80% of the Black population, with a disparity as great as 25 times in areas that were disproportionately Black.

The 1954 case, *Brown v. Topeka Board of Education*, which was initiated by the Black community, served as a cumulative landmark on behalf of Black children. The Supreme Court ruled that schools segregated on the basis of race were inherently unequal. Although court-directed school desegregation was instituted to attempt the encouragement of equity, it brought forth a multitude of long-term discriminatory educational practices. These include the examples stated previously (e.g., inappropriate ability tracking, false placement into special education classes, and the nonempowerment of Black parents). The African American community tenaciously challenged and legally resisted such institutional racist practices. *Hobson v. Hansen* and *Larry P. v. Riles* are two examples of court cases associated with this resistance. The former case focused on tracking in the Washington, D.C., school system, and the latter dealt with placement into classes for students with mental retardation on the basis of inaccurate psychological assessment tools (Jones & Wilderson, 1976). Subsequent federal legislation (Public Law 94-142, The Education for All Handicapped Children Act of 1975 [now IDEA]) responded to the arguments embedded within these kinds of cases. The act includes specific due process and nondiscriminatory assessment requirements to combat negative practices surrounding assessment and placement of youth from culturally and linguistically diverse backgrounds.

Despite federally mandated assurance of an appropriate education, the goal of quality programming for African American students with exceptionalities remains a major unresolved issue. The interwoven and deeply ingrained barriers to equitable services have yet to be systematically and effectively addressed (Ford, 1992; Ford Foundation et al., 1989; Gay, 1989; Johnson, 1976; Jones, 1976; Obiakor et al., 1993; Ogbu, 1978). These inhibitors include political and economic factors; negative attitudes and low expectations by many school personnel for Black youth; and culturally restrictive curriculum paradigms, pedagogy, materials, and reward and behavioral systems. Today, in reaction to the continuous academic failure, underachievement, and special education placement of Black students, especially males, there has been an increase in the number of independently operated Black schools and many are calling for public schools for Black males only (Ascher, 1991).

The Special Education System and African American Youth

Recent data reconfirm the overenrollment of Black youth in remedial special classes and disproportionate underrepresentation in gifted and talented classes (Chinn & Selma, 1987; U.S. Department of Education, Office for Civil Rights, 1993). Black males and youth from poor communities are especially vulnerable to misclassification and other forms of negative differential treatment. The problems associated with special education placement are further exacerbated by the high dropout rate of students within these classes. During the 1986–1987 school year, "41 percent of the special education students exiting schools did not receive a diploma or certificate" (National Education Association [NEA], 1990, p. 16). Research documents the various adverse consequences for these adolescents (e.g., pregnancy, underemployment or unemployment, involvement in the juvenile justice system, substance abuse) (Berry, 1989; Jones, 1989; NEA, 1990).

The lack of affiliation with community resources is cited as one of the many variables related to the school dropout rate for Black adolescents (Jones, 1989). Mickelson and Smith (1989) reported the conclusions from Coleman and Hoffer's analysis of differential dropout rates in public and Catholic schools (i.e., the rate was considerably greater in the public schools), which illustrate the importance of the community in reinforcing academic norms and sustaining Black children's schooling.

Summary

Although primary and shared school responsibility undertakings by the African American community are well documented, the general and special education systems have failed to constructively recognize and systematically capitalize on the strengths of critical African American community and family involvement processes. Even when these strengths have been acknowledged, they have been improperly used.

PERCEPTIONS BY THE SCHOOL TOWARD THE AFRICAN AMERICAN COMMUNITY

African Americans constitute approximately 12% of Americans, making them the largest ethnic minority group in the United States (U.S. Bureau of the Census, 1990). There is no one homogeneous or monolithic group of Blacks or Black community; Blacks are diverse relative to factors such as family units and composition, religious affiliations, economic resources, socialization practices, social and political orientations, and geographic location (Billinsley & Caldwell, 1991; Boykins & Toms, 1989; Parham & Parham, 1989; Sanders-Phillips, 1989). However, despite varying degrees of within-group diversity, historic and present-day experiences resulting from institutional racism compel African Americans in general (African American community-at-large) to be mutually supportive in combining and contributing significant resources (involvement processes) for the welfare of all African American youth.

Traditionally, educational institutions projected a "deficit-disorganized-pathological-dysfunctional" model (Barnes, 1991; Jenkins, 1989; Ogbu, 1978; Sanders-Phillips, 1989; Slaughter & Epps, 1987) on Black communities. Still present, this deficit paradigm is most often used by educators to define the lower socioeconomic class or "underclass" African American communities. A large percentage (82%) of African Americans live in cities, and the masses (60%) of these individuals reside in central cities with low economic resources (Edelman, 1985; Jenkins, 1989; Parham & Parham, 1989; Slaughter & Epps, 1987). The majority of children within these communities attend public schools. Such communities are generally plagued with a horde of social problems, including ill-equipped schools with inferior educational services and inexperienced teachers, high rates of poverty, unemployment, health and environmental problems, drugs, incarceration, and criminal victimizations. These communities and the families within them are presumed to be directly responsible for the academic failure and social-emotional problems of their youth. According to Slaughter and Epps (1987), in the perception of school personnel, the "community and family" replaces "IQ" in determining these children's learning potential. Too often, the guiding hypothesis is that these communities and families have little or nothing constructive to offer to effect positive educational outcomes of their young. Therefore, the schools must attempt the insurmountable job of changing and resocializing the youth from these communities.

Consequences of the Deficit Model

As discussed by Sanders-Phillips (1989), the above-described environmental realities can, and do in a cumulative fashion, decrease the probability that Black children who live in these troubled communities will be able to realize and achieve their full academic potential. However, the unquestionable acceptance of the lower class Black community as "a culture of poverty—nothing more" frame of reference by school personnel is both misguided and dangerous for numerous reasons. Three of the most prominent follow.

First, the destructive educational consequences of the deficit model are extensive. Studies point out that incorporation of a deficit mindset by school personnel contributes to negative attitudes and low expectations, which lead to differential treatment of Black students within general and special classes. By ascribing the principal cause of school difficulties of African American learners to external, out-of-school factors (e.g., community and family), school personnel are justifiably relieved of accountability and responsibility pertaining to their attitudes, quality of teaching, and overall services to Black youth. Family background does play a role in accounting for academic variance, yet research delineating factors that make a difference in the provision of quality programming and student outcomes specifically emphasizes the determinant effect of school-related variables, such as teacher expectations, teacher–student interaction, curriculum, classroom climate, and parental involvement (Bates & Wilson, 1989; Comer, 1985; Croninger, 1990; Cummins, 1986; Hale-Benson, 1989; Wang, Haertel, & Walberg, 1993–1994).

Second, a predominant deficit viewpoint of economically poor African American communities overlooks the traditional and contemporary pockets of involvement processes within these communities that provide the support needed to positively impact educational outcomes of students (Barnes, 1991; Billinsley & Caldwell, 1991; Haynes & Comer, 1990; Jones, 1989; Nettles, 1991; Sanders-Phillips, 1989). Slaughter and Epps (1987) and Stevenson (1990) respectively stated that African American families at all levels of social status have been remarkably effective and resilient at helping their children cope with the schooling process and that there exists within African American communities a reservoir of untapped strength. Parham and Parham (1989) called attention to the fact that many of the Black youngsters who are succeeding at rates equal to if not greater than their Anglo peers are reared in the same environment within which the vast majority of their African American peers are failing. Sanders-Phillips (1990) recommended the serious study of the mechanisms within low economic resource communities that produce competence in Black children despite destructive environmental conditions. Given the current emphasis on community involvement in the schools, I strongly agree that such mechanisms and their educational implications merit conscientious examination.

Third, a deficit perspective of the lower class Black community and its resources consciously dismisses the cumulative historical and present-day experiences resulting from the dynamic interplay among the perpetual political, social, and economic forces impacting on and within African American communities (Slaughter & Epps, 1987). As explicitly discussed by Ogbu (1978), schools are microcosms that reflect the attitudes and institutional practices and policies of society. Consequently, the conducting of serious analyses of the factors that create and reinforce the detrimental social obstacles accompanied by policies and structural changes leading to real equities in opportunities is being strongly recommended (Ford Foundation et al., 1989; Slaughter & Epps, 1987).

Based on his research with predominantly Black schools from the Yale Child Study Center School Development Program, Comer (1985) concluded that "schools attuned to black community history and needs represent one of the best opportunities to prepare more black youngsters for successful performance in school and life" (p. 138). Henry Levin's Accelerated Schools model also stresses instructional practices that tie lessons to students' own culture and everyday experiences as well as the use of community resources to heighten learning (Ascher, 1993). However, Comer further stated that, in actuality, research and evaluation in education are based on current conditions, with little appreciation for the effects of past conditions on school staffs, parents, and community.

Summary

The pathological model makes the misleading assumption that Black communities and families simply mediate and reflect societal influences without actively filtering and thus protecting their children from perceived threats to the children's images of themselves as learners and persons (Barnes, 1991; Sanders-Phillips, 1989; Slaughter & Epps, 1987). Coinciding with Cummins's (1986) recommendation that school personnel redefine the way they interact with African American communities in which they reside, educators (Boateng, 1990; Ford, 1992; Gay, 1989; Hale-Benson, 1989; Johnson, 1976; Lockwood, Ford, Sparks, & Allen, 1991; Obiakor et al., 1993) have highly recommended two basic requisites:

1. Systematic and monitored exposure of all school personnel working with African American youth to self-awareness activities concerning their attitudes and expectations for Black youth

2. Knowledge of accurate information about African Americans relative to historical and contemporary contributions, life-styles, value systems, interpersonal communication patterns, learning styles, and parental attitudes about education and disabilities.

The exposure must be purposeful, interactive, and monitored by well trained and knowledgeable individuals who possess positive frames of reference about African American youth, their families, and communities. Also, educators and administrators should be held accountable for translating the acquired knowledge into appropriate services.

Schools forming a "connectedness" to the African American community require the identification of mechanisms to serve as authentic and productive pathways into the community. The use of school-based community outreach specialists is one avenue. In addition, a more inclusive mechanism would center around networking with community-based educational programs. The nature of African American educational community programs makes them very functional networks. These programs generally bring together community-identified leaders, parents, local organizations, volunteers with various experience, and outlets for financial resources. A primary advantage is that the individuals involved have an understanding of the local community. To truly comprehend and capitalize on the benefits of establishing mutual support systems with community leaders and organizations that sponsor educational programming, the school professionals must:

- Individually develop a collaborative orientation frame of reference regarding local African American communities and families

- Be aware of and knowledgeable about African American community–sponsored educational programs within the school districts they work

- Understand the relevance of community–sponsored programs for Black youngsters with disabilities

- Become proficient in incorporating knowledge and resources (human and materials) acquired from community programs within the classroom

- Be willing to recommend to other school personnel and African American parents the participation of individual children into appropriate community programs

- Obtain experiences in learning how to expand their roles as collaborator or consultant beyond the school doors

- Use collaborative leadership skills to establish functional networks with significant African American community resources (e.g., individuals, organizations, programs, and social agencies)

AFRICAN AMERICAN COMMUNITY-BASED EDUCATIONAL PROGRAMMING

African American community–sponsored programs are constructed and implemented through a variety of traditional and contemporary secular and nonsecular organizations. For many, the Black church remains an important leadership institution within the African American community. It extends a host of outreach programs to support education at levels ranging from early childhood to adult. Individual churches may assume total responsibility or establish networks of collaboration with other churches, businesses, and community agencies, including the public school. Billinsley and Caldwell (1991) and Walton et al. (1991) provided in-depth discussions and descriptions of historic and contemporary community involvement processes of Black churches.

Black fraternities and sororities, professional organizations, civic and service organizations (e.g., National Association for the Advancement of Colored People, National Council of Negro Women, Black historical societies, African American creative arts groups), numerous local social clubs, and grassroots organizations also offer a multitude of ongoing educational programs to foster the healthy development of African American youth. Furthermore, social agencies, such as the Urban League, and local community centers provide a combination of support and information. Walton et al. (1991) presented an example of a successful collaboration between an Urban League agency and a public school. Collectively, African American individuals from different backgrounds volunteer for participation in community–sponsored educational programming. This group of volunteers comprises parents, professionals, skilled and semiskilled workers, business persons, performing artists, elected officials, and other community leaders.

Programmatic Topics of Community-Sponsored Programs

The programmatic topics and areas commonly addressed in African American community–based programs include but are not limited to the following (for more detailed information, see Ford & McLittle-Marino, in press):

- Academic motivation and advancement
- Self-development and cultural group identity
- Decision-making skills (e.g., school survival skills, drugs, alcohol, teen pregnancy, future planning)
- Goal setting
- Job-related skills (vocational/career)
- Self-advocacy, life survival skills, and "how to access" information skills
- Community responsibility
- Varying degrees and systems of mentoring by adults (short term and long term)
- Usually active involvement of parents is an integral component of community programs

Formats of Community Programs

Several formats of community programs are employed. Table 9.1 provides some examples.

Advantages of Community Programming for Students with Disabilities

Although African American youth with mild disabilities may be incidentally involved in regular community programs, those mani-

TABLE 9.1. Formats of Community Programs

- After-school tutoring
- Latchkey programs
- In-school tutoring (by individual volunteers)
- Saturday programming (e.g., independent program topics or extension of specific school objectives)
- Field trips (e.g., cultural or career oriented)
- Workshops (e.g., job fairs, career information seminars, health-related topics)
- Weekend retreats focusing on a specific topic (e.g., sexual responsibility, decision making)
- Gender-specific programs (e.g., female or male Rites-of-Passage Programs[a])
- Peer group activities
- Specially funded research projects
- Short-term programs (e.g., summer reading programs, educational programs designed to aid students in passing state proficiency tests, programs limited to a specific number of weeks or months)
- Long-term programs (offered by churches, service organizations, and certain community centers or social service agencies, such as Urban League)

[a]"Rites-of-Passage are those structures, rituals, and ceremonies by which age-class members or individuals in a group successfully come to know who they are and what they are about—the purpose and meaning for their existence, as they proceed from one clearly defined state of existence to the next state or passage in their lives" (Hill, p. 62). These programs may not be appropriate for some youth with very limited cognitive and/or social-emotional abilities. However, a particular benefit of Rites-of-Passage Programs is the emphasis on "heterogeneous group learning" and the practice of the ideas inherent in the "there are no gifted, average, and impaired grouping" concept (Hill, 1992, p. 66). For more detail concerning these programs, see Hill (1992) and Kunjufu (1989).

festing moderate to more severe levels of difficulties (e.g., those enrolled in self-contained classes for students with mental retardation or behavioral disorders) are not routinely involved. Yet, as listed in Table 9.2 and discussed below, several distinct benefits justify the planned and active inclusion of youth with exceptionalities.

Accessible Adult Role Models and Mentors

An important outcome of community programming for learners with exceptionalities centers on the increased interactions with appropriate and accessible adult African American male and female role models, which may result in long-term mentoring relationships. The majority of teachers and administrators do not reside in the

TABLE 9.2. Benefits of Participation Within Community Programs for Exceptional Learners

---

- Increased interactions with appropriate and accessible adult role models and potential mentors
- Observation of their parents and neighbors in education-oriented roles
- Reinforcement of academic skills
- Exposure to critical cultural information and activities to develop or enhance positive self-images and holistic understanding of self and cultural group identity
- Concrete practice in decision making
- Direct instruction in functional life survival skills

---

community of the vast number of African American students they serve. As pointed out by Gillis-Olion, Olion, and Holmes (1986), the past experiences and cultures of most special educators do not coincide with the social and economic conditions and cultures of African American students and their families. Demographic school data indicate that 80% of current elementary teachers are female and White (Ascher, 1991).

Teacher employment and student enrollment trends reveal that by the year 2000, African American teachers will make up barely 5% of all teachers (National Clearinghouse for Professions in Special Education, 1988). Unfortunately, this serious decline will occur at a time when projected data indicate that over one third of the students in the public schools are likely to be ethnic minority. Presently, 23 of the 25 largest school systems are heavily composed of minority students, with 75% being primarily African Americans (Bates & Wilson, 1989; National Clearinghouse for Professions in Special Education, 1988). Because African American school personnel frequently serve as significant role models, mediators, and mentors for students, the loss will impact Black students immensely.

Participation by students in community programming would help address the deprivation described above. Youth who live in poor urban areas often have limited access to individual adults with resources that directly influence academic success (Ascher, 1991; Nettles, 1991; Parham & Parham, 1989; Sanders-Phillips, 1989). Therefore, ongoing involvement in community programming that systematically exposes youngsters to available role models, potential mentors, and essential life skills becomes imperative.

Parental Involvement

Parental involvement is often an inherent element in community-sponsored programming. This critical feature permits Black youngsters the needed opportunities to observe their parents and neighbors in roles that concretely reinforce the importance of education. The positive effects of parental involvement on African American students' motivation and academic attainment is well documented (Comer, 1989; Croninger, 1990; Cummins, 1986; Epperson, 1991; Parham & Parham, 1989). The School Development Program (SDP) is an example of a proven model for public education that includes meaningful parental involvement throughout the school environment (for detailed description, see Comer, 1985, 1989). Additionally, the SDP model was specifically designed to improve academic performance of low income minority group children.

As a result of school-imposed barriers, individual families within poor Black communities often feel powerless, alienated from and intimidated by the school system (Ascher, 1987; Comer, 1985; Croninger, 1990; Cummins, 1986; Gillis-Olion et al., 1986; Marion, 1980). The traditional welcome properly extended to other families is not automatically afforded. Because of this historical treatment, Black families may be distrustful of and reluctant to embrace involvement when it is offered. Conversely, individual families may also self-impose barriers that prohibit adequate family–school cooperation. More positive relationships between Black families and the school could develop as a result of schools forming linkages with African American community organizations that strongly endorse parental participation.

Reinforcement of School-Related Skills

Another obvious advantage for students with disabilities is the reinforcement of academic and other school-related skills. Academic tutoring is a significant segment of most community programs. Students with disabilities require a great deal of time on task, repetition, and practice in the transfer and application of skills. Supplemental experiences provided in community programs would intensify learning of skills introduced in schools. Furthermore, such skills would be augmented by community persons and parents, thereby strengthening the relevancy of school tasks within a "home-based" environment.

Exposure of African American Youth to Necessary Cultural Information

Often, a primary objective of community programming centers on helping Black youth gain a clear understanding of the destructive external and internal variables that cause them to not achieve at maximum levels. As stated in the previous Programmatic Topics section, important elements include concentration on self and group identity, values, and decision-making and other life survival skills.

In Lomotey's (1990) interview of a respected educator about African American students and the schooling process, the importance of "political education" for Black children is stressed. *Political education* is defined as "a broad term that is used to apply to the culture, the history, the desire and the aspiration of a child that has been shaped in great part by the parents, the grandparents and all of his or her environment" (p. 14). The concept of education for liberation, for citizenship, for personal and collective power, and for advancement has deep roots in the Black community (Ford Foundation et al., 1989). Black students with disabilities are impacted by many of the same societal barriers and personal problems as are their nondisabled peers. However, the special education curriculum generally does not address decision-making and other life survival skills from a cultural perspective.

Slaughter and Epps (1987) cited the research of Holliday in stating that in the Black subculture many children are socialized to assume a posture of persistence and assertiveness in relation to problem solving. In contrast, when this type of behavior is displayed by them in the classroom, these traits are rejected by teachers as being inappropriate for Blacks in America. The cumulative influence of these rejections "transforms young black children's achievement efforts into learned helplessness" (p. 12).

Community programming that provides realistic experiences in skillful decision-making (to one's fullest potential) is a necessity for Black students with disabilities. This is further evidenced by the current requirement of "transitional services planning" for adolescents under IDEA. Transitional planning is defined as "a partnership involving students with disabilities, their families, school and postschool service personnel, local community representatives, employers, and neighbors. Its purposes are to help the student choose a living situation and to ensure that the student graduates with community living skills and can access postsecondary education if that is a desired outcome" (West et al., 1992, p. 3).

Self-advocacy skills (e.g., "learning to speak up and ask for what you need on your own behalf . . . taking charge of your life . . . being more independent"; West et al., 1992, p. 7) and adequate decision-making skills are considered crucial student skills for effective transitional planning. West et al. further stated that, to integrate students with disabilities into school and community settings, the Individualized Education Program (IEP) goals should focus on the least restrictive environments for skill acquisition. They argued that "in many cases the community is the *only* suitable environment for learning transition skills" (p. 17). For African American students, structured involvement in African American community–sponsored programming may aid them in attaining those culturally oriented life survival and transition skills not offered and required in the classroom.

Collectively, participation of Black students with exceptionalities in community programming would afford them the needed practice in the transference of school behaviors and simultaneously expose them to critical survival and political skills required for healthy functioning as African Americans. At times, specific strategies that accommodate the needs of individual students with disabilities will be required (Ford & McLittle-Marino, in press). However, the overall teaching methods, interpersonal communications, materials, and behavioral systems utilized within community programs may be more familiar ways of learning for African American students and thereby increase motivation.

Problems in academic motivation reflected by low school self-esteem are constantly cited as main causes of academic failure by African American youth from poor backgrounds and those with disabilities. A confident cultural identity and the acquisition of coping skills strategies for confronting racism are positively associated with motivation and competence in school (Cummins, 1986; Hale-Benson, 1989; Johnson, 1976; Olion, 1980; Parham & Parham, 1989; Powell, 1989). The enhancement of understanding of self and cultural group identity is a common theme for community programs. Exposure to accurate historic and contemporary information about African Americans, planned participation in structured and informal cultural experiences, and direct instruction in effective strategies for coping with racism and its consequences assist students in the development of a healthy sense of their cultural heritage and identity. This, in turn, should lead students to a better understanding and perception of themselves. Individual educators may do an adequate job of educating Black exceptional youth. Generally, however, special education teachers have not been provided with the specific training necessary to create learning environments that systematically reinforce the development of a cultural sense of well-being to effect motivation and school performance (Berry, 1989; Ford, 1992; Fox, Kuhlman, & Sales, 1988; Gay, 1989; Obiakor et al., 1993).

The following two examples are ways in which community programs use cultural content, materials, and methods to promote the necessary "political education" of Black youth:

1. When working directly on *self-esteem*, programs may use a variety of culturally appropriate materials and functional activities:

- Nonfictional and fictional books, Afrocentric student self-esteem workbooks and other exercises, Afrocentric board games, culturally oriented computer software, toys (e.g., puzzles, dolls), audio and audiovisual materials, cultural reward artifacts, celebratory materials, and a host of other reinforcing materials found in African American book and art stores

- Field trips to African or African American museums and businesses

- Black "motivational" speakers

These resources also can be used to introduce or maintain basic academic skills.

2. Topics that may be addressed in community programs when facilitating the process of *positive decision-making* include the following: Confronting racism, community responsibility and citizenship, economics, health issues (e.g., drugs and other substances, sex, personal hygiene), interpersonal communication skills, environmental concerns, career planning, and global concerns. When guiding Black youth to make healthy decisions about these issues, adult African Americans are in a position to facilitate straightforward relevant discussions and offer realistic strategies. For

instance, activities to promote community responsibility and understanding of issues that impact daily healthy living for Black Americans may focus on students interviewing community elders, working on specific community projects, and outlining strategies to address community problems.

Culturally relevant curriculum content and pedagogy are discussed in depth in other chapters within this text. It is important to note here, however, that teachers should be aware that many topics, materials, and methods stressed within community programs are applicable for the classroom; thus, teachers should incorporate them to enhance learning within the school.

African American Community Programs: Benefits for Special Education Personnel

Table 9.3 lists several important benefits of involvement in African American community–sponsored programs for special educators. These advantages are infused throughout the discussion in the next section of this chapter, on teacher preparation. Structured and monitored teacher participation within community programming has the potential to contribute to the reduction of negative attitudes and low expectations for Black youth held by some school personnel. Direct observation of African American parents, other community volunteers, and paid adults working to heighten the academic and life skills of Black youth may lead to teachers' improved appreciation of these significant individuals as "partners and colleagues."

PREPARATION OF SPECIAL EDUCATORS

Linking Community-Based Programming to Teacher Training Programs

Inadequate training of teachers and administrators in the understanding and usage of community resources is cited as a reason that schools fail to acknowledge the existence of the community around

TABLE 9.3. Benefits of Involvement in Community Programming for Special Educators

- Increased accurate and holistic understanding of Black children, their families, and communities the educators serve
- Expanded knowledge about ways to reinforce academic self-esteem and overall sense of well-being of African American youth with exceptionalities
- Broadened understanding about culture-oriented teaching and learning techniques to enhance presentation of lessons, student response modes, and other variables associated with structuring the learning environment (e.g., curriculum content, instructional and physical arrangement, resource materials, interpersonal communications, and behavioral systems)
- Elevated awareness about the kinds of functional life survival skills needed by Black exceptional students
- More opportunities for positive interactions with parents and recognition of them as "colleagues" and partners
- Potential pool to recruit African American paraprofessionals as prospective special educators or educational assistants who are sensitive to the needs of African American students

them when planning educational programming (Mahan et al., 1983; Wikelund, 1990). Mahan et al. (1983) suggested the combining of "add-on" and "hands-on" approaches interwoven with specific community involvement assignments to teacher education programs. The add-on approach includes class assignments with direct community involvement and analysis modules, and the hands-on approach entails the actual practicum placement of students in nonschool community settings where they have the opportunity to work and interact with community members for long periods of time. Mahan et al.'s (1983) recommendation of coursework centering on community involvement assignments can be used as a framework to aid special educators in acquiring adequate knowledge bases about community resources. Using this approach as a foundation, I propose the Community Involvement Model, discussed in the following section.

A Community Involvement Model for Teacher Training Programs

If school personnel are to be encouraged to incorporate elements of community programming in the school environment, they first must be motivated to do so. Such motivation originates with the establishment of a positive mindset and philosophy about African Americans in general. Although a few special education training programs are beginning to seriously recognize African American students from a holistic, positive, and cultural perspective, this practice is neither systematic nor widespread. Thus, most personnel in both special education and general education are exiting teacher training programs without appropriate attitudes, skills, and knowledge needed to promote maximal learning in African American students in general, as well as those with disabilities and those who are gifted and talented (Fox et al., 1988; Gay, 1989; Wayson, 1988).

This lack of sufficient preparation demands that, as a prerequisite to community involvement activities, teachers in training participate in formal university courses or seminars designed to promote positive attitudes about ethnic minority groups. Such experiences should focus on preservice-level teacher trainees undergoing analyses of their attitudes and beliefs about African Americans and implications of these on their patterns of behaviors regarding African American learners. This more appropriately conditioned mindset is better prepared for further enhancement through African American community involvement assignments.

For prospective teachers and administrators to become committed to the study of community programs and to follow through by including relevant components within the school setting, community involvement activities must permeate their entire special education preservice training experience. To this end, knowledge of community programming must be explicitly emphasized in all coursework rather than a brief assignment in one course. At a minimum, community involvement assignments should be essential courses in methods, working with families, and administration. The movement toward site-based managed schools and increased parental involvement demands that administrators possess the kinds of leadership skills that support functional school–community liaisons. Therefore, administrator trainees should also be exposed to the type of experiences outlined below. I offer a three-phase community involvement model, presented in Figure 9.1, for use in teacher education and inservice training programs.

For assignments to be meaningful, teacher trainees must have a clear sense of direction as to the rationale of the African American community involvement activities. Specific course objectives and the expected level of performance must be precisely outlined. The sequence of phases depicted in Figure 9.1 may be accomplished by having students engage in the following noncomprehensive list of activities, which are discussed in detail in the next sections:

1. Computer-generated compilation of organizations that sponsor African American community programs

2. Direct participation in the local programs contained within the data base

3. Application of cumulative knowledge and experiences about community programming during the student teaching practicum

Community Programming Data Base

To obtain the knowledge base of information for Phase 1 of the model, teacher trainees can be placed into small cooperative groups. Each group would be required to create a list of easily accessible human and published resources to assist them in gathering information about national, local, and regional community organizations that sponsor programming for African American youth. These could include the *Blackbook/Black pages* (a city- or region-specific publication that lists Black-owned businesses and organizations, information about college scholarships, special celebrations and community events, etc.), Black newspapers, television programs, churches, directors of community centers in predominantly Black neighborhoods, members of fraternities and sororities, and African American professors and students at their college or university. In addition to obtaining information about traditional and contemporary organizations, trainees may also attempt to identify individuals or "subgroups" not formally organized but that informally provide invaluable mentoring to local Black youth and can be used as resources (e.g., respected "elders" who gather at the local barbershop).

After trainees acquire the above information, they would compile a computer data base containing the community organizations and significant individuals with their unique characteristics. A table might be set up for data with the following column headings:

PHASE 1

Knowledge Base About Community Programming
- Awareness of African American community-based educational programs
- Establishment of future personnel contacts
- Understanding of the benefits to special educators, students, and families

↓

PHASE 2

Application of Knowledge (In-Class Activities)
- Teacher trainees incorporate information acquired from Phase 1 into educational planning.
  - Preventive-level or referral stages (working with general education)
  - Intervention stage (IEP development, curriculum content, instructional strategies, resource materials, physical design of the classroom, behavioral systems, and interpersonal relations)

↓

PHASE 3

Student Teaching Experience and Practicing Special Educators (collaborative research among postsecondary institutions, public schools, and community programs is needed)
- Demonstrate competencies from Phase 2
- Monitor the effect of community programs
- Note changes in practicing special educators' behavior regarding the use of prevention and intervention activities outlined in Phase 2

FIGURE 9.1. Three phases of community involvement activities.

Name/Address/Phone, Contact Person(s), Purposes and Areas Addressed, Format, Type of Staff, Type of Parental Involvement, Benefits for Students with Disabilities, Weaknesses for Students with Disabilities, and Modification Required for Successful Inclusion of Exceptional Learners. Trainees could then select a community program and interview the program planner or other relevant staff member(s) to obtain the information needed to fill in the table. Finally, teacher trainees could, with permission from program directors, perform systematic observations. This observational experience should be designed to permit trainees opportunities to answer questions pertaining to an understanding of the program's benefits and disadvantages. A composite data base could be created from the cooperative groups. The basic information obtained in Phase 1 would be applied in other special education classes, student teaching, and in future teaching positions. An alternative to a computer data base is the construction of African American community resource portfolios, using programmatic categories such as education, culture, and health.

In addition, trainees could create a finished product that is practical and encourages usage. An example is a *Thematic Community Resource Calendar* (Blackwell, 1994). Each month is assigned a theme or topic (e.g., education month, nutrition/health month, self-awareness and family month), and African American community-based resources that provide services corresponding to the theme are described. For instance, education month would include programs and resources that offer tutoring or other academic-oriented activities; nutrition/health month would delineate resources providing food baskets, parenting fairs, health screening, and other health-related programs; self-awareness and family month may include resources providing cultural enrichment programs, family togetherness activities, African American big brother–big sister programs, male–female mentors, as well as services to assist families in need of support.

Direct Participation of Teacher Trainees in Community Programs

Field experience activities of teacher trainees in community programs would necessitate ongoing collaborative efforts between university-level special education instructors and community organizations. For maximal results, these experiences should coincide with specific academic courses. For instance, most special education methods courses require field experience hours in special educational settings. These hours can be expanded or modified to accommodate nonschool settings in the form of African American community programs. Working with community program planners, teacher trainees could be trained as volunteers and allowed to engage in activities that permit them to respond to the areas in Phase 2. Ideally, teacher trainees should be able to do the following:

1. Discern whether and how targeted African American community programmatic activities or individual resources can be used to prevent the occurrence of academic or social-emotional problems of Black students in the regular classroom, thereby lessening the chances of special referral and placement.

2. Discuss and illustrate how the content, materials, cultural activities, and teaching styles employed in the community programs can be positively infused into the school environment (e.g., as objectives on the IEP, as components of academic- or social-oriented lesson plans, in school use of cultural-oriented reward and behavioral systems).

It is important that teachers in training be given assignments that require them to interact with African American parents whereby the trainees are placed in progressive roles first as "learners," then as co-workers with parents. Such facilitated experience should assist future educators to positively engage in communications with African American parents.

Use of the Knowledge Base and Skills from Field Experiences During the Student Teaching Experience

Efforts to aid teacher trainees to apply knowledge and skills from Phases 1 and 2 should be integrated into the student teaching practicum. One way to accomplish this would be to have the student teacher monitor the progress of African American learners in the classroom who are participating in educational community-sponsored programming.

Several monitoring approaches can be employed. Trainees could focus on comparing baseline data (e.g., before student involvement in the community program/intervention) to combined intervention data (community program involvement and school). Student teachers would conduct observations of learners' attitudes and overall motivation, specific skill acquisition rate, and progress for skills and topics emphasized simultaneously in school and the community program. Other techniques could center on trainees observing and noting comments made by students and family members about the students' involvement in community programs that can positively influence school performance. Based on the results, trainees could make recommendations for the participation of other students with special needs in community programs. Utilizing information and skills from the previous phases, student teachers could also reinforce and incorporate relevant community programming content, materials, and strategies into the classroom.

The kinds of guided exposures discussed above increase the likelihood of special education personnel exiting teacher training programs with the necessary tools for designing and implementing productive learning experiences for African American youth. During the student teaching experience, it is crucial that the supervising teacher and university supervisor be competent in the community involvement skills requested of the student teacher.

Preparing Practicing School Personnel for Effective Involvement in African American Community Programs

With the encouragement and support of school administrators, special education teachers and other personnel can develop competency in establishing networks within the local African American community. School personnel can be provided with information about community-sponsored educational programs by the school's community outreach specialist or school–community liaison person. This sharing of information can occur as a building-level inservice program. Directors or coordinators of several local community programs could serve as speakers.

To increase the probability of meaningful application of the information from the inservice programs, a building-level team approach could be instituted. The direct involvement and endorsement of building administrators are prerequisites for success. In order words, the principal would be a participating member of the team, along with special and regular educators. This team would, in turn, outline ways in which identified community programs could be of value to the school environment and the African American pupils served. Next, the team would formally share this information with school personnel throughout the building as well as those itinerant personnel servicing the building. In addition, teachers could be provided with publications (e.g., the aforementioned *Thematic Community Resource Calendar*) about local African American community organizations that sponsor programming and names of contact persons.

Explicitly including aspects of school–African American community networking into regularly scheduled inservice training programs could further the creation or refinement of a positive frame of reference about school–community collaborations. As standard procedure, personnel designing and conducting inservice training for educators who work in school districts that serve large numbers of African American youth should critique the content of all typical inservice topics to determine how community information can be infused.

As recommended in the discussion pertaining to student teachers, practicing teachers must also directly participate in community programs if they are to take full advantage of the benefits delineated in Table 9.3.

Active involvement in local African American community-based programs by special educators affords them opportunities to extend their mentoring roles beyond the school doors into their students' homebase. In addition to the techniques outlined in this chapter, Garcia (1991, p. 59) described several relevant activities to assist teachers in studying the community of their students, such as teachers joining and developing friends in non-school–related community groups and surveying the community to obtain understanding and appreciation of it.

Table 9.4 lists several potential roles of special educators when linking community-sponsored programming to the school. With the exception of the special educator as collaborator or consultant, each of these has been previously discussed in this chapter. Through the establishment of school–community networks, the special educator is in the desirable position of being able to recommend students with disabilities for participation in African American community programs and to offer technical assistance in ways to accommodate the unique needs of such students.

I designed a collaborative university–African American community program targeting Black youth titled Project Well-Being (Ford & McLittle-Marino, in press). The program included a heterogeneous group of adolescents aged 11 to 15 years (e.g., gifted students and students with and without disabilities). It was specifically designed to identify the kinds of accommodative strategies that would facilitate successful inclusion of youth with disabilities into regular community programs without changing the programmatic goals. The primary topics of the program were understanding of self and ethnic group identity, positive decision making, and goal setting. Some examples of the general types of modifications that helped to increase successful participation of students with disabilities in Project Well-Being include the consistent use of both adult guided cooperative learning groups and peer–peer activities; direct instruction in self-monitoring of social behavior; and the varied repetition of programmatic concepts and skills (for more detailed information, see Ford & McLittle-Marino, in press).

School–community collaborative initiatives require the establishment of trust between school personnel and program organizers. Volunteer efforts by special education teachers in community programs as described above would assist in the development of trust. Working directly with the school's African American community outreach specialist, educators could construct a general information booklet or a list outlining the benefits of participation in community programming for Black exceptional learners, along with examples of the kinds of modifications that would improve their involvement level. This information could be shared with community organizations.

As requested, special educators could present informal workshops at local community facilities or the school to share information with community program planners. The need for information and the need to be valued and respected are cited as major factors for African American parents (Marion, 1980; Patton & Braithwaite, 1984). Through involvement in African American community programs, special educators are in a viable position to provide parents with information about legislation, educational services, and local organizations for families of children with disabilities. By interacting with parents in community environments in which the parents

TABLE 9.4. Potential Roles of Special Education in School–African American Community Programming Networks

- Establish information networks about local African American community–sponsored programs for the school building
- Share information with and sensitize other school personnel
- Incorporate information about community programs into the schooling process as needed:
  - To maintain and further enhance appropriate academic or social behaviors of African American students
  - As an element in the preventive strategies considered during the pre-referral stage to special education services and placement
  - During the intervention stage as an inclusive approach to effectively address the motivational, academic, personal-social, and career needs of African American learners
- Participate in out-of-school mentoring of students
- Collaborate or consult with African American community-sponsored resources
- Provide technical information concerning ways to promote better participation of students with disabilities in community programs
- Provide information beneficial to parents about community resources and special education services as applicable to their children

---

are clearly operating from an empowering capacity, educators should gain more respect and valuing of parents and their community resources. Recruiting minority teachers from the ranks of paraprofessionals is one strategy currently recommended to combat the serious issue regarding the low number of minority special educators (National Association of State Directors of Special Education, 1994). Community-based programs could serve as a rich resource pool in which to recruit potential candidates. This recruitment benefit could act as extra incentive for building-level administrators and state educational agencies to promote the establishment of and active participation within genuine school–African American community networks.

CONCLUSION

The present dismal and nonproductive state of affairs for African American learners demands that the educational system become serious about adopting policies and practices that result in quality programming and equity in educational opportunity for all African American youth. There is evidence that individual public schools can make a difference for African American youth. Given the significance of certain resources in African American communities on educational outcomes for Black youth and the current movement toward community–school collaborative systems, schools constructed to make a difference can no longer justifiably disregard relevant resources within African American communities. The formulation, ongoing utilization, and maintenance of effective collaboration between schools and local African American communities must become the rule rather than the exception.

REFERENCES

Anderson, J. D. (1988). *The education of Blacks in the south, 1860–1935.* Chapel Hill: University of North Carolina Press.

Ascher, C. (1987, December). *Improving the school–home connection for poor and minority urban students* (ERIC/CUE Trends and Issues Series No. 8). New York: Columbia University, Institute for Urban and Minority Education.

Ascher, C. (1991). *School programs for African-American male students.* (Contract No. RI88062013). New York: ERIC Clearing House on Urban Education (Trends and issues No. 15).

Ascher, C. (1993). *Changing schools for urban students: The school development program, accelerated schools, and success for all.* New York: ERIC Clearinghouse on Urban Education Institute for Urban and Minority Education (Trends and Issues No. 18).

Barnes, E. J. (1991). The Black community as a source of positive self concept for Black children: A theoretical perspective. In R. L. Jones (Ed.), *Black psychology* (pp. 667–692). Berkeley, CA: Cobb & Henry.

Bates, P., & Wilson, T. (Eds.). (1989). *Effective schools: Critical issues in the education of Black children.* Washington, DC: National Alliance of Black School Educators. (ERIC Document Reproduction Service No. 312 361)

Berry, G. L. (1989). Afro-Americans and academic achievement: Pathways to excellence. In G. L. Berry & J. K. Asaman (Eds.), *Black students: Psychosocial issues and academic achievement* (pp. 286–294). Newbury, CA: Corwin Press.

Billinsley, A., & Caldwell, C. H. (1991). The church, the family and the school in the African-American community. *Journal of Negro Education, 60*(3), 427–440.

Blackwell, B. (1994). An interview of Betty Blackwell, program coordinator for preschool–kindergarten programs in the Akron Public Schools about community networking and classroom teachers.

Boateng, F. (1990). Combating deculturalization of the African-American child in the public school system: A multicultural approach. In K. Lomotey (Ed.), *Going to school: The African-American experience* (pp. 73–84). Albany: State University of New York Press.

Boykins, W. A., & Toms, F. D. (1989). Black child socialization: A conceptual framework. In H. P. McAdoo & J. L. McAdoo (Eds.), *Black children: Social, educational and parental environments* (pp. 33–51). Newbury Park, CA: Sage.

Braddock, D. (1988). Challenges in community integration. In L. W. Heal, J. I. Haney, & A. R. Novak-Amado (Eds.), *Integration of developmentally disabled individuals into the community* (2nd ed.). Baltimore: Brookes.

Brown v. Topeka Board of Education. (1954, May 17). 347 U.S. 483.

Chinn, P. C., & Selma, H. (1987). Representation of minority students in special education classes. *Remedial and Special Education, 8*(4), 41–46.

Coleman-Burns, P. (1989). African-American women–Education for what? *Sex Roles, 21*(1–2), 145–160.

Comer, J. P. (1985). Empowering Black children's educational environments. In H. P. McAdoo & J. L. McAdoo (Eds.), *Black children: Social, educational and parental environments* (pp. 123–138). Newbury Park, CA: Sage.

Comer, J. P. (1989). The school development program: A psychosocial model of school intervention. In G. L. Berry & J. K. Asaman (Eds.), *Black students: Psychosocial issues and academic achievement* (pp. 264–285). Newbury Park, CA: Corwin Press.

Croninger, B. (1990). African-American parents . . . Seeing them as colleagues, neighbors, and friends? *Equity Coalition for Race, Gender and National Origin, 1*(2), 8–9.

Cummins, J. (1986). Empowering minority students: A framework for intervention. *Harvard Educational Review, 56*(1), 18–35.

Edelman, M. W. (1985). The sea is so wide and my boat is so small: Problems facing Black children today. In H. P. McAdoo & J. L. McAdoo (Eds.), *Black children: Social, educational and parental environments* (pp. 72–82). Newbury Park, CA: Sage.

Epperson, A. I. (1991). The community partnership: Operation rescue. *Journal of Negro Education, 60*(3), 454–458.

Ford, B. A. (1992). Multicultural education training for special educators working with African-American youth. *Exceptional Children, 59*(2), 107–114.

Ford, B. A., & McLittle-Marino, D. (in press). Successful inclusion of youth with disabilities in regular African-American community-based programs. *The Journal of Negro Education.*

Ford Foundation and John D. & C. T. MacArthur Foundation. (1989). *Visions of a better way: A Black appraisal of public schooling.* Washington, DC: Joint Center for Political Studies. (ERIC Document Reproduction Service No. ED 312320)

Fox, L. C., Kuhlman, N. A., & Sales, B. T. (1988). Cross-cultural concerns: What's missing from special education training programs? *Teacher Education and Special Education, 11*(4), 155–161.

Garcia, R. L. (1991). *Teaching in a pluralistic society: Concepts, models, strategies.* New York: Harper Collins.

Gay, G. (1989). Ethnic minorities and educational equality. In J. A. Banks & C. A. McGee-Banks (Eds.), *Multicultural education: Issues and perspectives* (pp. 167-188). Boston: Allyn & Bacon.

Gill, W. (1991). Jewish day schools and Afrocentric programs as models for educating African-American youth. *Journal of Negro Education, 60*(4), 566–580.

Gillis-Olion, M., Olion, L., & Holmes, R. L. (1986). Strategies for meeting with Black parents of handicapped children. *Negro Journal of Educational Review, 37*(1), 8–16.

Hale-Benson, J. (1989). The school learning environment and academic success. In G. L. Berry & J. K. Asaman (Eds.), *Black students: Psychosocial issues and academic achievement* (pp. 83–97). Newbury Park, CA: Corwin Press.

Haynes, N. M., & Comer, J. (1990). Helping Black children succeed: The significance of some social factors. In K. Lomotey (Ed.), *Going to school: The African-American experience* (pp. 103–112). Albany: State University of New York Press.

Hill, Jr., P. (1992). *Coming of age: African American male rites of passage.* Chicago: African-American Images.

Jenkins, L. E. (1989). The Black family and academic achievement. In G. L. Berry & J. K. Asaman (Eds.), *Black students: Psychosocial issues and academic achievement* (pp. 138–152). Newbury Park, CA: Corwin Press.

Johnson, J. L. (1976). Mainstreaming Black children. In R. L. Jones (Ed.), *Mainstreaming and the minority child* (pp. 159–180). Reston, VA: Council for Exceptional Children.

Jones, R. L. (1976). *Mainstreaming and the minority child.* Reston, VA: Council for Exceptional Children.

Jones, R. L. (1989). *Black adolescents.* Berkeley, CA: Cobb and Henry.

Jones, R. L., & Wilderson, F. (1976). Mainstreaming and minority children: An overview of issues and a perspective. In R. L. Jones (Ed.), *Mainstreaming and the minority child* (pp. 1–13). Reston, VA: Council for Exceptional Children.

Kunjufu, J. (1989). *Critical issues in educating African-American youth (a talk with Jawanza).* Chicago: African-American Images.

Lockwood, R., Ford, B. A., Sparks, S., & Allen, A. (1991). *Cultural: Differences? Diversity!* Columbus: Ohio Department of Education.

Lomotey, R. (1990). An interview with Booker Peck. In K. Lomotey (Ed.), *Going to school: The African-American experience* (pp. 13–30). Albany: State University of New York Press.

Mahan, J. M., Fortney, M., & Garcia, J. (1983). Linking the community to teacher education: Toward a more analytical approach. *Action in Teacher Education, 5*(1–2), 1–10.

Marion, R. L. (1980). Communicating with parents of diverse exceptional children. *Exceptional Children, 46*(8), 616–623.

Mickelson, R. A., & Smith, S. S. (1989). Inner city social dislocations and school outcomes: A structural interpretation. In G. L. Berry & J. K. Asaman (Eds.), *Black students: Psychosocial issues and academic achievement* (pp. 99–119). Newbury, CA: Corwin Press.

National Association of State Directors of Special Education. (1994). State agency strategies for recruiting culturally and linguistically diverse special education professionals. *Liaison Bulletin, 22*(1), 1–5.

National Clearinghouse for Professions in Special Education. (1988). *Information on personnel supply and demand: The supply of minority teachers in the United States.* Reston, VA: The Council for Exceptional Children.

National Education Association. (1990). *Academic tracking: Report of the NEA Executive Committee/Subcommittee on Academic Teaching.* Washington, DC: Author. (ERIC Document Reproduction Service No. ED 322 642)

Nettles, S. M. (1991). Community contributions to school outcomes of African-American students. *Education and Urban Society, 24*(1), 132–147.

Obiakor, F., Algozzine, B., & Ford, B. A. (1993). Urban education, general education initiative, and service delivery to African-American students. *Urban Education, 28*(3), 313–327.

Ogbu, J. (1978). *Minority education and caste.* San Francisco: Academic Press.

Olion, L. (1980). *Strategies for meeting the needs of the mildly handicapped Black adolescent.* Paper presented at the Annual Council for Exceptional Children Conference, Philadelphia.

Parham, W. D., & Parham, T. L. (1989). The community and academic achievement. In H. P. McAdoo & J. L. McAdoo (Eds.), *Black children: Social, educational and parental environments* (pp. 120–137). Newbury Park, CA: Sage.

Patton, J. M., & Braithwaite, R. L. (1984, August). Obstacles to the participation of Black parents in the educational programs of their handicapped children. *Centering Teacher Education,* pp. 34–37.

Powell, G. J. (1989). Defining self-concept as a dimension of academic achievement for inner city youth. In G. L. Berry & J. K. Asaman (Eds.), *Black students: Psychosocial issues and academic achievement* (pp. 69–82). Newbury Park, CA: Corwin Press.

Ratternay, J. D. (1990). African-American achievement: A research agenda emphasizing independent schools. In K. Lomotey (Ed.), *Going to school: The African-American experience* (pp. 197–208). Albany: State University of New York Press.

Sanders-Phillips, K. (1989). Prenatal and postnatal influences on cognitive development. In G. L. Berry & J. K. Asaman (Eds.), *Black students:*

Psychosocial issues and academic achievement (pp. 18–39). Newbury Park, CA: Corwin Press.

Slaughter, D. T., & Epps, E. (1987). The home environment and academic achievement of Black American children and youth: An overview. *Journal of Negro Education, 56*(1), 3–20.

Stevenson, H. C. (1990, January). The role of the African-American church in education about teenage pregnancy. *Counseling and Values, 34,* 130–133.

U.S. Bureau of the Census. (1990, March). *U.S. population estimates, by age, sex, race and Hispanic origin: 1989* (Current Population Reports, series P25, No. 1057). Washington, DC: Author.

U.S. Department of Education, Office for Civil Rights. (1993). *1990 elementary and secondary schools civil rights survey: National summaries.* Washington, DC: U.S. Government Printing Office.

Walton, F. R., Ackiss, V. D., & Smith, S. N. (1991). Education versus schooling—Project LEAD: High expectations! *Journal of Negro Education, 60*(3), 441–453.

Wang, M. C., Haertel, G. D., & Walberg, H. J. (1993–1994). What helps students learn? *Educational Leadership, 51*(4), 74–79.

Wayson, W. (1988). Multicultural education in the college of education: Are future teachers prepared? In C. Heid (Ed.), *Multicultural education: Knowledge and perceptions* (pp. 39–48). Bloomington: Indiana University–Center for Urban and Multicultural Education.

West, L. L., Corbey, S., Boyer-Stephens, A., Jones, B., Miller, R. J., Mickey, & Sarkees-Wircenski, M. (1992). *Integrating transition planning into the IEP process.* Reston, VA: The Council for Exceptional Children.

Wikelund, K. R. (1990). *Schools and communities together: A guide to parent involvement* (Contract No. 400-86-0006). Washington, DC: Office of Educational Research and Improvement.

PART IV
Alternative Models

CHAPTER 10

Two Examples of Existing Schools

1. The Foreign Language Immersion and Cultural Studies School: An Alternative Public School in Detroit, Michigan

Ineala D. Chambers

All children are born geniuses. . . . It is what [educators] do that will either manifest or inhibit that genius. (Hilliard, 1990)

It is with this assumption that parents, students, and staff of the Foreign Language Immersion and Cultural Studies School (FLICS), with its 98% African American student population, embark upon their "faith journey" to excellence.

Effective education for African American students is probable where there are high expectations (within a meaningful curriculum), parental involvement, and teacher autonomy. If all students are born with the capacity for success, then the responsibility of all educators is to design challenging educational programs that will cultivate the genius of all children. The visionary parents and educators in 1984 who began the Foreign Language Immersion and Cultural Studies School had this insight.

This school is an empowered public school of choice in Detroit, Michigan. It is a site-based managed school with local school autonomy over curriculum. FLICS has as its mission and goals the production of students who are globally aware and functionally bilingual in either French, Spanish, or Japanese upon their completion of the 9-year, kindergarten through eighth-grade program. The educators seek to produce youth who are knowledgeable about their own cultural heritage and who are sensitive to the language and culture of others. All students begin the program in kindergarten or first grade. During this time, they receive all of their instruction in their selected target language.

HISTORICAL OVERVIEW

Since 1984 the Detroit public school system has offered the Spanish Language Immersion Program. Starting in kindergarten or first grade, *English-speaking students* are taught exclusively in Spanish by native-speaking Hispanic teachers or educators with near-native fluency. Not only does this program produce fully bilingual students, but these children continue to test at superior levels of achievement in English and other content areas.

The 1988–1989 school year marked the expansion of this program into a citywide school of choice, at a new site: FLICS. Presently, the FLICS features three immersion programs, French, Spanish, and Japanese, taught to English-speaking children in a multiethnic, multicultural setting. As students gain global awareness and proficient second-language skills, they experience enhanced appreciation of their own language and culture, along with heightened self-esteem.

The Immersion School is distinctively different from any other school in Michigan. As indicated above, it aims to stimulate cultural awareness through the predominance of teachers whose home language is French, Spanish, or Japanese. Spanish was chosen in 1984 for the immersion program because Spanish-speaking people form the fastest growing minority in the United States, with increasing political and economic importance. French not only has value for relations with our immediate northern neighbor, Canada, but is also spoken across the African continent. The French language is taught with emphasis on African and Caribbean cultures, and has special ability to foster pride and cultural awareness for African American children as they contact African and Caribbean teachers. Japanese is offered because the Japanese are the top foreign investors in the state of Michigan, and competency in Japanese represents a critical economic and commercial requirement for U.S. business and industry.

When students are accepted into FLICS in kindergarten or first grade, parents are expected to commit to the entire 9-year (K–8) sequence of immersion classes and are expected to become active participating members of the school. Parents are a vital and necessary part of the program. They contribute 2 hours of voluntary service by working on a Local School Community Organization committee (LSCO), attending LSCO meetings, or working with other teachers.

PHILOSOPHY OF EDUCATION: HIGH EXPECTATIONS FOR STUDENT SUCCESS

As an urban institution that serves a large African American community, the Detroit Public Schools has as its mission becoming the first urban school district to successfully educate all of its students. To achieve this goal, there have to be underlying assumptions about expectations of excellence for African American students.

One of these assumptions, teaching for negative skewness (Chambers, 1990), is an integral part of the leadership of FLICS. The idea of negative skewness is in contrast to the bell-shaped curve philosophy that assumes success for only a small percentage of students. Negative skewness is the statistical distribution frequency that would group *all* students on the success curve. It is the belief of FLICS that most children, even those classified as in need of special education services, can benefit from the curriculum and the immersion learning process at FLICS. A small number of FLICS students have been diagnosed and classified as having specific learning disabilities or attention deficit disorders. These students are an integral part of the entire program at FLICS. As indicated by their Individualized Education Programs (IEPs), their unique needs are being successfully addressed by the general education staff. They receive no direct special education services.

TEACHER AUTONOMY

The philosophy of education at FLICS also embraces the concept of teacher autonomy. The leadership at FLICS believes that teachers will become creative risk-takers in developing educative experiences for their students when student outcomes are clearly defined; when teachers are free to choose the methods, strategies, and materials; and when they are held accountable for getting their students to the terminal objective or outcome. Anticipated benefits for teachers are the freedom to try new things and feelings of ownership for the curriculum. A subsequent benefit for students is enthusiastic teachers.

The monitoring process includes both formative and summative evaluation procedures. Currently, FLICS is in the process of developing a self-evaluative peer-coaching model (e.g., teacher–teacher) through language and grade curriculum clusters. In addition, weekly reviews of lesson plans, several informal evaluations, and at least one formal evaluation are conducted by the building principal.

THE CURRICULUM

The curriculum at FLICS is the same as at other public schools in the district: The Detroit Strands and Objectives. However, at FLICS the curriculum is dynamic, undergoing constant revision through evaluations from instructional staff as well as parents and the community.

It is the *delivery of instruction* that is significantly different. Students are taught in a foreign language. All of the curriculum content, concept and skill development, even disciplining are in the target language. Students acquire the target language in a natural way. Therefore, the foreign language is the medium rather than the object of instruction.

The immersion model used at FLICS is called *Early Total Immersion*. By definition language immersion is an approach to second-language instruction in which the usual curriculum activities are conducted in a second language. In the Total Immersion model, the second language is used for the entire school day during the first 2 years (kindergarten and first grade) and reading is taught through the second language. Instruction using English is introduced gradually and the amount of English used in the classroom is increased until the sixth grade. At this time, about half the day is spent in English and half in the second language (Curtain & Pesola, 1988). The challenges to teachers using this model are twofold. First, negotiation of meaning must take place as teachers and students communicate in the targeted second language. Second, teachers must create an environment for communication.

Cultural studies is another integral part of the curriculum. Global awareness and appreciation of other cultures are important goals if students are to function successfully in the 21st century. They also are outgrowths of understanding and appreciation of one's own history and culture. FLICS has a student population of 98% African Americans. The students are from varied socioeconomic statuses (low to upper middle class) and experiential backgrounds. An African-centered curriculum complements FLICS's language program. African and African American cultures are infused into the curriculum starting in kindergarten, as evidenced mostly through art and social studies. An annual African fest is held at FLICS where students, staff, and parents, regardless of their ethnicity, wear African clothing. Students perform songs and dances reflecting African culture, display their artwork, and take visitors on a tour of various African countries featured in different classrooms. A street fair is also held with vendors hawking their wares. Of course, there is food: African as well as African American samplings for all to enjoy.

All students from grades 3 through 8 receive intensive African and African American studies in a special class. They study the African Diaspora, which includes history of Africa from 40,000 B.C. to present, and the African American and Caribbean experience. Students in grades 5 through 8 are given the option to travel to Africa for a month-long home-stay and study tour after completing at least 1 year in this program.

By design the science curriculum is strong. Beginning in second grade, all students receive their science instruction in English from specialists. This hands-on program has made science the favorite subject for most students at FLICS and has won numerous awards for students as well as schoolwide recognition for excellence in science.

THE INSTRUCTIONAL STAFF

One of the greatest strengths of FLICS is the instructional staff. Teachers and educational technicians either are native speakers of the target language or have near-native fluency in French, Spanish, or Japanese. To teach at FLICS, teachers must be elementary certified and prepared to teach all subjects. Educational technicians must be fluent in one of the languages and have completed at least 2 years of college. Parents and staff, along with the administrator, interview and select the instructional staff.

The instructional staff at FLICS has traditionally been international, multicultural, and multiethnic. Teachers and technicians in the Spanish program speak various dialects that reflect their Central American, South American, Mexican, and Caribbean origins. French immersion teachers are Franophones from France, Belgium, Lebanon, and West African Countries such as Benin. Also in the French program are some Americans who are fluent speakers.

The Japanese immersion program has brought together an interesting mix of teaching staff. Two of the teachers in the Japanese immersion program are African American. One lived for several years in Japan and then completed graduate studies in the language and culture; the other studied the language for several years and was an exchange teacher. The staff also consists of Japanese and Chinese natives. A conscious effort has been made to recruit male staff members, especially African Americans.

PARENTAL INVOLVEMENT

Offering choice to African American families enhances parental involvement. Regardless of their educational or socioeconomic status, parents, given information and options in choosing educational programs for their children, can be made to feel that they can become powerful allies in promoting success for their children. They can be helped to feel and believe, through their involvement, that they do make a difference. This is evidenced at FLICS by the many parent volunteers in the school daily and by their involvement in several parent organizations that meet regularly in the evenings. At FLICS, parental involvement originates when parents take a 2-hour orientation tour, given twice a week during winter months. This tour, conducted by parent volunteers, is the first step in the application process and provides prospective parents with an opportunity to see the program in action. Classroom visitations, as well as question-and-answer periods with administrators and FLICS parents, are the highlight of the tour.

A packet of written information about the school mission (see Appendix 10A), curriculum, foreign languages, history, parental involvement, public relations, and policies and procedures, is distributed and discussed. Parents are advised that they must make a 2-hour commitment each month to give volunteer service to the school, either directly or indirectly; to give service to the parent organization of record and its various committees; or to attend the monthly parent meetings.

Applications to FLICS are mailed to persons who complete the tour, and are available to the general public at the school and at various offices throughout the district. Parents must indicate a first, second, and third choice of the language they target for their children. This is an important decision because students will remain in that language program from kindergarten through the eighth grade. Applications are then returned to the school in person or through certified mail beginning in April.

Students are not screened for this program. Applications are accepted on a first-come, first-served basis, with preference given to students who live in the immediate school neighborhood, and to siblings of students currently enrolled. Because FLICS is a citywide magnet school, there is limited involvement from the surrounding community; however, FLICS has established and maintains a good relationship with neighborhood schools and their parent organizations.

Parents perform diverse activities to fulfill their volunteer commitment. They have planned parent-sponsored language clubs corresponding to each of the three languages. These clubs are under the auspices of the parent organization of record; however, they function independently to provide many out-of-school activities that enhance the use of the target language as well as understanding of diverse cultures. Students take field trips to restaurants and businesses, or interact socially with other ethnic communities where the languages are spoken. They sponsor foreign language book fairs and bake sales to raise money for curriculum materials.

Parents play a significant role in the FLICS Travel Club. It is the goal of the school to produce students who are language proficient and globally aware. Therefore, having real travel experiences to other countries is important. The Travel Club, which is co-sponsored by the parent organization, plans trips to many countries throughout Latin America, Europe, and Asia. The first project was a month-long trip for upper elementary students to Senegal and The Gambia in West Africa.

Parents share their talents with the school. They make international flags and cultural costumes that adorn the building or are used in the many student performances. They share their careers as guest speakers or mentors. Several parents have written grants to secure funding for special projects.

Many parents prefer leadership roles. They attend board of education meetings as advocates for immersion, empowerment, and schools of choice. They form committees that work in conjunction with the school on curriculum development, school improvement, school climate and beautification, and site-based management (empowerment).

At least 88% of the parents at FLICS attend one or more parent–teacher conferences each year. African American families are concerned about their children's education and, when given a choice and real opportunities to become involved, they respond.

ASSESSMENT: NOW AND THE FUTURE

Assessment of student achievement at FLICS is varied. This includes formal and informal assessments that are norm referenced or criterion referenced.

Formal norm-referenced assessments are conducted annually, using the reading and mathematics sections of the *California Achievement Test.* This test, in English, is given to all students in the Detroit Public Schools, kindergarten through twelfth grade and special education. The anticipated results are that students in the lower grades who have had no formal instruction in language arts in English will not score well, but that students in upper grades will score above the district norm. Research has shown that students in immersion programs score higher on norm-referenced achievement.

Students in select grades are also involved in the *Michigan Educational Assessment Program,* a criterion-referenced test. Fourth- and seventh-grade students are assessed in reading and mathematics. Fifth- and eighth-grade students are assessed in science. As implied previously, FLICS is not an exclusive public school for students identified as "gifted." Yet, historically, FLICS students have scored above district and state averages.

Reporting student progress has been done using the traditional report card with the grading scale A through F. The district and administrators and staff at FLICS are researching alternative performance assessments. The ultimate criterion-referenced assessment will be tailored to the classroom instruction and will be based on products (e.g., portfolios, videotapes) and performance (e.g., teacher observation logs, student self-assessments). Such alternatives provide valuable information to parents, students, and teachers.

LATCHKEY PROGRAM

FLICS offers an after-school latchkey program which addresses communication skills, self-development, cultural pride, and cross-cultural appreciation. Activities include sign language, Swahili, Black English and African American culture, supervised free play with emphasis on positive conflict resolution and development of social skills, and a homework center.

MULTICULTURAL PRESCHOOL (AT THE COUZENS COMMUNITY SCHOOL)

A preschool opened in the 1988–1989 school year which focuses on providing children with a holistic view of the world. The preschool is conducted in English, but offers many opportunities for children to practice the foreign languages used in FLICS and to become acquainted with members of other cultures. Preschool attendance does not guarantee admission to kindergarten at FLICS.

THE FINISHED PRODUCT: FLICS'S VISION

The student who completes the 9-year immersion program at eighth grade is one who is proficient in two languages, as documented by a portfolio of formal, informal, and alternative assessments. This student, using modern technology, has written and illustrated two books, copies of which are housed in the school library. One of these books is in the target language in which the student has been versed; the other is in English. The student has constructed a videotape that highlights his or her oral proficiency in both English and the target language. Additionally, this student has evidence of excellent achievement in science.

This student is culturally sensitive and globally aware, having had much contact with other cultures, partially through exposure at school and partially from travel experiences. Included in the student portfolio is a journal that details cultural awareness. Finally, this student is confident and exemplifies high self-esteem with a sense of purpose. The student displays a great deal of pride because of the knowledge acquired about his or her own cultural heritage, and recognition of that genius mentioned by Hilliard at the opening of this chapter.

This is the vision.

REFERENCES

Chambers, I. D. (1990). *Teaching for negative skewness.* A lecture included in a class taught at Wayne State University, Detroit, MI.

Curtain, H. A., & Pesola, C. A. (1988). *Languages and children: Making the match: Foreign language instruction in the elementary school.* Reading, MA: Addison-Wesley.

Hilliard III, A. G. (1990). Series of seminars in Educational Leadership Conference, Oakland University, Rochester, MI.

APPENDIX 10A

Foreign Language Immersion and Cultural Studies School Mission Statement

The Foreign Language Immersion and Cultural Studies School (FLICS) is a citywide empowered school of choice that successfully educates its students as they acquire second-language proficiency through the immersion process.

In addition to gaining global awareness and an appreciation of ethnic and cultural diversity, FLICS students are enriched in a positive learning enviroment that promotes and encourages self-respect, fellowship, and harmony within the child–home–school triad.

2. Marcus Garvey School, Los Angeles, California

Anyim Palmer

At the Marcus Garvey School, fourth graders regularly work from 12th-grade textbooks, and academic excellence is the rule rather than the exception. The school day begins with a choral recitation of the school's teacher-created chants, such as "Hey Black Child" or "Ode to the Ancestors." This aloud and collective recitation creates an affirmative frame of reference for students to approach the formal learning process.

Three elements are essential for any successful inner-city educational program. Fundamental is a talented, energetic, creative, and dedicated staff. The second element is a curriculum that is academically sound and challenging, yet contains a high degree of excellence for its captive audience. The third element is that parents must be an essential, involved, and participating link between the school and the students. In addition to understanding the policy and goals of the school, the parents must be supportive of them. It also is critical to the success of both students and the school that the parents and the educational institution function as allies, not antagonists. Marcus Garvey School is fortunate to have been endowed with all of these critical elements from its inception to the present.

BACKGROUND

On June 6, 1972, the *Los Angeles Times* carried McCurd's article titled "Minimum Reading Levels for Los Angeles Schools Ordered by Board: Members in Unprecedented Move Tell Superintendent Johnson to Establish Definite Goals and Draw Up a Plan of Action." The unprecedented action was aimed at raising reading levels among Black and Mexican American children, who comprised most of the low-achieving students in the district. The Mexican American Education Commission proposed a goal that no school would have an average reading score below the 25th percentile by 1974. In 1972, most of the minority (i.e., African American) schools in the district scored below the 25th percentile. However, yearly comparative data revealed that the academic performance of children in the targeted schools worsened from 1972 to 1974 to 1976.

Obviously, what was needed was an effective model. In an attempt to address this problem, I decided to establish a school in the inner city that could serve as a prototype for public school districts with large inner-city populations. At the time I was a professor at the California State University in Los Angeles, with an extended and diverse background in education. Through collective effort, the Marcus Garvey School was created in September of 1975.

In January 1985 the Marcus Garvey School moved into a two-story, multimillion dollar, newly constructed facility housing kindergarten through grade 9. The school managed to achieve this tremendous feat exclusively through its resources. Monies were generated by tuition and a 3-year program of vigorous fund-raising events by parents, staff, and various supporters of the school.

Since its infancy the school has been known for its uncompromising academic excellence. This excellence is so renowned that recently two major school districts asked Garvey to train selected teachers for them. By law, each public school teacher, no matter what his or her field, must have at least a bachelor's degree. Yet, in spite of all the legal and formal qualifications met by their instructional personnel, these districts, by their own admission, have failed. Tragically, the failure extends far beyond the state line of California. It extends to each of the 50 states. The inequity of this dire state of affairs is resident in the fact that school districts annually receive prodigious sums of money from state governments, buttressed by additional revenues from local governments, various business foundations, the federal government, and private sources, yet these districts continue to proceed on an uninterrupted course of abysmal failure.

In view of Garvey's continued positive impact on both the cognitive and affective domain of its students, I believe that the school is clearly a standard of educational excellence to be exemplified. It has won the right to be one of several models for California and the nation.

The role of the administrator is crucial in the quest for maximum parental involvement in the alternative school. In view of the socioeconomic status of the typical African-centered alternative school parent, maximizing parental involvement poses a formidable challenge. Due largely to the multiple factors responsible for their existence, most African-centered alternative schools are in the inner city, a circumstance obviously compounding an already difficult task.

Nevertheless, some techniques to reach parents over the years have empirically been demonstrated to be of more use than others. Some of the more successful approaches have involved citing the long-term benefits certain to accrue in both the short and the long run as a result of parental involvement; convincing the parent of the mutual interest shared by him or her, the child, and the school; and finally mentioning the long-term economic benefit likely to accrue to the child should involvement be sustained, consistent, and nonsuperficial.

The primary figure of the African-centered alternative school most often has the prerogative of selecting inservice programs from a literal host of choices. The items usually selected for staff development are found to be contingent on the needs of the institution, the bent of the primary figure, and of course the availability of resources. The school's philosophy or ideology is also very pertinent when staff development is considered.

MARCUS GARVEY CHILDREN

The Marcus Garvey School has been in existence almost 18 years. A great many misconceptions and myths have developed concerning Marcus Garvey children. They are said to be gifted and their parents high professionals. This is an absolute falsehood: Most parents' incomes are in the median range and their occupations range from janitor to physician.

After its third year, the school began to be marked by two distinct phenomena. One was a constant upward curve regarding growth in student body size; the other was the presence each year of at least two students who had been formally and officially labeled "retarded" by the traditional system. At no time were any of these children placed in special classes or made to feel different. The school's standard technique consists of love, discipline, and consistency. The educators would begin the students' resurrection by making them accept the beauty of their physical features. After the young person no longer felt he or she was ugly, the educators then had to find how best to restore their withered spirit and rekindle the flame of confidence that once burned high but was now only an ember, faint and nigh expired. To reduce these children to the pathetic state in which they arrived at Garvey, no holds had been barred. At Marcus Garvey School, no holds were barred to salvage them.

Several years ago the student population was approximately 250. About 8% of these young people were formerly classified mentally retarded. Many others had been diagnosed as having a number of academic handicaps, from cultural deprivation to slow learning skills. We found these children to be neither culturally deprived, nor slow, nor retarded. However, they had gone to schools that are culturally deprived, slow, and retarded. In most instances, through the application of Garvey's standard technique, educators were able to restore these children to grade level and above. These young people now feel very good about themselves, enjoy doing school work, and love both Africa and their ancestors.

CURRICULUM AND PEDAGOGY: MODEL FOR A NEW EDUCATION

Marcus Garvey's instructional staff was relentless in its determination to create an institution that would stand as a model and a beacon for countless generations to come. During the formative years, Marcus Garvey teachers typed their own materials, created their own textbooks, and constructed and typed their own tests. Despite an obvious need, the school possessed neither copying machines nor heaters for individual rooms. An open classroom arrangement was used, and classrooms were not separated by doors or partitions, but neither teachers nor students were distracted. Many teachers had not been adequately trained to provide educational service from an "Afrocentric" theoretical framework; however, they developed the necessary attitudes and additional competencies.

Today, the Marcus Garvey faculty is a very special group of people. The energy they display when selling dance, fashion show, or raffle tickets is surpassed only by the energy exhibited in their classrooms. Their academic competency, creativity, dazzling energy, and above all dedication to the educational excellence of their students are apparent. Marcus Garvey teachers are a unique breed. Without them, Marcus Garvey would be merely another of the numerous private schools steeped in mediocrity.

The school's philosophy is grounded in the history and experience of African America. This philosophy assumes the following:

1. The internal development of the African American community is dependent on the achievement of its children.

2. African Americans should reflect and reinforce their own history and culture as a corrective for the racist oppression of the African American community.

3. Education is both vital and necessary for preparing Black people to meet the needs and challenges of the future. The locus of the school within the Black community and its subjective approach to education allow for pedagogic breadth in a specific African American context.

Garvey has been the subject of six television documentaries, numerous term papers, and at least two dissertations for advanced degrees. An article in the *Los Angeles Times* (Smith, 1983), entitled "Myths Don't Add Up But Students Do," offers an excellent opportunity to gain insight into the Garvey mystique. Smith offered an excellent overview of student life at Marcus Garvey:

> In addition to speaking English, Spanish, and Swahili, children ages five and six can add, subtract and multiply, and spell all of the days of the week, and all the months of the year. The Garvey pre-school is the most exciting in the nation. As a matter of routine, they perform academic tasks sixth and seventh grade children in traditional inner-city schools are not able to do. Four year olds, in addition to reading from second and third grade books, are able to name all of the planets and describe the dominant characteristics of each of them. Additionally, they are able to state the relationship of each planet to the earth. (pp. 3–4)

This article was written over 10 years ago. In the ensuing 10 years, as one can imagine, the school has accelerated tremendously with reference to academic levels. Two-year-olds in the preschool program are now able to name all of the parts of the body in Latin and 4-year-olds read third- and fourth-grade texts and are able to perform second-grade arithmetic.

MARCUS GARVEY'S TEACHERS SPEAK OUT

The following are abbreviated first-person accounts of various classroom procedures and activities of three classroom teachers.

Teacher 1

The first day of school, I welcome my students, introduce myself, and have them introduce themselves. Next, I give the class our rules and regulations, in addition to the kinds of penalties to be imposed should they be violated. Some of the rules by which they will be guided the remainder of the school year are as follows:

- We will not talk without permission.
- We will not get out of our seats without permission.
- We will maintain order and control at all times in class, out of class, and at home.
- We will study hard and do our work each day.
- We will not laugh at each other.

I use "we will" to create collective involvement of all, a concept familiar to our ancestors. At some point, we discuss what I expect from the class, what their parents expect from me, and what our community expects from each of us. I then explain to my students that I will give my best and, therefore, I have the right to expect the best from them. I further explain that our subject matter for the year is quite simple and easy to understand. To facilitate understanding, after the introduction of each new mathematical or science concept, the class responds to a lengthy series of why or why not questions. Children who are not attentive do not do well in these drills. Students unaware of why or why not are unable to apply the correct process in the event of problem solving. I have found over the years that this technique is most effective in enhancing both listening skills and the realization that they must understand what they are hearing.

African American children must have a sense of competence if they are to evolve into dynamic and focused young people who possess self-worth. To its everlasting shame, Western civilization generally, and the United States particularly, deliberately and systematically stripped Africans of their connection to the past. I attempt to counter this by teaching my students salient elements of the history of math, science, and languages. When they learn that their ancestors were the fathers of math, science, language, writing, literature, and astrology, they approach their task from an entirely different perspective. Their attitude becomes "give me more." It may be said that from this point math and science are demystified. As an addendum, I demonstrate to them how important math, science, and health are in our daily lives. By the conclusion of the school year, my second graders will have completed algebra 1 and geometry and my third graders will have completed algebra 2 and geometry and will have begun the study of trigonometry. I demand that my students achieve to their full capacity; therefore, I push them. I categorically refuse to allow my students to do as they often wish to do; neither will I accept them as they are. Translated, this means that my pushes often become violent shoves.

More often than I would like to say, parents deny their children the opportunity to experience growth by doing the child's work for him or her or, if the assignment was not complete, providing the child with an excuse. During the initial weeks of each new school year, I invariably receive notes from parents stating, "My child did not complete the homework because he did not understand it" or "My child failed to do the homework because she was with me." The excuse that always elicits a chuckle from me is, "My child completed her homework, but forgot to bring her notebook." Once I accept any of the above excuses, or any excuse for that matter, for nonperformance, for all intents and purposes the school year is over. However, upon noting the phenomenal progress of their child, the parents usually begin to push them as vigorously as I do.

Should all go according to plan, and it usually does, by the beginning of the second month, my students will no longer dread the introduction of challenging concepts and the opportunity of solving so-called difficult problems. They actually welcome them. It is at this point that I refer to them as seasoned Marcus Garvey students.

Teacher 2

Marcus Garvey School has always had quite an extensive, demanding, and comprehensive curriculum. In the 2 years I have taught here, I have learned to teach the 14 subjects not only for the benefit of the students' general knowledge, but to maintain a most important goal in my classroom as well: for students to know and love themselves in as many aspects as possible. This is enhanced through intensive academic study, consistent discipline, and the continuing development of social skills. Academically, my fourth-grade class is far more advanced than any other fourth-grade class I've seen or heard of outside of Marcus Garvey School. We study numerous subjects, among them spelling, phonics, African American history, reading, English, math, algebra, health, science, geography, history, African history, Spanish, Swahili, and penmanship.

Using African history as the basis for many of our studies, we build self-esteem and confidence in ourselves. We learn that our foremothers and forefathers had built a foundation for us centuries ago in letters, arts, and sciences. Contrary to what society has told us for so many years, we begin to eradicate the many fears and feelings of inferiority that have been instilled in us. Practice in overcoming the fears comes with learning the other subjects. Swahili is a language from Africa that is widely used; knowledge of it and its value is important in reaching our goal. Knowing how to speak and write standard English, and knowing basic conversational Spanish hones our communication skills and puts us in touch with still other cultures. My students are currently spelling and defining words that are comparable to those found on the *Scholastic Aptitude Test* and *Graduate Record Examination.* . . . Our reading level is that of 12th grade and beyond. In terms of reading, what is important to us at the present time is to fully comprehend the written word; to understand not only what is written on the page, but also that which is implied "in between the lines." My 9-year-olds are learning to look at the context in which subjects are written, and to interpret and critique the various texts they read. This is a step beyond merely reading the words and looking for facts—a concept that even many of the greatest scholars are hard pressed to master. But this is another crucial step in knowing, understanding, and accepting ourselves.

My fourth graders know with confidence all aspects of basic arithmetic: properties of addition, subtraction, multiplication, long division, fractions, decimals, and the operations concerning these properties. In fact, they knew all of this by the time they came to me in the third grade. With this very solid foundation, my students are well into their second year of algebra. We know exponents, how to factor numbers and variables, how to combine like terms, how to solve and check for variables in algebraic equations, and so on. Currently my class is learning linear equations and plotting the answers on graphs. By the end of the academic year, my students should have a very strong foundation in algebra, so that next year they will be able to move on to geometry and trigonometry with ease.

All of our academic work shows important strides toward our goal: to see ourselves as the great people we really are—intelligent, proud, creative, strong—and not like the images that society has impressed upon us. Learning about our great heritage facilitates this process. We must learn to think for ourselves, to read between, over, and under the lines. We must know how to communicate among ourselves and with other peoples.

Teacher 3

For the past several years, I have had the good fortune of teaching high school algebra to 9- and 10-year-olds. This of itself would seem a miracle of academic achievement, but at Marcus Garvey School such is expected. My students, like all Marcus Garvey students, fail to see anything out of the ordinary with respect to their high achievement in science and math. Last year I taught fourth-grade math, science, and health. For nearly the entire term, one of my students tutored his cousin in algebra. A fourth grader capable of tutoring anyone in algebra is in itself considered greatly removed from the ordinary. But what made the circumstances even more remarkable was the fact that his tutee was an 11th-grade student in the Los Angeles public school system.

My fifth-grade students have covered the following areas in math: linear equations, polynomials, angles and their properties, similar triangles, trigonometry, and analytical geometry. None of the above areas presented any undue difficulties from my fifth graders. All of my students are aware of the African origins of math and science and perhaps feel that their ancestors have given them the power to master their own creation. Presently we are in calculus l, and I will have completed it by the end of the school year. Contrary to what is heard in other circles, the appetite of Marcus Garvey students for math and science is voracious. I cannot recall ever hearing them use the word "difficult" within the context of their math and science studies.

SUMMARY: INNER-CITY AFRICAN AMERICAN CHILDREN

Each year Marcus Garvey School blazes new paths and sets forth new challenges. At this point, it is necessary to take a cursory look at the inner-city African American child. It is that child whose so-called failure is most dramatic and pronounced in the school. Although the remarks about the inner-city child will be brief, I hope they will be definitive. The child's importance is obvious. Without the child's so-called failure, there would have been no need for this chapter, or this book, to have been written.

The inner-city child should be a topic piece, not because of the failure to do well in school, but rather because he or she managed to survive unbelievably harsh environmental handicaps to attend school to be a failure. It should also be noted that the word failure with respect to his or her progress in school must be used with a great deal of caution.

Hardly anyone would question the fact that the United States is a racist society. The inner-city or African American child overall is the victim of the historical and contemporary racial policies and practices that impact every aspect of life. The tremendous adverse effects of the deficit model and how it retards the cognitive ability and social-emotional status of African American children are discussed in other chapters. Because a significant number of African American youth attend public schools, it is imperative that I reiterate the impact of racism with respect to the negative teacher attitudes and the delivery of inferior educational services to Black children. Such practices must be precisely defined, eliminated, and replaced by effective models.

Black children cannot continue to be subjected to such substandard treatment. If success in educating Black youth can be demonstrated in schools such as Marcus Garvey, similar innovating methods can be incorporated into curricula in public schools, especially those servicing predominantly Black students.

The questions that need answers are how and why the Marcus Garvey School is successful in educating Black children when the standardized test data suggest that Black children are either more difficult to teach or have a lower capacity for learning. The near absence of literature concerning alternative education in the African American community and contemporary Afrocentric pedagogy requires exploration in both areas. This discussion seeks to explicate important aspects of the Marcus Garvey School. It will provide a deeper understanding of alternative education in the Black community. Further hypotheses from which to pursue a more comprehensive, comparative study of public education and the Marcus Garvey School can be developed.

Education in the African American community has developed along two divergent paths. While the Eurocentered path would come to dominate the education of the African Americans following World War II, the Afrocentered path has continued to flourish. The Marcus Garvey School is a good example of the continuity in community-based Afrocentered education. A comparison of the Marcus Garvey School and public schools is needed to assess the interplay of factors, the cross-cultural applicability of the factors, and the possibilities and implications this study may have for public education.

At the Garvey preschool 11 teachers are on staff. None has a college degree. Four-year-olds who have been in attendance for over a year are able to read from third- and fourth-grade books. At the elementary school, second graders regularly work math problems from 10th-grade algebra texts. At the end of the school term, third graders will be working problems in 11th- and 12th-grade math, and fifth graders will have completed a course in high school calculus. However, only two teachers at the elementary school have college degrees.

Conversely, consider the state of affairs within the traditional system where degrees, credentials, and certificates abound. Nonetheless, many of the students who are twelfth graders in the traditional system are unable to perform academic work that Garvey kindergarteners perform as a matter of routine. The reference of course is to the inner city. The outer city would not tolerate such failure even for a moment.

Taylor (1992), in a paper entitled "A Solution to the Problem of the Miseducation of the African Americans: Marcus Garvey School," elaborated on the theme of young people of African descent not being educated, but miseducated. Her paper was presented to a professor of race and racism in satisfaction of the writing requirement in the Spring 1992 session of the Texas Tech School of Law. Taylor began her paper by quoting Woodson's (1933) *Miseducation of the Negro*:

> When you control a man's thinking you do not have to worry about his actions. You do not have to tell him not to stand here or go yonder. He will find his "proper place" and will stay in it. You do not need to send him to the back door. He will go without being told. In fact, if there is no back door, he will cut one for his special benefit. His education makes it necessary. History shows that it does not matter who is in power. . . . Those who have not learned for themselves and have to depend solely on others never obtain any rights or privileges in the end than they had in the beginning.

Although Woodson was writing and lecturing about the failure of the schools over half a century ago, his message is as timely and relevant now as it was in 1933. I would submit that the relevancy of Woodson's work has heightened during the course of the years in that education in the Black community during the past decade has reached a crisis undreamed of during this era. During the life and times of Woodson, there were hundreds of excellent Black schools in the South that were producing scholars and academicians who had positive impacts on their entire generation. However, these Black schools that were once community centered are now integrated. The products they are producing are much like the products being produced in the inner cities of New York, Chicago, Los Angeles, Boston, and Kansas City.

Woodson is one of the primary figures taught at Marcus Garvey School. Within the context of his teachings, Garvey teachers make every attempt to dissuade children from cutting back doors. Instead, teachers instruct the students to tear down back doors upon finding them, no matter what the circumstances, and to never erect one.

Other works of great importance to us are *Garvey and Garveyism* (Garvey, 1970), *Black Power and the Garvey Movement* (Vincent, 1972), *Garvey, Lumumba and Malcolm: Black Nationalist Separatists* (Maglanqbayan, 1972), *The Destruction of Black Civilization* (Williams, 1987), *Notes for an African World Revolution: Africans at the Crossroads* (Clarke, 1991), and *Stolen Legacy* (James, 1988).

Teachers at Marcus Garvey School accept the dictum of Woodson as correct and daily attempt to influence the students' perception by consistently presenting to them edited and corrected history. Teaching the young people about the great and illustrious past of their ancestors serves a twofold purpose: They are motivated to learn about Africa, the land of their ancestors, and their curiosity generalizes outward. To cope with their boundless curiosity, the teachers must often do extensive research. Thus, all parties are enriched.

In 1992, Malikah Hanan Salaam authored a doctoral dissertation titled "The Relationship of African Cultural Consciousness and Self Esteem on the Academic Achievement of African American Students." At the time of her dissertation, Salaam was a student at the University of California, Los Angeles. She examined the degree to which the school's cultural sensitivity influenced the self-esteem levels of African American students, and how the self-esteem levels impacted academic performance. Salaam proposed to examine three major questions:

1. How is a particular African cultural program defined and translated into a specific school program, particularly as reflected in a school's curriculum and its instructional process?

2. To what degree do elementary school students exposed to an Afrocentric or a Eurocentric program show different levels of African cultural consciousness (as defined by the school)?

3. If African cultural consciousness is higher among one group of students, what is the relationship of this African cultural consciousness, self-esteem levels, and academic achievement to participating students?

These research questions resulted in the development of several hypotheses. One of the most important was whether African American students exposed to a curriculum with an African cultural component would show higher levels of self-esteem than those African American students who were not exposed.

Two schools were chosen as research sites for the study. Both schools were located in south central Los Angeles within a 3-mile radius of each other. The first school is a public elementary school with a traditional curriculum. Enrollment at the traditional school was 1,500 students, with 53% being identified as African American. The second school is an independent Black institution—the Marcus Garvey School—that is referred to in the study as the independent school. Whereas each educational unit offered reading, mathematics, science, social studies, music, and art, the independent school also offered African history, African American history, Swahili, Spanish, geography, geology, American history, sociology, psychology, European history, and advanced mathematics through calculus.

The curriculum at the independent school was Afrocentric, a factor totally separating it from the traditional school. According to Salaam, students in the African school environment showed more positive feelings about themselves when compared with the students in the traditional public school environment. She added that students at the independent school conclusively demonstrated the exposure to positive images added to students' feeling good about themselves. She went on to explain that many pictures and images of outstanding African and African American leaders surrounded the students attending the independent school. The school was named after a great African American leader, and to the exhilaration of the children, pictures of African American scientists, authors, engineers, explorers, and musicians were constantly in full view in the corridors and classrooms of the two-story building.

Social and peer groups at the African-centered school were characterized by excellent relations and cooperative learning styles. Salaam stated that at the independent school she observed neither fights nor confrontation between students. Although she listened intently to playground conversations, she failed to hear a single negative racial remark between students. Although in some instances play was rough, the players involved inevitably parted with laughter.

Salaam's research seemed to strongly suggest that African American students do not appreciably differ from other students when it comes to their culture. They feel a great deal better about themselves when they have an understanding of who they are and of the contributions African and African Americans have made to both America and the world. Within the same context, African American students excel as readily as other students when the learning environment is culturally conducive and the expectations of the teachers are high. Salaam concluded by stating that American public schools could benefit by observing the schooling process of independent African American schools.

Marcus Garvey School is an institution of many components. It seems clear, however, that its most exciting component is the academic achievement of its children. In 1975, a vision of African American children learning *true* world history was actualized through the establishment of the Marcus Garvey School. These same inner-city children who had once been considered to be mentally retarded, slow learners, or unable to learn, are now excelling two to three grades above what is normally required. The reason for the success of the Marcus Garvey School is so simple it escapes the experts, yet it can be stated in two words: The teachers!

REFERENCES

Clarke, J. H. (1991). *Notes for an African world revolution: Africans at the crossroads.* Trenton, NJ: African World Press.

Garvey, A. J. (1970). *Garvey and Garveyism.* New York: Collier Books.

James, G. G. (1988). *Stolen legacy.* New York: The African Islamic Mission Publications.

Maglanqbayan, S. (1972). *Garvey, Lumumba and Malcolm: Black Nationalist Separatists.* Chicago: Third World Press.

McCurd, J. (1972, June 6). Minimum reading levels for Los Angeles schools ordered by board: Members in unprecedented move tell Superintendent Johnson to establish definite goals and draw up a plan of action. *Los Angeles Times.*

Salaam, M. H. (1992). *The relationship of African cultural consciousness and self esteem on the academic achievement of African American students.* Unpublished doctoral dissertation, University of California, Los Angeles.

Smith, D. (1983). Myths don't add up but students do. *Los Angeles Times.*

Taylor, C. (1992). *A solution to the problem of the miseducation of the African American: Marcus Garvey School.* Unpublished paper, Texas Tech School of Law, Lubbock.

Vincent, T. G. (1972). *Black power and the Garvey movement.* San Francisco: Rampant Press.

Williams, C. (1987). *The destruction of Black civilization.* Chicago: Third World Press.

Woodson, C. G. (1933). *The miseducation of the Negro.* Washington, DC: Associated Publishers.

Subject Index

AAE. *See* African American English (AAE)

Active listening, 81–82

Adolescence
dropout rates during, 243–244
goal of, 166
Project Well-Being, 266
traditional secondary SED classrooms and, 158
transitional planning and, 254

Advanced Progressive Matrices, 37–38

Africa. *See* African culture

African American church, 34, 35, 54, 55, 249

African American community. *See* Community involvement

African American English (AAE). *See also* Language of African Americans
assessment and, 111–115
clinical-educational program on, 105–111

code switching between African American English and Standard English, 117–118
collaborative model on, 106–107
and culturally relevant themes, 115–117
educational versus clinical issues in, 103–105
intervention goals concerning, 114–115
legitimacy of, 119
linguistic features of, 95–96
and Standard vs. Nonstandard English, 93–94, 97–98, 102
stigma against, 97–98, 102–103, 119
treatment approaches and, 115–119
use of, as term, 93
whole language method and, 107–111, 115

African American families. *See also* Parent involvement

Author Index